ALSO BY
ROBERT KANIGEL

HEARING HOMER'S SONG
The Brief Life and Big Idea of Milman Perry

EYES ON THE STREET
The Life of Jane Jacobs

ON AN IRISH ISLAND

FAUX REAL
Genuine Leather and 200 Years of Inspired Fakes

HIGH SEASON
How One French Riviera Town Has Seduced Travelers for Two Thousand Years

THE ONE BEST WAY
Frederick Winslow Taylor and the Enigma of Efficiency

THE MAN WHO KNEW INFINITY
A Life of the Genius Ramanujan

APPRENTICE TO GENIUS
The Making of a Scientific Dynasty

VINTAGE READING
From Plato to Bradbury, a Personal Tour of Some of the World's Best Books

YOUNG MAN, MUDDLED
A Memoir

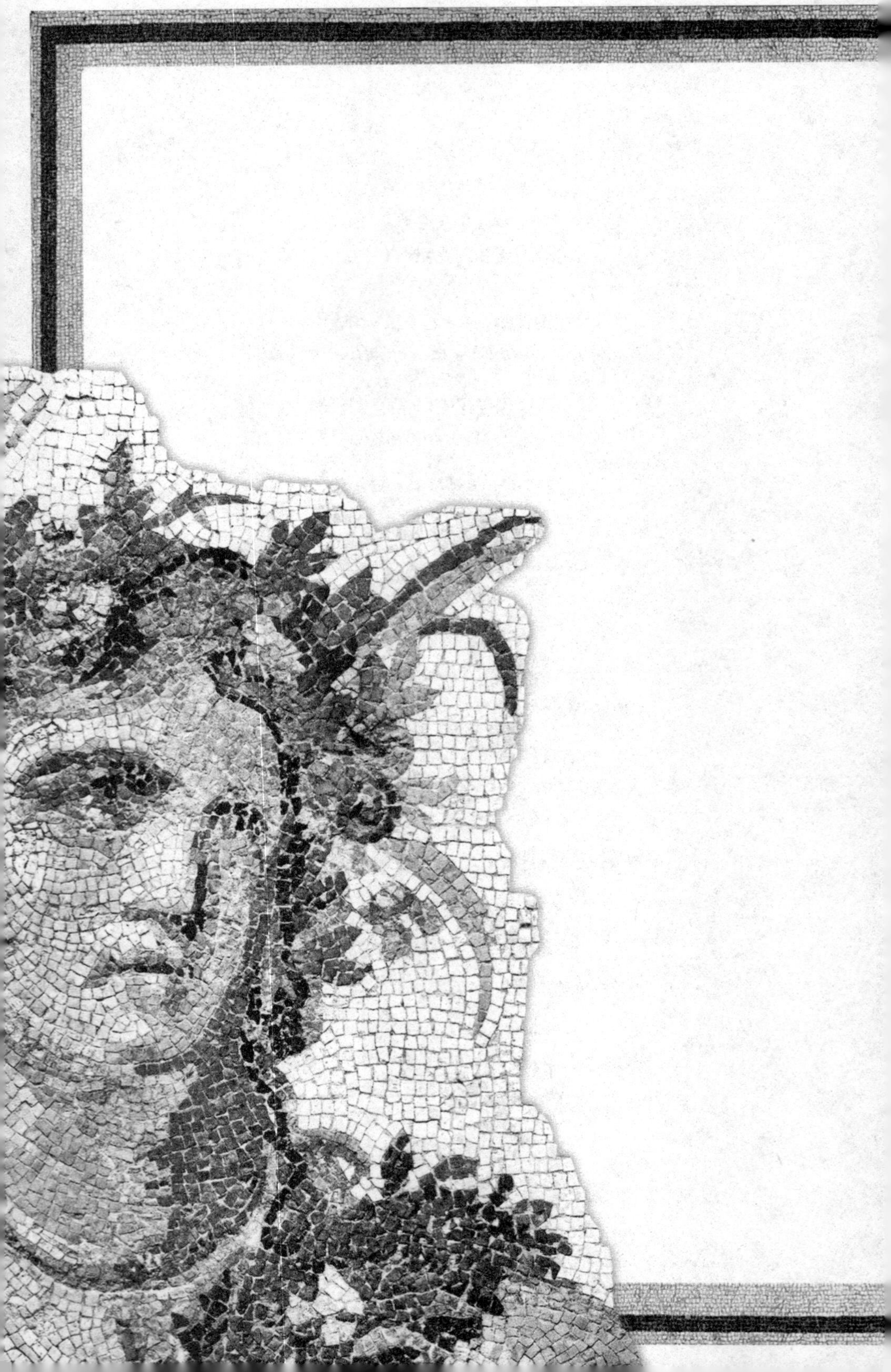

UNCOVERING ANTIOCH

The Ancient City and Its Lost Treasures of Mosaic Art

ROBERT KANIGEL

SIMON & SCHUSTER
New York Amsterdam/Antwerp London
Toronto Sydney/Melbourne New Delhi

Simon & Schuster
1230 Avenue of the Americas
New York, NY 10020

First Simon & Schuster hardcover edition August 2026

SIMON & SCHUSTER and colophon are registered trademarks of Simon & Schuster, LLC

Interior design by Lewelin Polanco

Manufactured in the United States of America

1 3 5 7 9 10 8 6 4 2

Library of Congress Control Number is available.

ISBN 978-1-6680-0625-2
ISBN 978-1-6680-0624-5 (ebook)

For wounded Antakya

CONTENTS

PART III

West

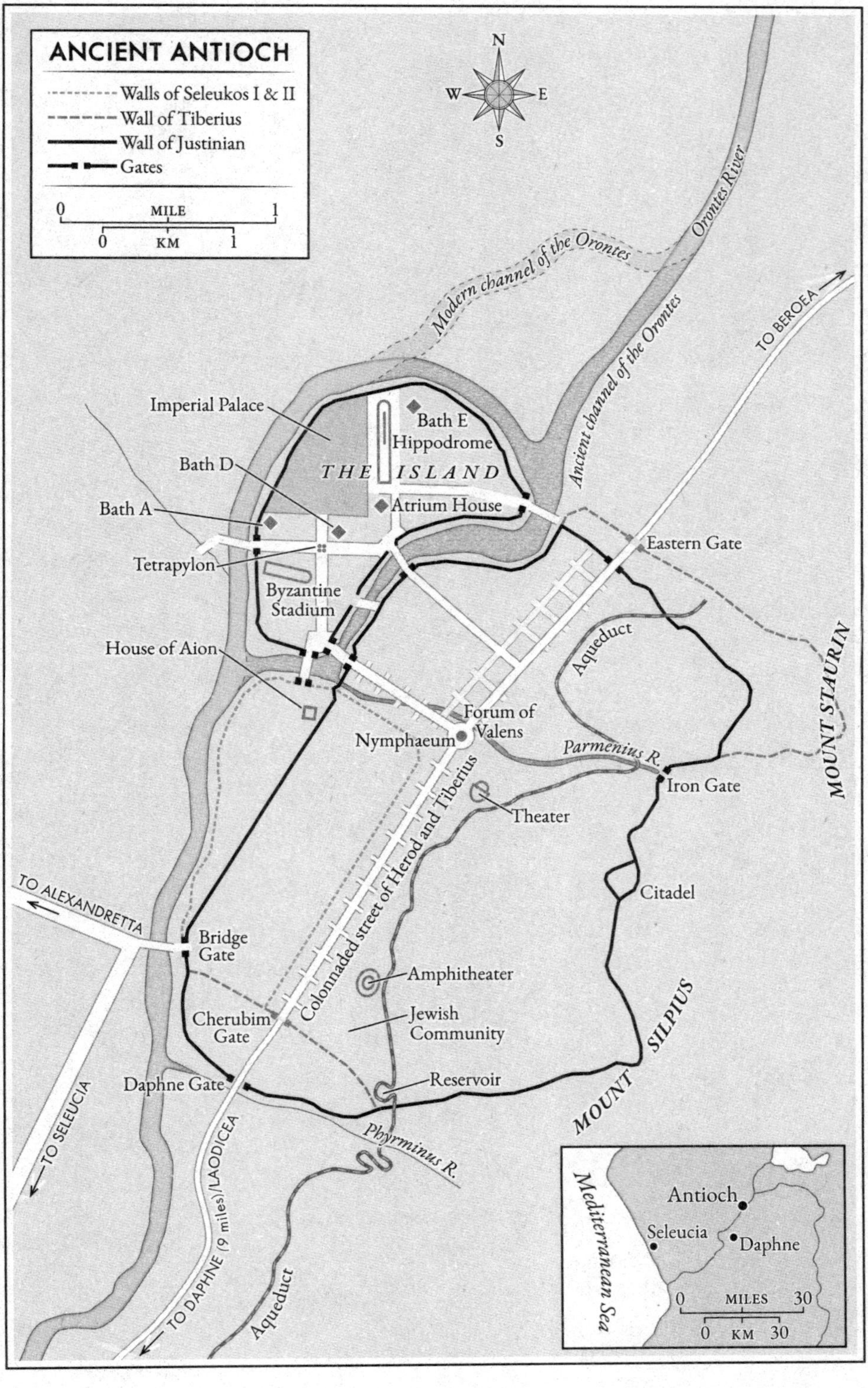
ANCIENT ANTIOCH
Walls of Seleukos I & II
Wall of Tiberius
Wall of Justinian
Gates
0 MILE 1
0 KM 1
N
W
E
S
Orontes River
Modern channel of the Orontes
Ancient channel of the Orontes
TO BEROEA
Imperial Palace
Bath E
Hippodrome
THE ISLAND
Bath D
Bath A
Atrium House
Tetrapylon
Byzantine Stadium
Eastern Gate
House of Aion
Aqueduct
MOUNT STAURIN
Forum of Valens
Nymphaeum
Parmenius R.
Iron Gate
Theater
Colonnaded street of Herod and Tiberius
TO ALEXANDRETTA
Bridge Gate
Citadel
Amphitheater
Cherubim Gate
Jewish Community
MOUNT SILPIUS
Daphne Gate
Reservoir
TO SELEUCIA
Phyrminus R.
TO DAPHNE (9 miles)/LAODICEA
Aqueduct
Mediterranean Sea
Antioch
Seleucia
Daphne
0 MILES 30
0 KM 30

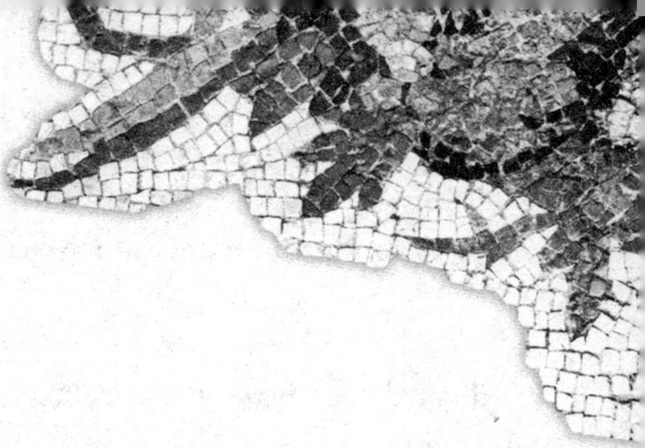

PROLOGUE

Eros and Psyche

There are some three hundred of them, these mosaics from the Roman metropolis of Antioch in ancient Syria—chiseled fragments of stone and glass heaped up into visions of gods and goddesses, glories of color and design. Many are vast, room-sized tableaus, commissioned by wealthy Antiochenes for their baths and villas. They depict banquets, drinking contests, olive harvests; lions, leopards, peacocks, and gazelles; scenes from mythology, Cupid and Psyche, Narcissus and Dionysus.

Though dated to early in the Christian era, they are unabashedly pagan, scarcely a Christian image in the lot. The animals and plants they represent are so lifelike that scholars can often identify them by species. Their dazzlingly intricate geometries fairly burst into three dimensions. Together, the Antioch mosaics represent a vast, collectively obsessive outpouring of art and artisanship. They stand for beauty, the will to make it, and the need to knit it into our lives.

Through them, we glimpse something of what men and women long ago cherished, what tugged at their imaginations, how they were like us, and how they were not. While some mosaics were damaged over the ages, some destroyed altogether, many had lain undisturbed for all the intervening centuries, their stones impervious, their luster little dimmed, looking much as they had when first laid down, forming an almost direct, unmediated, uncorrupted window into the past.

—

I don't think Charles Rufus Morey of Princeton University gave much thought to mosaics. Not at first, anyway. Not in 1927, when he first learned of French interest in mounting an archaeological dig in Antioch. Or over the next few years as he begged and bargained to get the expedition going. Or even by 1932, when the first astonishing mosaic treasures were unearthed. In his early proselytizing on behalf of an Antioch venture, Mr. Morey had nothing to say of mosaics, couldn't have imagined them so ardently admired, haggled over, studied and scrutinized, then bought up or traded by Harvard University, Boston's Museum of Fine Arts, New York's Metropolitan, Paris's Louvre, or any of the more than twenty other museums that house them today.

In his 1938 book, *The Mosaics of Antioch*, Mr. Morey couldn't always be counted on even to *call* them mosaics. They were "pavements," because they'd been found not on walls but on the floors of public baths and private villas. Or they were "paintings," because he was comparing them to other works of art that really were paintings, familiar subjects and themes of Greek and Roman art expressed now in bits of stone and glass. Only rarely did he nod to some feature that emerged from the little tiles that *made* them mosaics, the tesserae: He noted the masterly technique of one mosaic devoted to the Roman god Neptune, its marble squares of such "minute dimensions for the subtle flesh shades and features of the faces." He saluted the special crew of workmen charged with lifting the mosaics from the earth, setting them on beds of concrete while never, presumably, losing a single precious tile.

It might be churlish to suggest that Mr. Morey couldn't at first accept that the big finds coming out of Antioch weren't sculptures, inscriptions, busts, palace walls, and frescoes; they weren't the trove he "knew" would be found there. They were, rather, products of a medium often overlooked, deemed lesser in the precincts of high art. In his book, Morey had to take them seriously because, spanning five hundred years of late antiquity, they gave evidence for some of his pet notions about how classic Greek art had shape-shifted into the Byzantine art of the Middle Ages; that they were mosaics could seem an afterthought.

Not here, though, not in this book.

—

Lucky to grow up in an era during which the crafts in America have flourished, I came to care about mosaics perhaps more than Mr. Morey did, or at least differently. It began in 2014 when I took a single introductory class in mosaics at the American Visionary Art Museum in Baltimore. At the end of the day, I had produced a paperback-sized thing—about all I dare call it—built up from small pieces of blue, green, and white glass, sprinkled with adorable little mirrors, glued down onto a board.

How to explain why glass and stone should attract me, but not charcoal or acrylic or the rest of the myriad of materials with which we make art? Why did I early give up on the possibility of drawing a graceful line, yet happily embrace—both in writing books and making mosaics—the challenge of making graceful compositions? As a mosaicist I am still every bit the amateur, a hobbyist. Still, with smalti and stone, broken teacups, hammers and cutters, glue and grout, by now I've made a couple of dozen mosaics. At first, with much confusion, ineptitude, and an obvious deficit of training and experience. Later, some small gains—works larger and more complex, experiments in color and design, maybe a little more interesting. So much to get wrong—the natural consequence of seeing too indistinctly, of rendering too crudely. But also pleasure and some little pride when my mosaics worked out well, or well enough. None of them will ever grace a gallery or museum. Yet by now I've put enough time and energy into their making that I'm moved to ask what I find so satisfying in them; how, for example, they can be seen as "paintings," as Mr. Morey did, yet in their stony permanence, transcend painting. Certainly, my hands-on experience, coupled with visits over the years to the serene and stunning Antioch Court at the Baltimore Museum of Art, where mosaics from Antioch have been exhibited since the 1930s, left me susceptible to every turn of the aesthetic, cultural, and human story I undertake to tell in this book.

Though a working writer for decades, I've had a long, if intermittent, relationship with crafts, too, and the material and tactile world of which they are a part. My father and grandfather ran a shop in Brooklyn where dull, gray steel emerged from steaming tanks of chemicals electroplated in yellow brass or silvery chrome. In college, I studied to become a mechanical engineer, and for a few years afterward I worked as one. I was drawn to the sheer *thinginess* of the physical world, to the smell of hot metal chips coming off the lathe; to novel objects and working mechanisms that had never before *been*, yet now, occasionally through my contrivance, *were*. Then, for a time, in my twenties and thirties, I worked in leather, making bags, purses, and bicycling gear, even shoes, always relishing leather's soft touch and tactile presence.

Later, I read C. P. Snow's famous "Two Cultures" lecture, his lament for the ungainly gap among intellectuals between the humanities and the sciences, between Shakespeare's tragedies and the second law of thermodynamics. I came to see another such split, an analogous one, between art, words, and ideas on the one hand and the often overlooked or denigrated realm of steel and stone, tools and machines, objects and their makers, studios, factories, and shops, artisans and craftsmen, on the other.

In the reflected glow of the ancient metropolis upon which the Antioch mosaics throw such warming light, those who made them can recede into the background. The mosaics about which Mr. Morey wrote in 1938, that hundreds of art historians, classicists, archaeologists, and other scholars have studied since, and that countless museum visitors have admired close-up over the years were the work of human hands, eyes, and minds. This book delves into realms of art, myth, history, religion, and human striving. But I hope, too, never to neglect for long the sound of hammers hacking limestone, marble, and glass into tiny tiles, the feel of them in the fingers as they're laid into wet mortar, the satisfaction gleaned by artists and ordinary workers as they stood back to look at what they had made, and would then leave to us.

—

Before the mosaics there was Antioch.

Along with Alexandria, Constantinople, and Rome itself, Antioch was one of the four great cities of the ancient Roman world. For three centuries, it had been the capital of the Seleucid kingdom, largest of the fragments into which Alexander the Great's empire broke up after his death in 323 BCE. In 64 BCE it was absorbed by Rome. It was in Antioch—third-largest city in the world, "up-to-date, amusing, elegant, wicked"—that St. Paul preached the new religion, Christianity. There, it is recorded in Acts of the Apostles 11:26, Christians were first called Christians. At its height in the fourth century, it was home to perhaps half a million people.

Lying near the border of today's Syria and southern Turkey, twenty miles back from the shores of the eastern Mediterranean, the dart-shaped island of Cyprus pointing straight at it, Antioch was a polyglot jumble of Greek and Roman, East and West, Christian, Jew, and pagan. It was an immigrant city, alive with foreign ways, proudly cosmopolitan, home to merchants and traders, scholars and soldiers. From Antioch, in 361 CE, the emperor Julian the Apostate waged his brief, bold, unsuccessful campaign to turn back the new state religion, Christianity, and welcome back Athena, Dionysus, and the other Greek and Roman gods. "From all the corners of the world," asserted the fourth-century orator Libanius, a son of Antioch and among its most ardent champions, the city's leaders "collect fine marble of all descriptions, and this they use upon beautiful buildings which illumine our city like stars." He loved the place, in all its unbridled urbanity. "Every part teems with human beings." This, for hundreds of years, was the capital of Roman Asia.

Then, in 526, Antioch was struck by an earthquake that took a quarter of a million lives; it was one of many that racked the city over the centuries, both earlier and since. A quake in February 2023 left large parts of modern Antioch and surroundings in ruins and killed more than fifty thousand people across Turkey and Syria; in a few terrifying moments of hellish shaking, collapse, dust, and death, it called up the whole awful story in a way history books never could. After past disasters, Antioch had each time been rebuilt, one emperor after another restoring the crippled city, erecting new walls, laying out new imperial ways, aqueducts, and baths. But after 526, and especially after the Persians sacked what remained of Antioch in 540, the city never came back, or not to what it was. Absorbed by the Ottoman Empire in the seventh century, this ancient city of vast historical, religious, and cultural importance was reduced to a cheerless backwater, all but lost to the world. By the 1930s, it was a town of perhaps thirty-five thousand "huddled on a fraction of the ancient area of the city," as one visitor noted, its past underground, obliterated, invisible. Though alive in the awareness of archaeologists, classicists, art historians, and biblical scholars, who'd grown into intellectual maturity with its past splendor secure in their minds and imaginations, physically speaking, ancient Antioch was lost.

But in 1927, the French, who during this time presided over Syria as something like a colony, aimed to find it. Just before Christmas, Rufus Morey, chair of the Art and Archaeology Department at Princeton, received roundabout word from René Dussaud, curator of Near Eastern art at the Louvre, that it and the Musées Nationaux de France would look with favor on a Princeton archaeological dig at Antioch.

It is not clear whether the French acted on their own to approach Princeton, or whether their overture followed some discreet informal inquiry, possibly from Morey himself. But invitation it surely was. It went from the Louvre to Bayard Dodge—the well-connected president of the American University of Beirut, scholar of Islam, and Princeton grad—thence through a colleague in the Princeton history department, Dana Munro, and finally to Morey. Ten days later, Morey wrote to Dodge. "As you probably know, we have had this project as a dream for some years." Now word from Dussaud meant the dream might yet be realized.

No one, it should be said, was talking about mosaics.

—

Today, the great floor mosaics recovered from Antioch bear names like Mosaic of the Striding Lion, the Rams' Head Mosaic, or the Mosaic of

Briseis's Farewell. Some of them are known simply for the ruined villas in which they were found, like the House of the Calendar or the House of the Drunken Dionysus. These names didn't originate in ancient times. Or in the Princeton expedition's later excavation diaries, or in the crude sketches and raw scribbles of each day's field books. Before a mosaic emerged into the light, after all, it had no name, for the excavators didn't always know what they'd found. Their accounts sometimes sag under vague, equivocal references to "one section of a large villa," or "a pavement of large marble and limestone tesserae," or "figure panels . . . arranged toward the entrance from the hall." Only later did the mosaics get the more picturesque or fanciful names by which they're known today.

One of them would be called the Mosaic of the Boat of Psyches. In a story going back to the second-century Roman writer Apuleius, a beautiful princess, Psyche, was loved by Eros (Cupid, to the Romans), son of the goddess Aphrodite. The mosaic, found almost wholly intact, shows Eros driving, as if a chariot or boat, two butterfly-winged Psyche figures (the myth itself speaks of but one); another scholar's preferred name was Eros as Charioteer of Souls. In any case, the ruined third-century villa where it was found in 1934 took the name of this find, becoming the House of the Boat of Psyches.

But this was just one of many mosaics found on the site in Daphne, an elite suburb a few miles up into the hills outside Antioch. The more the team explored the villa, which had been rebuilt in the fifth century, the more they found. "The rest of the pavements [floor mosaics] in this area were so numerous and of such outstanding quality that we decided to excavate the whole building."

Another mosaic found was a bust of Tethys originally thought to be Thalassa, both of them being sea or water goddesses. In the ancient Greek creation story going back to Hesiod, even before Homer, Tethys was one of the Titans, beings that preceded the rest of the Greek pantheon. Wings erupting from her brow, she was the sister and wife of Okeanos, who represented the great river thought to encircle the world. "Modelled in light red with white highlights and shadows of grey and yellow-grey," the expedition's published account describes Tethys: "Pupils of eyes, black under light red eyelids and grey-blue eyebrows. Wing-like antennae, yellow, shaded green and grey . . ."

In a book normally consulted only by scholars, its photos rendered in muddy black and white, so dutiful an accounting of color might be necessary. But the humdrum detail cheats us, too, the Psyches and winged Erotes of the Greco-Roman tradition, the sea goddesses and Titans, a little lost to us. Better to pull up close to Tethys and really *see* her.

On a wall at the Baltimore Museum of Art she stands about six feet high, four and a half wide. We need no lessons in mythology, from the mosaic itself or its interpreters, to enjoy her; like some other mosaics from the House of the Boat of Psyches and elsewhere in Antioch, this one is a hoot. In her iconic head wings, Tethys appears about life-sized, turned a little to one side, a riotous tide of marine life around her. She looks out from her perch on the museum wall, a dragon-headed sea creature around her neck, swarmed by fish, crabs, and wiggling, slithering eels. And by an Erote—a winged infant representing Eros or an aspect of him, a fixture of Roman art—plump thighs wrapped around a dolphin, cruising along, fishing. Fishing fruitfully, in fact, actually landing a fish; there it is, dangling from a line suspended from its pole. In its freshness, its sweet, unlikely playfulness, it reminds me of the early Beatles, with their *marmalade skies, tangerine trees, sea of green.*

Tethys shows up in another mosaic from a different room in the same complex, this time with her husband, Okeanos; crab claws erupt from his forehead, framed by hair in unruly wavelets, all in reds and yellows, beside a trio of peacocks. Other mosaics from room 8 of the House of the Boat of Psyches also bear a watery flavor; water looms large in Antioch's own view of itself, splashing down mountain slopes to the sea or channeled through aqueducts, its fresh, plentiful flow a source of civic pride.

Many of Antioch's mosaics are awash in water, stocked with deities of all things wet and wonderful. Yet, abiding in stony perpetuity with meanings contested, secrets unrevealed, they resist any too facile an interpretation. A mosaic allowing just a single reading was like a bad poem, one that "means" some one thing, tedious and dull. The Antioch mosaics are usually better than that. They could provoke thoughtful interpretation—or squeals of delight. Some of the geometric mosaics, in their convoluted symmetries, their recurring forms and folds, defy words altogether, leaving a viewer to wander happily within their intricate visual landscapes.

The cool floors of mosaics afforded relief from the Mediterranean heat; that was one reason they were so popular in Antioch and throughout the region. A bigger factor was that they wowed visitors, gave patrons a chance to show off their wealth, their taste, their embrace of the storied Greek past. And the breadth of interpretation they could inspire suggests their worth, too, as spur to an evening's fine conversation, like a good book.

Like any work of art, a mosaic could also be enjoyed for its sheer artistry, embodied in every grouping of tesserae—the tens or hundreds of thousands of small square-cut tiles, in color sometimes limited to a narrow palette, yet representing so wide a range of subject matter and vision. Viewed up close, clumps of tiles could arrest the eye's attention and distort; but at any little distance they all but disappeared, revealing the goddess, the plate of food, or the crab scuttling across the sand.

Through its mosaics, a myriad of such surprising and alluring moments emerged from the great dig at Antioch; indeed, an undercurrent of *number*, an exultant too-muchness, runs through our story. The first few mosaics were something of a surprise. Then others were dug up. And they kept on coming, big, beautiful, and many, from all over the city and its hinterlands, from Daphne to Seleucia, the old working port, a few miles down the Orontes river. Their excess and opulence tallied with many an account of Antioch itself: "Fashion was the only law, pleasure the only pursuit, and the splendour of dress and furniture was the only distinction of the citizens of Antioch." So wrote Edward Gibbon, in *The History of the Decline and Fall of the Roman Empire*, of Antioch during the reign of the emperor Julian. "The arts of luxury were honoured; the serious and manly virtues were the subject of ridicule; and the contempt for female modesty and reverent age announced the universal corruption of the capital of the East." Gibbon's pronouncement might be overdrawn, but it spoke a partial truth of Antioch during the final five hundred years of its imperial life.

When the mosaics did start coming out of Antioch in 1932, many of them already had takers: First in line were the original subscribers, the institutions that had ponied up for the costly, yearslong effort; the mosaic finds had first to be apportioned among them. But which ones? And just how? In the end, some stayed in Antioch, some went to France, some to America. Then, later, other museums and arts institutions wanted some for their own collections, buying, trading, sometimes pleading for coveted specimens.

—

Newspapers of the day would style the Princeton excavations as "The Dig of the Century"—a considerable claim given Howard Carter and Lord Carnarvon's discovery of the tomb of Tutankhamen in Egypt in 1922. The story of the dig, its impact on Antioch in the minds of scholars and thinkers and on our understanding of late antique art, and on mosaics as its own distinctive way of making art, are the subjects of this book. So, too, is the subsequent fate of the mosaics, once they were unearthed—their sometimes tortured passage from the East, where they'd lain untouched for 1,500 years or more, to new lives in the cultural and art capitals of the West.

Part I, "This Big Thing," tells how the Antioch excavations came to be in the first place, the forces converging on them, the exasperating search for funding and support, all before the team from Princeton ever reached Antioch. They were bound for a place where most of them had never been and which they knew, if they knew anything, only from books, New Testament references, and scattered historical accounts.

Part II, "East," embeds the reader in the eight years of excavations. We encounter the early disappointments, the persistent ignorance about where anything was to be found in the ancient city, the thrill of the first mosaic finds, the divisions, frustrations, and resentments among the expedition's shifting staff, and the civil strife and threat of war that finally forced them out of Antioch.

Part III, "West," tells how half or more of the recovered mosaics were dispatched to museums in America and France; what they revealed about the progress of Western art and the making of the later Byzantine and medieval eras; how the mosaics were subsequently bought, sold, traded, conserved, and exhibited; what we know of how they were made, and how later generations of art historians and other museum professionals brought to the mosaics new insight and understanding.

This sort of familiar three-part scheme—roughly before, during, and after the excavations—makes for a kind of road map to *Uncovering Antioch*. But a perhaps equally useful way to navigate the book's varied territory, heedless of chapter-and-part, is to anticipate some of the recurring themes wending through it.

This book can be seen, first, as the biography of a great expedition, one conceived, lived, experienced, witnessed, and influenced by many people, their voices sounding together here, bringing to life an adventure of art and intellect. The dig recovered ancient art. It could sometimes seem like the work of science. But in the end it was a human undertaking.

In *Uncovering Antioch* we meet an interwoven skein of archaeologists and excavators from the Louvre, Princeton University, Massachusetts, Baltimore, Beirut, and all through the Near East. These ambitious, sometimes prickly men—almost no women yet—worked the dig through the 1930s and up to the onset of World War II. For the most part they were serious intellects, knowledgeable professionals. But that, as we'll see, didn't shield them from confusion, mistrust, and mistake.

We meet Morey, the dig's original mastermind; affable Sandy Campbell; the haughty young Frenchman Jean Lassus; the eccentric field excavator Clarence Fisher, bearer of secrets. They planned, they erred, they feuded, they found. Later, we see the mosaics through the probing intellect of Italian art historian Doro Levi, victim of Mussolini's racial laws, marooned in America during the war. We peer over the shoulder of the driven and innovative art historian Christine Kondoleon, determined to see the mosaics through new eyes. Together, they pilot us through the story.

Uncovering Antioch, too, is a story never entirely removed from the unholy realm of money and grasping want. The theme crops up first in the "Hard Money" chapter of Part I, which tells of early efforts to fund the expedition and so bring it into being. Here was a seductively attractive and ambitious venture that for four years didn't actually exist, and at several desperate turns looked like it never would. It needed money, a certain amount of it, and couldn't get it. The theme surfaces again in Part II, in the chapter titled "Divvying Up the Spoils"; and again in Part III, "For Sale or Trade," as the mosaics are dispatched to distant places and seemingly unlikely institutions. Museums cared for their mosaics, studied them, exhibited them. But first they had to *get* them, which often meant dealing and wheedling for them.

The Antioch mosaics are profoundly physical objects—fifty or a hundred thousand, say, pieces of stone, each the size of a fingernail, gathered and set down on a heavy concrete base; they are *things*, not just images—big, awkward, sometimes fragile, stone and glass essences-of-earth, physical facts, impossible to take for granted. Drawn up from underground only with great effort, often coming to the surface ravaged and broken, they demanded restoration and loving care, though they didn't always get them.

Many of the mosaics can be esteemed as major works of art; some, certainly, cannot. Often, they were the work of men we might not today term artists at all. To get at something of the nature and conditions of their work, whether seen as art, craft, or something else, is part of what I've tried to do in *Uncovering Antioch.* Typically, we lack first-person accounts and are often left at the thresholds of the great villas and baths in which the mosaics were conceived and laid down, at tantalizing remove, peeking in from outside. But at a few junctures, I hope, readers will gain satisfying glimpses of what lies within and come away moved to imagine more.

Today, the mosaics unearthed from Antioch take up breadths of wall and floor in the museums of Paris, Baltimore, New York, and numerous other American cities, as well as in the great halls of the new archaeological museum in Antioch, which is now part of Türkiye and known as Antakya; the 2023 earthquake seems to have spared most of them. They are almost always the big guy in the room: In their size, bulk, and weight, in the thousands of small acts of art, care, and patience embodied in their close-packed tiles, they rarely strike me as decorous or reserved. They are many and large and they cut across centuries. They offer no modest snapshot of the past, no meek insight, but together an arresting tableau of a former world.

Conceived and created in the age of the Empire, lost underground for a thousand years and more, largely forgotten, then uncovered and raised in the twentieth century, laid before us now in the twenty-first, they command our attention, just as they finally did Mr. Morey's.

PART I

This Big Thing

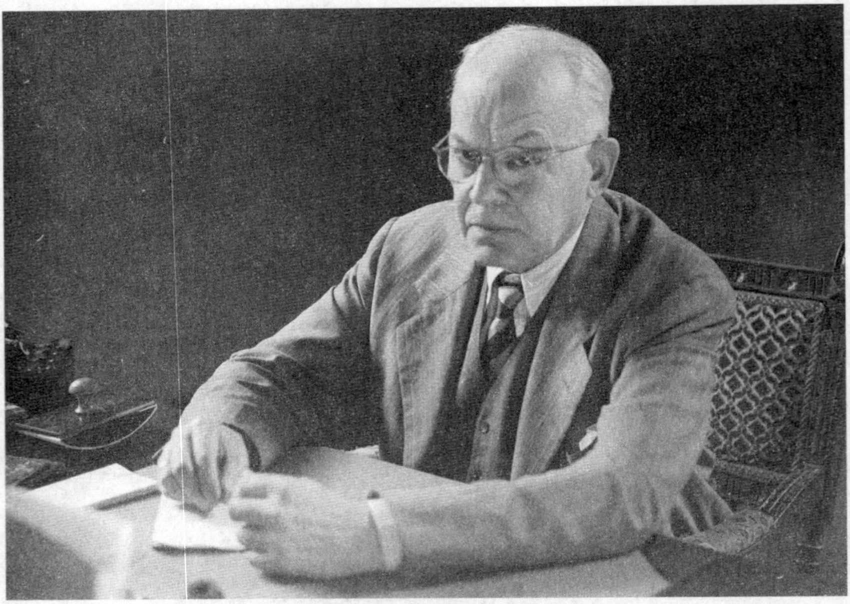

Charles Rufus Morey, the irresistible force behind the Antioch expedition.

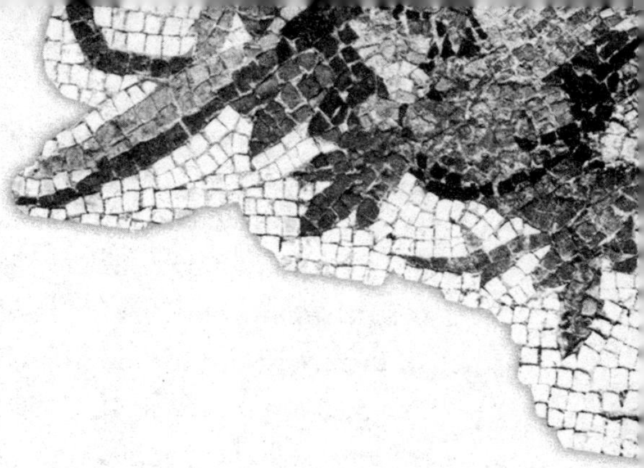

CHAPTER ONE

Mr. Morey

The invitation to excavate Antioch reflected the new realities of the postwar world. It came not from Syria, of which Antioch for centuries was a part. Nor from the new Turkish republic, just across the border, all that remained of the Ottoman Empire. In the Great War, the Ottoman Turks had joined Germany in the titanic struggle against Britain, France, and their allies; Germany lost, and so did the Ottomans. Their empire, intact for centuries, had extended along both the northern and southern shores of the Mediterranean, including Antioch, the Holy Land, and ranging east toward China. Now it was dismantled. The French and the British split the Near East between them, each enjoying a "mandate" over part of it. Britain got Iraq, Palestine, and Jordan. France got today's Lebanon and Syria, including at its northern border Antioch, abutting the new Turkish republic.

Charitably, this big-power chess play might be seen as a healthy rejection of the old prewar colonialism; after all, Britain and France were now merely temporary trustees. Syria was in French hands only for the time being. But France's writ extended to the control of archaeological digs; it could say yea or nay to any proposed excavation. Mostly it said yea. The Ottomans, through laws enacted in 1884 and 1894, had sharply restricted removal of any of their own rich archaeological heritage. France now proved far more liberal. It could do as it pleased, and what pleased it was to make Syria and Lebanon its own archaeological boomtown; a French map of Syria and Lebanon from 1936 shows them fairly littered with sites, three dozen of them, awarded to American, British, and French teams.

"It seemed opportune in 1922–1923 to open new archaeological sites in Syria," wrote Charles Virolleaud, then director of the French antiquities service. The time had come, he declared, "to organize, in conformity with the unanimous wish of the scholarly world," new expeditions "having for their goal the cities most celebrated in ancient Syria, Antioch and Palmyra." In 1924, two French archaeologists set off on an exploratory tour of Syria, returning again the following year; soon they realized that making a dent in Antioch would require resources beyond anything that France, in the wake of the costly, crippling Great War, could manage.

But America had come out of the war rich. So now, most of the way through the rollicking twenties, it was to America that France, through the overture of René Dussaud, linchpin of its archaeological ambitions in the Near East, made its appeal, reaching Professor Morey one day in December 1927.

—

Fifty years old at the time he heard from Dussaud, Morey—Mr. Morey to his students, Rufus to his friends—came out of America's upper Midwest. He was born in Hastings, Michigan, in 1877, descendant of a pioneer family. His father, a Civil War veteran, died when Rufus was nine. His mother, Addie, who lived to the age of ninety-four, worked for much of her life as a teacher and school principal. She was a charter member of the local Shakespeare Club, active in the church. And she did nothing to crimp the ambitions of her children. She had two boys besides Charles Rufus, the youngest; one became a lawyer, politician, and judge, the other a successful silent film actor.

Rufus attended high school in Charlotte, Michigan, went off to the University of Michigan, where he studied classics, graduating Phi Beta Kappa, in 1889. He earned a master's degree the following year, then won a three-year fellowship to the American School of Classical Studies in Rome;

at the time, a PhD was not the required calling card for a place in academia, and Morey never got one. He steeped himself in the Latin classics, but soon gravitated to a later epoch, the Middle Ages.

In Rome, at age twenty-three, where he apparently cut something of a romantic figure, he met Allan Marquand, by one account his "spiritual father," founder of the Art and Archaeology Department at Princeton over which Morey would later preside. Rome became profoundly part of Morey's life, the city to which he would return at the end of World War II, as cultural affairs officer at the U.S. embassy there. "Exploring the rest of Italy by train and bicycle," friend, colleague, and admirer Erwin Panofsky would write of him, "Morey experienced with his eyes a past long familiar to his mind and imagination—and realized that this past had never died." It was all around him, in the monuments, museums, galleries, and archaeological ruins of Rome and the rest of Italy.

Morey became entranced by one great overarching question: Greek and early Roman art was one thing, Christian and Byzantine art quite another. How, through what steps and under what influences, had one been transfigured into the other? He would devote his energies and intellect to this question for most of his life.

He became less the classicist of his college years than art historian, when that discipline itself was only a generation or two old. He had plenty of ideas about art, including those he hoped an Antioch expedition might resolve. He was well-read, much published. And yet his résumé little hinted at what he was to become, the steady crackling fire beneath the Antioch expedition over the next dozen years. For a dig at Antioch to happen, a scholar never happier than while left alone in his study wouldn't do. It needed a go-getting middle-American entrepreneur to gather money and resources, override objections, push the damn thing through. Morey could ruminate with exquisite focus on the finest details of medieval art. But he could push things through, too.

As an outgrowth of his early work, Morey had developed a scholarly tool on which his reputation rested as much as on any art-historical book or paper—not an insight, not a theory, not a neatly marked-off question, but a real *thing*. As one look back at early art history in the U.S. baldly put it, he "invented" it, as if it were the next light bulb or telegraph. This was the Index of Christian Art, which is still going strong at Princeton today as the Index of Medieval Art.

Since before the twentieth century, the use of photographic and other imaging technologies to record works of art had flowered; Morey transformed these early aggregations of images, this heaped-up visual data, into a powerful humanistic research tool. The Index was a way to assign to any work of art a subject, a style, and some brief, ordered way of describing it that scholars could relate to works of their own special interest. With it, any religious scene, symbol, ornament, piece of furniture, or utensil could be fruitfully compared with others like it around the world. At first the Index covered the period from 300 CE, when the first identifiably Christian art appeared, to 700 CE, and then later extended into the Renaissance. It materialized first as file cards that would ultimately fill rooms, lined with banks of drawers, on the third floor of the university's McCormick Hall; today it is largely digitized.

Cataloguing systems had been developed before, but invariably were given up for lack of funds or a flagging of will. Morey's will never flagged, from the Index's creation in 1917 and for the rest of his life. It was his own "accumulation of such data and its subsequent waste after the immediate purpose was served, that first suggested the Index," Morey wrote later. You'd track down the arcane details of a Roman sarcophagus, and nobody else could readily benefit from what you had found. No more. The Index grew, becoming useful to more and more scholars, firmly establishing its inventor in the art-historical world.

Morey, Panofsky said of him, "could not prevent the force of his personality from acting upon his surroundings, much as the force of gravity operates in the physical world." He was something like that rarity in science where a physicist, say, is both a brilliant theorist and gifted experimentalist; such an amalgam was as rare in the arts and humanities.

In the classroom Morey was not "brilliant" in ways that might leave undergraduates in awe. He did not, quite, charm. One colleague, Donald Wilber, would call him "a man of no idle talk and with no visible sense of humor; colorless, even dull in his lectures, but awe-inspiring in his learning."

He could get so caught up in his own lecture he'd forget everyone else present. Once, giving a lecture at the Morgan Library in New York, a detail in the image thrown up on the screen arrested his attention. "He meditated about it in silence," as Panofsky told the story, until a note, slipped to him discreetly, invited him to "share his thoughts with his audience."

He was a heavyset, bald, blue-eyed man who reminded some students of a much revered Renaissance cleric, Nicholas Albergati, both in looks and in his "spiritual qualities." In photos taken of Morey across the years, both before and after the Antioch excavations, mouth, lips, and set of jaw project a sternness, even belligerence, but in any case seem never much to change. On the other hand, his hands, arms, legs, and torso seem never idle. At a table with colleagues, chin in hands; or on the steps of a building in Rome, leaning forward, elbows thrust onto his knees; or one arm thrown around the chair of his wife; a cigarette between two fingers never far from his lips; or, in successive snapshots, hands first set demurely in his lap, then an instant later folded across his chest. . . . It is as if his body chafed at confinement, needed to push out into the world around him.

It is unfashionable these days to place much stock in the Great Man theory of history; the notion goes back to 1840 and a lecture by Scottish essayist Thomas Carlyle. The great road of history and progress, so goes the idea, is cut by the Napoleons, Einsteins, Picassos, and Churchills of their age. Today, we're more apt to observe that whatever they achieved owed as much to the times in which they lived, the spirit of their age, and to coincidences, chance encounters, and all the men and women, high and low, who came before them.

The 1930s excavators would themselves nod to the French expeditions to Syria of the early 1920s and to those of Marquis Charles-Jean-Melchior de Vogüé back in the 1860s and 1870s. Princeton's own Howard Crosby Butler, revered among his colleagues, had likewise led expeditions to Syria in 1899, 1904, and 1909. In 1910 the retrieval near Antioch of a mysterious "chalice," bruited about by some as the true Holy Grail, helped edge Antioch itself back into the limelight. By the 1920s and '30s, then, a major archaeological expedition there could seem almost inevitable.

Yet saying so does little to explain just how and why, and through what trouble and pains, circumstances converged on Antioch in the spring of 1932. The dig in Antioch was not just Rufus Morey's doing. But whether or not we choose to picture him among Carlyle's "great men," it is hard not to think that he made the Antioch excavation happen. His name was all over it, like an artist's signature scrawled at the bottom of a painting.

—

What did he think, Morey wrote Bayard Dodge, of Dussaud's solicitation, of the feasibility of such a venture, the expense involved, and its formidable logistical challenges? If Princeton responded to the invitation, could it count on the French as true partners, or would Princeton wind up having to deal "with the Italians or somebody else" later on? And where would the money come from? Their plans, this early on, were not well formulated, he allowed, but

> as I see the project, it would involve the appointment of an experienced excavator such as Clarence Fisher, who would have the assistance of young men with less training in field work who we could send out from the Department. The financing of the expedition would be a difficult matter, because it seems to be a particularly expensive site to excavate.

Ten days after hearing of the French interest, Morey was on the case.

It was five years, however, before the first spade dug into the ancient earth of Antioch. For much of that time it seemed it would never happen at all.

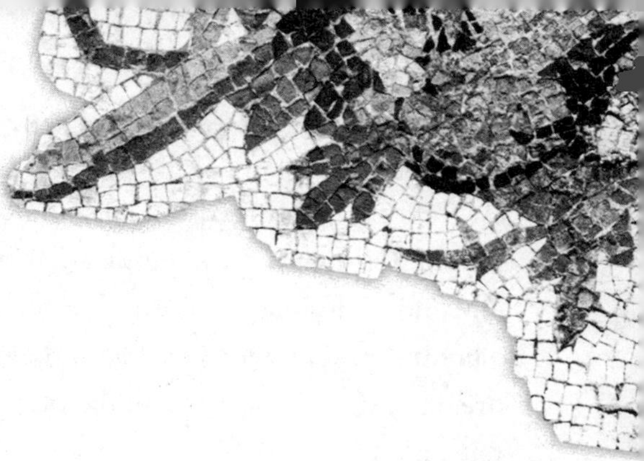

CHAPTER TWO

Hard Money

It would edge up and down a little with tweaked estimates and new economic realities, but the figure that consumed Rufus Morey during the late 1920s and early 1930s as he tried to get Antioch off the ground was $220,000. This was the amount thought necessary to sustain the excavations for five years.

The number can seem ludicrously small, a miserable pittance, the world today awash in millions and billions. Trifling even back then, maybe, for Rockefellers, lushly endowed Princeton, and the other communities of wealth to which Morey turned. Yet the number distracts us, masking the magnitude, worry, and frustration of Morey's task. A young secretary starting out in a New York office in 1931 might make $12 a week, an assistant professor at Harvard $2,000 a year. A Model A Ford could be gotten for $650. We can work backward, turn to standard tables comparing the worth of a dollar then and now, and calculate that, by the roundest of reckonings, the money Morey needed for Antioch might be worth five million today.

That helps a little. But not much, because the story we tell here, reaching back most of a century, vaults the cataclysmic economic fissure that was the stock market crash of October 1929. The ensuing worldwide economic depression, which coincided almost exactly with the years of the Antioch excavations, overturned the meaning of a dollar, a French franc, a Syrian pound. Otherwise meaningful numbers offered to satisfy a modern reader's understanding mean ever less set against the crippling economic fragility inflicted by the Depression, the uncertainty, worry, and fear. Money dried up. Its disappearance undid plans and projections, twisted lives, shattered hopes.

It is 1929, 1930, and 1931, the world spins, markets churn, men and women scramble for a share of the world's food and shelter; more than at any other time in living memory, they fail to get it. For the moment, our story lies caught up in a thicket of harsh dollars-and-cents truths from which scholarship, art, and culture might be imagined exempt, but never are.

—

A year before the Crash, on December 15, 1928, Morey wrote Horace Oakley, a wealthy, well-connected trustee of the Chicago Art Institute, the city's premier art museum, suggesting collaboration on Antioch; the idea had apparently been broached at a "little dinner party during the meeting of the Visiting Committee" at Princeton. The French, he wrote, welcomed an excavation in Antioch: "I have received word . . . that the French archaeological authorities in Syria are under fire" from the League of Nations, leaving them amenable to a more liberal "division of finds" than otherwise—that is, more willing to share the archaeological fruits of an excavation. With this hopeful prospect, might the Art Institute wish to meet with Morey's Art and Archaeology Department to discuss the possibilities?

Morey would write dozens of letters like this over the next few years, seeking affiliations, advice, promises, and money from his connections in academia, archaeological and art institutions, philanthropies, anybody he could think of. He was exploring leads, trying to make something solid of that invitation from Dussaud. His missives were rarely about art or science, always in the end about money. Most led to nothing at all.

An early draft for one such letter, which may have been a collective effort among Morey and his colleagues, reaches us through the Princeton archives full of cross-outs, hesitations, and emendations, author and recipient never indicated. Drafted late in 1929, as it plainly was, it referred to a "group of wealthy men in Chicago, who are members of the visiting committee" of the department and had expressed interest in the new venture. These "Chicago gentlemen," as the draft letter called them, thought they could raise the required sum for the first year's work—but not beyond the first year. Needed first was support for Princeton's ambitions from the French Ministry of Foreign Affairs; with that, the needed funds "could be raised in Chicago."

Later, some of this draft letter's wording made its way into a letter to Eustache de Lorey, a French archaeologist and diplomat who had recently visited Princeton. Plainly, Morey and Co. hoped he would function as their sympathetic emissary to the French. If not artfully, the draft letter flattered de Lorey, French scholarship, and all things French. Princeton, the letter insisted, sought only "scientific results," not publicity, but hoped "our French friends will agree with us that the work be carried on as 'the Howard Crosby Butler Memorial Expedition in Syria,'" in honor of the Princeton scholar. The university claimed no exclusive rights, had no wish to duplicate work undertaken by French scholars. Nor was it "interested in the acquisition of any objects of art or other finds." Or so Princeton was saying in 1929.

Six months earlier, a year and a half after first hearing from Dussaud, Morey had written a U.S. State Department official, Gardiner Howland Shaw, chief of its Near Eastern division, to suggest the State Department approach the French for a "concession," a formal grant of rights. Morey worried the French might have in mind an essentially French expedition, Americans relegated to a subsidiary role. He pitched a Princeton-led expedition, citing philanthropists and others who favored it. But, he admitted, "the money . . . has not yet been raised." Concession in hand, he was sure, the money would materialize. But just now, he didn't have it.

In December, soon after the stock market crash, Morey wrote Henry J. Patten, another Chicago philanthropist, about whether he thought the Art Institute could help finance Antioch. No, Patten replied three days later, he didn't think so. Nor did he think the Art Institute's vice president, Frank G. Logan, could contribute much on his own; he was already overextended. As for himself, he was helping Chicago's Presbyterian Theological Seminary with an expedition to Palestine and had contributed to three other expeditions. So he couldn't help, either, "except to a very moderate amount." Finally, the recent death aboard a ship bound for Naples of Horace Oakley, whom Morey had approached the year before, seemed to further wall off Chicago money from Antioch.

—

In March 1930, Morey was in Florence, at the Villa San Giorgio, just back from Paris, where he had worked out with the French the terms of the concession: Syria, under the French Mandate, would physically protect the dig, in and out of season, and claim for itself half the finds, the physical discoveries. One-quarter would go to France itself, 5 percent to Princeton, 20 percent to other American subscribers, none of whom were yet in hand; Chicago, as we've seen, had come to nothing.

From Florence, Morey wrote Fiske Kimball, a leading architectural historian and director of the Pennsylvania Museum (now the Philadelphia Museum of Art), with news of the concession and a detailed "preliminary budget" for Antioch. Each of four American contributors would sign on for $7,500 per year for five years. At the bottom of the first page, Morey made his pitch:

> Would the proposition interest the Pennsylvania Museum to the extent of one or more shares? The finds should be numerous and interesting, and perhaps 5% of them would be worth more to the Museum than any objects of Early Christian or late antique art that it tried to buy in the open market for $7500, besides being securely documented.

"Documented" meant that whatever they found would have a secure provenance, traceable to the excavation itself and not to some anonymous forger or tomb robber. If Kimball was interested he should write back as soon as possible. Once the Art Institute of Chicago was out of the picture for sure, as now seemed likely, "it would be, so far as I can see, first come first served, if any come at all." He was making similar offers, Morey advised Kimball, to four other potential funding sources.

Kimball didn't hesitate. "This letter," he wrote Morey, "is to ask you to hold the place for us as long as you can," and in any case not "give us up without a final cable"; its telegraphic urgency might be "the very thing needed to help me with our trustees." It was as if Morey were hosting a ball, its appeal uncertain, and now the local grandee was begging to be invited. Three weeks later, Kimball wrote Morey that the museum had voted a $10,000 subscription to Antioch. Yes, some of his trustees wondered about what they, the museum, would get out of the dig. But "we are proceeding with the gamble nevertheless." Morey had landed his first real commitment.

Only, he didn't know it—because just then, traveling from city to city in Europe, he'd received none of Kimball's letters.

And on June 29, when they did finally reach him, Morey couldn't revel in the good news. For by now, impossibly, out of the blue, the whole project seemed undone. Kimball had idly wondered whether he might mention the museum's pledge in its upcoming annual report. No, Morey had to say, better not:

> LETTERS JUST RECEIVED PLEASE WITHOLD ANY STATEMENT ANTIOCH LETTER FOLLOWS

His letter bore the awful, infuriating news: Some of Morey's own Princeton colleagues, three senior faculty, were holding out against the allure of Antioch: "I have not been able at this distance to convince my colleagues that [the language of the concession] does not mean that the French will run the dig."

Back in March, one of the three, Baldwin Smith, had written Morey that he was "exceedingly sorry" Morey was trying to work things out with the French. Doing so was futile. "All collaborative excavations with the French have led to misunderstanding and to unsuccessful results. Furthermore, I don't like what I hear about de Lorey," who represented the French national museums. “My own feeling would be—either Princeton or nothing.” Besides, how could they sign on to *anything* when they had no field director and no money to pay him even if they did?

To this catalogue of what Smith himself termed “disagreeable matters,” he added one more, this one verging on outright criticism of Morey:

> I would like to point out that there is even a limit to the number of things that you can keep alive. You have tremendous vitality and power, but even those powers can be strained to the breaking point, and the rest of us [in the department] cannot undertake anywhere near as much as you can put through.

Morey was pushing too far, too fast.

So he had to go back to the French, hat in hand, and request a delay. To him, a place for the French at the Antioch table seemed only natural. It was they who had most recently explored Syria, and it was their League of Nations mandate governing it. Besides, as Morey read it, American say-so over the dig was built into the concession document itself. Still, he had to write Kimball that, just then, “I do not feel very confident as to Princeton’s acceptance of the concession.”

When Morey first bought into Antioch, in the late twenties, the economy was buoyant, brimming with energy and optimism. But now, in early 1931, prospects for Antioch looked grim. The Art Institute had said no. So had New York’s Metropolitan Museum of Art, Harvard’s Fogg Museum, and the Ny Carlsberg Museum of Copenhagen. “I am sorry that there could not be a more enthusiastic view taken of the Antioch dig,” wrote another potential resource a year after the Crash, but “in these trying times” you couldn’t get money out of anyone for anything, unless it was “giving employment to the unemployed and feeding the hungry.”

Among those to whom Morey turned for help was Robert Schirmer, the thirty-one-year-old son of Gustav Schirmer, the classical music publisher, and a devoted Princeton alum, class of 1921. But he, too, had nothing good to tell Morey. He had approached Brown University’s wealthy founding family; Mr. Brown said no. George Blumenthal, a wealthy banker and trustee of the Metropolitan Museum of Art, "also turned us down. . . . He felt in these times of depression and unemployment he could only contribute to strictly charitable humanitarian causes rather than those of an educational or scientific nature."

Morey's money problems threatened the very birth of an Antioch expedition. But they challenged its integrity, too: "I don't know if the dig will ever come off and, if it does, if I shall be in charge," Morey had written Fiske Kimball a few months earlier. But if it did, and if he was, he would proceed only once the money for all five years was pledged. No one imagined getting into Antioch for a few months in the spring and coming back with the ancient metropolis all dug out; the project needed five years, ten, maybe more. Limping along from year to year, Morey felt, would distort the dig, turning it toward "objects that will excite interest and further contributions. This would mean a dig to raise money, and not one whose sole principle would be the scientific exploration of the site."

The stock market crash had delivered a few days of bold headlines, and a shock. But it did not instantly subvert the American economy. In that first year, average weekly earnings in American manufacturing, to use one measure, slipped from $27.36 a week to $25.39. But already by 1932, the equivalent figure was $18.18, unemployment 25 percent. The Depression infiltrated every recess of American and European life. Those with money in hand had better uses for it than digging up buried palaces halfway across the world.

This was no unreasonable position to take. But Morey's well-off friend in Baltimore didn't hold to it.

—

Robert Garrett was a scion of one of Baltimore's wealthiest and most prominent families; his grandfather was, back in the 1850s, the first president of the Baltimore and Ohio Railroad.

After his father died at age thirty-nine in a boating accident, Rob's mother took him and his two brothers for a tour of Europe and the Near East that extended over the next two years. This was 1889; Rob was fourteen, and he kept a journal. "We visited Egypt one winter and also Palestine

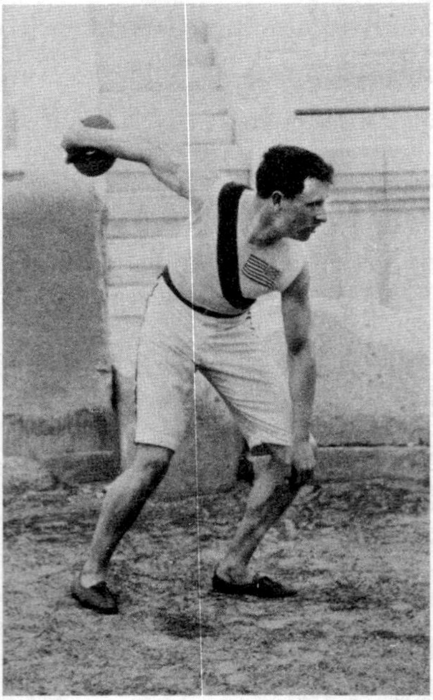

Forty years before he almost single-handedly secured the support of the Baltimore Museum of Art for the Antioch expedition, Robert Garrett had traveled through the Near East, begun collecting rare manuscripts, and won a gold medal in the 1896 Olympics.

and Syria," his most memorable experience of many being a three-week trip by horseback from Damascus to Jerusalem. They were joined by a private tutor as well as a professional guide, who spoke many languages and could quote Bible verses bearing on the historical sites they visited. "It was marvelous."

All his life Rob would retain vivid memories of how they'd camped on the shore of the Sea of Galilee, visited Nazareth. "How," he'd ask in an essay years later, "could one fail to take up some special interest as a result of such experiences."

He did not fail. He retained an active interest in the lands of the Bible, the Levant, and the larger Near East all his life. From early on, he collected rare books and manuscripts that, long before his death, he'd bestow on his alma mater, Princeton University, on Johns Hopkins University, and on other institutions. After graduating from Princeton in 1897, and over the next three years, he would join expeditions to Syria with Howard Crosby Butler, who'd graduated from Princeton five years before him and whose name Rufus Morey would use to invoke the almost mystic ties between Syrian exploration and Princeton.

Nowhere else had the architectural monuments of antiquity been preserved in such numbers, perfection, and variety as in Syria; so Cindy Kelly, then director of Evergreen House, the Italianate mansion in which Rob Garrett grew up, now a museum, told a Baltimore audience in 2001. The Butler expedition of 1899, which twenty-four-year-old Garrett helped finance, followed in the steps of the French explorer the Marquis de Vogüé, who'd ranged through this territory, then terra incognita, forty years before. Theirs was not an excavation but a survey. Butler, Garrett, and the others took down inscriptions from ancient structures, photographed some of the same buildings de Vogüé had seen, prepared maps, and, in Rob Garrett's case, kept a diary.

> It was then five o'clock in the afternoon, and we hurried down that exceedingly long stretch of road to Antioch. The moon came up in all her glory at 6:20 and we pushed steadily on, passing a few travelers, a caravan encampment with beasts and men taking their evening meal—and saw a fox scamper off into the sagebrush.

That evening, in camp, beside the tents, they enjoyed "a four-course affair good enough to delight the most particular epicure." They went to bed late, only to be woken by an early-morning storm, "the rain beating a tattoo on the fly of the tent." Garrett registered frank wonder at how each day, after full early breakfasts, they could be back on the road with their tents and pack mules, a team of fifteen or so men loading them up each morning, in twenty minutes flat.

> We form an absorbingly interesting sight for the natives of Antioch, and they seem to look upon us as a travelling circus would be looked upon by the rabble at home. They stare and turn about to look after us, and many of them actually follow us along the street. . . . The people are a very simple and ignorant lot, and the town is filthy in the extreme.

One of four scholarly reports issuing from the expedition, published only in 1914, was given over to the expedition's *Topography and Itinerary* and was written by Garrett, who could be notably clear-eyed about what he saw.

> The famous Antioch, variously known as the "Queen of the East," "Antioch the Beautiful," the "City of God," and by still other

> glorious names, was once considered the third city of the world, only less than Rome and Alexandria in size and splendor, and until the rise of Constantinople was actually the chief city of the East, but it is now a squalid town. . . . Only a few shapeless traces of its great buildings of early days are to be seen.

Now, three decades later, Garrett, a tall, upright, balding man in his early fifties, presided over the investment house of Robert Garrett & Co. He had become a power in the cultural and civic world of Baltimore. Back in 1896, he had won gold medals in the first modern Olympic Games, in the discus and shot put, financing the trip for himself and three Princeton classmates; in later life, his interest in fitness and physical activity matured into support of the Young Men's Christian Association and of public recreation broadly. In the 1920s, when the Baltimore Museum of Art was the barest wisp of an idea in the minds of a few civic leaders, he helped make it real and establish it where it stands today, in its growing, ever-morphing home beside the Johns Hopkins University campus.

Since at least 1925, Garrett and Rufus Morey, in easy assumption of their mutual interests in ancient art, had maintained a comfortable correspondence—on rare manuscripts Garrett had seen, those he planned to buy, what he might perhaps soon bestow on Princeton. On October 31, 1930, he advised Morey, "I am taking up with several Baltimore associates, in connection with the museum, the possibility of cooperating with you in the exploration of Antioch."

Just maybe, then, it would be the Baltimore museum, along with Princeton, the Louvre, and Fiske Kimball's Pennsylvania Museum, that would get Antioch going.

—

Another route to funding Antioch passed through a city still more set off from the cultural capitals of the world than Baltimore. Worcester was a small industrial city, halfway across Massachusetts from Boston, with a population of about 190,000. Its little jewel of an art museum, which went back to 1898, had a new director, twenty-eight-year-old Francis Henry

Taylor, three years out of grad school and brazenly ambitious. As assistant curator of medieval art at the Pennsylvania Museum, he'd be remembered for having managed to import, rebuild, and install a French Romanesque cloister from the eleventh century.

A former student of Morey's at Princeton, Taylor had traveled with him to Greece to study ancient ruins. He was a quarter-century younger than his sometime mentor, inevitably the junior figure. Now, in the summer of 1931, Taylor scarcely having had time to unpack and assume his new office, Morey was on him: Might he, at the helm of the Worcester Art Museum, want a piece of the Antioch dig? For 5 percent of what was sure to be a rich haul of sculpture, marble, and bronzes and a chance to participate in the archaeological resurrection of Antioch?

Taylor held back.

Morey pressed. The Antioch digs would be "the greatest archaeological proposition in existence," he wrote Taylor. "I will do anything to get this big thing started. It simply must not fall through." To help make sure it didn't, Morey invited Taylor, along with the Worcester museum's board, Baltimore's Rob Garrett, and other potential subscribers, to a weekend at Princeton in late October. They'd meet first in the Hall of Casts, a bright open space in McCormick Hall given over to white plaster replicas of ancient sculpture. T. Leslie Shear would talk about his excavations in Athens. The following noon, just before the Princeton-Michigan football game, they'd gather again in the Hall of Casts for a buffet lunch. In the evening, Morey would have them to dinner at his house on Broadmead Street, off Prospect Avenue.

"Our little Antioch dinner went off very well," Morey wrote Fiske Kimball a few days later, "and both Garrett and Francis Taylor seemed to be very enthusiastic for the project." It now seemed likely that Worcester would come aboard.

Not so fast. First, Taylor needed Morey's help with his own board of directors. At some point, he'd had to report that they'd struck "a snag on the Antioch proposition, so I prevented it from coming to a vote at the last meeting. The committee feel that the guarantee of objects is not great enough." Well, then, Morey arranged for Taylor to receive letters from senior figures in the world of art and archaeology that he could brandish to his board, attesting to the veritable "harvest of art objects" Worcester was sure to reap.

One came from Leslie Shear, veteran of Athens and Corinth: Excavations in rich cities like those and Antioch invariably turned up buildings, statues, "inscriptions of great historical interest, much pottery, quantities of lamps and terracotta figurines and great numbers of coins, glass bottles, small bronzes, ivories, etc." And beyond such routine finds, there was "the chance of coming on a great work of art, and every Greek site which has been extensively excavated has yielded one or more of such masterpieces. They existed once at Antioch," he declared, "and sooner or later the excavations will uncover them." Why, the first problem they would face would be devising means of "handling and housing . . . the great number of objects which will begin to come in just as soon as the excavations start."

On November 19, a few days after Shear's letter, Taylor wrote Morey that his museum board had come around, voting to subscribe to a share in Antioch.

On November 27, Morey wrote George Wintringer, the Princeton University comptroller, with the good news. "All we have to hear from now is Baltimore," whose pledge was not yet quite definite. "As soon as that is settled, I will let you know."

—

But that same day Morey got shocking news from Philadelphia. We know this because, obviously alive to its import, Fiske Kimball, from the Pennsylvania Museum, noted the fateful moment in the margins of another document: *Told Morey. Nov. 27, '31.* What he told him was that the museum was backing out.

Earlier that fall, Kimball had written Morey, sounding peeved at having heard little from him: "Will you let me have a line outlining the present status of the Antioch matter?" Last he'd heard was back in February. He needed to know "what financial calls we shall have to meet this year, being of course prepared to proceed on our understanding, if the work is going ahead."

Of course it was going ahead, Morey shot back, adding that Baltimore and Worcester were by now good bets. Once they were locked in they would formally organize what he proposed to call the Committee for the Excavation of Antioch.

A few days later he relayed to Kimball a letter from Bayard Dodge, through whom the original French overture had come, about a hypothetical French withdrawal from Syria that could, in principle, leave any excavation in progress to an unreliable successor. Not to worry, was how Morey read Dodge's note.

But Fiske Kimball did worry. About this and about how his museum would fare with Antioch. "You probably are not unaware," he wrote Morey, "that the general view is that the French have driven a very hard bargain with you on this point." He felt that too small a share of "the spoils" would go to America; and the chances any museum's 5 percent share might include finds of real importance "would seem to be almost insignificant." Penn was still committed, he assured Morey, but not because he had much confidence it would pay off. Could Morey go back to the French for better terms?

Morey wrote back right away, and with unaccustomed vehemence: "I don't agree with you at all, but am very glad to have the expression of your opinion." Kimball's concerns, said he, were groundless. As for being snookered by the French: "I was not aware that the general view is that the French have bested us in the bargain with regard to the division of spoils, and as a matter of fact, have been congratulated by persons familiar with excavations in the Near East"; our Mr. Morey was sounding defensive. And he didn't think a 5 percent share of the take was insignificant. Of course, "an excavation is a gamble, and you may turn out to be right. I do not think you are."

In any case, it hardly mattered now, since Penn had opted to pull out of Antioch altogether.

"The Philadelphia share for the Antioch excavation has broken down," Morey had to explain to Taylor in a letter on December 2. Ravaged by the Depression, the City of Philadelphia had cut off its appropriation to the University Museum, which now had "to close the museum one day a week, cut salaries, and let go some of its staff." Kimball's Penn Museum, in part also supported by the city, had suffered similar cutbacks. "All this I learned last Friday, and since then have been very busy endeavoring to repair the damage."

Actually, it was worse even than it first seemed. Kimball had made his museum's bid for a share of Antioch jointly with the University of Pennsylvania Museum, under its director, Horace Jayne; the two together had committed to $30,000 across five years. At first Morey thought only Kimball's museum was pulling out, the University Museum presumably good for its original pledge. But no, it was both of them.

By now, Morey sounds desperate, to the point of raising the possibility, broached previously but never with any real prospect of success, of Taylor and Worcester pitching in for a second share. In the Antioch archives at Princeton, this letter exists in two forms. In one, it ends with Morey assuring Taylor that a second share would deliver "the best pieces in the American portion" to Worcester. In an earlier draft, he first advises Taylor that news of "the Philadelphia debacle" was confidential. He had not informed Garrett. "I do not want him to begin to get worried again until this Philadelphia matter is cleared up."

Morey turned to everyone he could think of to fill the hole left by Philadelphia. "Last chance for Antioch subscriptions," Morey advised Paul Sachs of Harvard's Fogg Art Museum. "Doesn't the Fogg want to put in a couple of thousand a year with proportionate returns in find?" No, Sachs wrote back, "I have no money for this purpose in hand." And so, as one later account would put it, "Harvard missed the early train."

Morey had applied to the Rockefeller Foundation. But it, too, now turned him down. "As I indicated to you during our recent conversations, needs growing out of the present depression" had sapped their resources, Thomas Appleget, Rockefeller's vice president, wrote him. Money for archaeological digs could go only toward current excavations, not for new ones.

Morey was not ready to give up. Rockefeller wasn't funding new expeditions? Well, then, what if the Penn applied for Rockefeller support not for Antioch, but "as an aid to its [own] purchasing power and its cooperation in a scientific enterprise," of which a portion might go to Antioch? In this genially Machiavellian scenario, the emphasis would be on the museum and its needs, "without too much talking about the excavation per se."

So maybe there was a way back in. Morey wrote Robert Garrett on the last day of 1931 that there was still some "slight chance of something to be done with the University Museum's pledge."

—

For the past year, since first advising Morey of his wish to help with Antioch, Robert Garrett had pressed ahead.

Baltimore, that midsized industrial and port city on Chesapeake Bay, a bit past its prime, had only in the past few years hatched its own proper art museum. But as recently as 1929 the museum's endowment stood at just $19,000, and by now it was caught in the coils of the Depression like everyone else. Rather than fire anyone, its executive committee would decide to spread the pain: The director's salary was cut from $6,300 a year to $5,400, a curator's from $2,700 to $1,500, a guard's from $889 to $780, a telephone operator's from $780 to $520. Somehow, against the backdrop of such Depression-era belt-tightening, Garrett hoped to extract a commitment to Antioch of $6,000 a year for five years. When he approached fellow board members, he'd recall later, several "just vanished into thin air."

Garrett was buoyed by deep wells of family money, but yet deeper resources of energy and will. "I am pushing things here as hard as I can," he wrote Morey on December 1, 1931, busy cajoling the few wealthy men and women in the orbit of the museum who might care about Antioch. But what availed in the end was his promise that, if all else failed, he was prepared to surrender his own priceless personal treasure.

Back on that first trip to Europe with his mother when he was fourteen, Rob Garrett had drifted into an objets d'art shop in Rome and, seemingly on his own, if that was possible, purchased a rare fifteenth-century "book of hours," a Christian devotional volume with gorgeous painted miniatures. It was, he'd gush, "the most beautiful book I had ever fondled."

It had no binding and came with no information about its origins; he worried it had been stolen. But now, almost half a century later, it was worth a fortune; the Morgan Library in New York valued it at $25,000, perhaps half a million today. With prospects for Antioch uncertain and the museum board otherwise resistant to his pleas, Garrett offered it up as pledge and guarantee, adorned with a tincture of melodrama: His written agreement with the museum, "in regard to the use of a certain French manuscript of his as a guarantee for the Museum's share in the Antioch project," got its own safe-deposit box.

In the end, sixteen wealthy Baltimoreans chipped in to make up the first year's $6,000. Garrett himself contributed $1,000. Baltimore's pledge was redeemed.

—

The way it all turned out could seem like some smoke-and-mirrors scam: The same economic crisis that made raising funds for the expedition so difficult reduced the need for them. Withdrawal of the Philadelphia institutions cost the Antioch dig $30,000. But three conversations with three Near East experts with impeccable credentials—a Danish museum director, a Chicago philanthropist, and Bayard Dodge, as versed in the day-to-day moods of the Near East as anyone—had now convinced Morey that the dig could manage on $50,000 less.

What they all said, Morey informed George Wintringer, was that the established estimate for the wages of unskilled workers in the Near East, eighty cents a day, was way too high. It had been based on past digs around Athens. But they wouldn't be digging in Athens, they'd be digging in Syria, where thirty to fifty cents a day was more like it. Using this new figure cut the cost of the whole venture, over five years, from the long-established $220,000 to $170,000. And that was enough to make Antioch work.

Morey had included the Philadelphia museums among sources of support he'd listed for Wintringer. But now, even with their loss, the dig would have enough. The imminent confirmation of Baltimore and Worcester, coupled with a small grant Morey expected (and would receive) from the

American Council of Learned Societies, made it all but certain the excavations could begin, as earnestly hoped and long planned, in the spring of 1932.

Now, and really for the first time, the problem Morey and his friends faced was not getting numbers to come out right, but digging down into Antioch and finding treasure that might justify all the worry, trouble, and expense.

CHAPTER THREE

Excavation's Eve

Morey was no field archaeologist. No one was in Princeton's Art and Archaeology Department. They'd need an experienced hands-on field director to take charge.

James Montgomery, a sixty-three-year-old Old Testament scholar and president of the American Schools of Oriental Research based in Baghdad and Jerusalem, put in the name of Clarence Fisher, "who has longer experience in Oriental excavation than any other American." He lived in Ramallah, on the West Bank, north of Jerusalem, and had worked under Montgomery's auspices on several digs. Just then he was between jobs, and might be glad for the opportunity. Well, Morey wrote back, Fisher was the first name he'd thought of, too. Could Montgomery sound him out?

An architect by training, Fisher had no formal education in archaeology. Yet for three decades, since an early stint working on excavations at Nippur, in today's Iraq, he had led excavations around the Near East. He and George Reisner, an older man, had pioneered a new approach to excavations. Rather than dig straight down through multiple layers of a site, they'd excavate a large open area, lightly dig, uncover objects in their original settings, closely record what they found, only then go down deeper. At Giza, he'd excavated cemeteries near the Pyramids; at Memphis, a pharaoh's

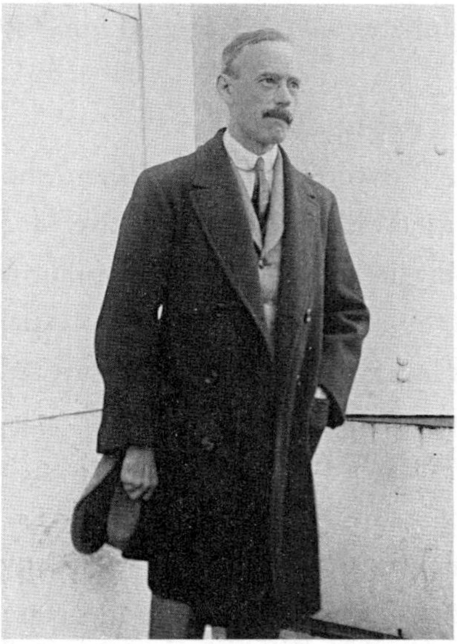

Clarence Fisher, a veteran archaeologist with much experience in Egypt and elsewhere in the Near East, served as field director for the expedition's first two seasons, inspiring strong reactions from the rest of the team.

throne room. This last caused a stir; headlines intimated that he had uncovered the site where Moses pleaded with Pharaoh to "let my people go." Fisher was on hand for the 1923 opening of Tutankhamen's tomb, into which he was personally led by Lord Carnarvon and Howard Carter, its discoverer. In 1924, he'd been appointed curator of the Egyptian section of the University of Pennsylvania Museum. But the following year, brought low by malaria and thoroughly exhausted, he'd had to resign.

So Fisher, just Rufus Morey's age, had plenty of credentials and was a good bet for the job. And yet, an air of mystery clung to him. He was, at least, a complicated figure. He provoked rumors. He was said to be difficult, prickly, paranoid, and quick to clash with colleagues. At one site, his second-in-command asked for breakfast at 6 a.m. and to hold church services each morning. We are not missionaries but archaeologists, replied Fisher; and as for him, it would be breakfast at seven. Fisher rarely published. Unlike many archaeologists, he refused speaking engagements; he suffered from a severe stutter. And he was supposed to be an incorrigible procrastinator.

Fresh concerns surfaced after Fisher, not yet formally awarded the position, had money released to him for a survey of potential dig sites. When the survey failed to materialize, his once-probable appointment seemed to derail. By October 22, 1930, when it still hadn't come in, Morey proposed an up-and-coming younger man with experience at excavations in Greece, Carl Blegen, professor of classical archaeology at the University of Cincinnati. But then, on November 18, Fisher finally supplied his report. It was brief, but thoroughly competent. Morey offered him the job. Fisher accepted.

Yet one final insinuation had to be cleared up first.

"He was a delicate and a sensitive man," it would be said of Fisher, who made "considerable sacrifices to live the kind of life he wanted to live." He was married, and was said to miss his family in America during his sojourns in the Near East. But it could be heard, too, that he formed homosexual attachments, infatuations, and that back in Egypt he extravagantly favored a certain young Greek man. Later, in Antioch, he typically shared his quarters with his longtime secretary, Adib Ishak, a Palestinian man, though what this meant, if anything, no one could say.

In late 1931, with the Princeton team set to converge on Antioch early the following year, Morey felt obliged to ask Fisher's advocate, Montgomery, about yet another rumor. He'd been told "that Fisher or his wife is involved in some affair with a Turkish officer." Mere unseemly gossip? Some little nothing blown out of all proportion? Still, Morey had to know. "I hate to make a query of this sort, about anybody, but the circumstances make it necessary."

Montgomery replied: "I think I can deny the incipient scandal. The lady is in this country and is not inclined to *affaires*."

Johns Hopkins University biblical scholar and archaeologist William F. Albright was similarly dismissive. "You may rest assured that there is no truth" to the story of the Turkish officer, he wrote Morey on October 29, "nor in any similar tale which may circulate." Fisher was "secretive by nature and . . . picks his own friends, both qualities which lead to gossip on the part of those who are excluded from his confidence or from his friendship. . . . I have never seen anything like the loyalty which he inspires in his Egyptian surveyors, assistants, and foremen." Some of them had worked under Albright, too, so he felt qualified to conclude as he had.

Fisher's selection was made all the more inevitable by what he would bring to the job—his personal corps of expert assistants. Late in the interval between when Fisher was first bruited about for the job and when he accepted it, he'd written Morey about how circumstances had forced him to "split up my own trained body of workmen and loan them to other expeditions." Still, he added, "I hope to be able to arrange for two or more of our skilled Egyptian foremen" for Antioch. "We will need these as a nucleus for future gangs of local workmen."

These men were known as *reises*. Visit a dig, look down from ground level, and you'd likely spot them from among dozens or hundreds of laborers, marked off by their proud posture, long white or black robes, and swagger sticks. Their skill in handling men, their care in overseeing their work and upholding the archaeological practices of the day, made them essential to Near East excavations. Some of the best of them were Quftis, from the otherwise poor, undistinguished town of Quft, in southern Egypt. Fisher had developed long, close relationships with a select body of them; they were "his," and figured large in his reputation.

By the end of 1931, Fisher had taken up his new position. Princeton had signed on to the French concession. Its finance committee had approved Morey's newly trimmed budget: "You are therefore now in a position to proceed with your plans," comptroller Wintringer wrote Morey on December 24.

Merry Christmas.

—

It had been four years since Morey had learned of the French interest in an Antioch expedition. Antioch had become his great project, the "big thing" on which he'd focused his prodigious energy and will. The letters, phone calls, meetings, proposals, and deals among men—and pretty much only men—at the highest reaches of the American cultural and philanthropic establishment—read like the classic old boys' club at work. They talked much of money, connections, and deals, little of hands-on art or archaeology.

This began to change in the early months of 1932, once field director Clarence Fisher assumed charge. Now the scene shifted from the hulking Gothic campus of Princeton University and the boardrooms of foundations and museums to the scraggly streets of Antioch and the dusty fields and orchards around it. There they would face the hard business of digging down beneath them in quest of archaeological treasure.

It was all set to begin in early spring, with Fisher to arrive in Antioch by January 15, two months before the main crew from Princeton was due in Beirut. "The time left us for preparation is rather short," Fisher wrote Morey from Jerusalem on December 17. But he had already fashioned a general scheme for the work, prepared lists of equipment needed, and ordered supplies, which he planned to pick up in Beirut on his way north to Antioch; certain specialized surveying equipment would come from London and New York.

Money went further these days, wrote Fisher, corroborating Morey's own assessment. The Syrians were hurting; "the expedition, therefore, will be a Godsend to them," and much appreciated by the French authorities. He planned to rent an American car for $45 a month and reckoned he could hire an experienced chauffeur-mechanic for $25 a month. He needed a specialized drafting implement known as the universal proportional divider, which could only be gotten from Keuffel & Esser, the famous slide rule maker, in New York; "it is absolutely necessary for drawing pottery, etc., and cannot be obtained here or in England." And oh, perhaps they could take out subscriptions "to a few good weeklies and monthlies" he and his colleagues might appreciate at idle moments. "I myself will have the *Saturday Evening Post* and the *Literary Digest*." Staff new to the East, Fisher recommended, should plan on wearing either riding breeches or shorts, khaki shirts, and their old clothes. "You might send out with them a large American flag and some Princeton pennants for our headquarters." Fisher noted that he normally did business through Barclays Ltd., but that revered old company had branches only in British dominions; so, he'd work through Banque de Syrie, which had branches in Antioch. His long letter bore the mark of a man of rich experience laying out not wisdom, really, but simply his own established practice, built up over the course of years.

A few days later, Morey replied to Fisher with capsule biographies of Fisher's new colleagues, some of whom would remain key figures in the excavations of Antioch through their entire course. "Elderkin, I suppose, is the only one well known to you." He meant George Wicker Elderkin, fifty-two, senior among them, director, in overall charge. A Chicagoan, graduate of Dartmouth College, he had gotten a PhD in classics from Johns Hopkins and joined the Princeton Art and Archaeology faculty in 1910, and had written a study of early religions in 1924 that proposed that the Greek Jove and the Hebrew Jehovah shared similar roots. Morey had known him for years. Elderkin was general editor of the *American Journal of Archaeology* and considered an expert in Hellenistic art. Before that, it seems, he'd had another life—as the composer of "Draw Me Nearer, Blessed Jesus," "Love One Another," and other Protestant hymns. Nominally, Elderkin was to preside over Princeton's excavations in Antioch, but had little practical experience in working archaeological digs. "With reference to the main excavation," Morey wrote Fisher, "Elderkin wishes me to state that he intends to leave that to you, with Campbell as your assistant."

William Alexander Campbell—"Sandy" to all—had enrolled in the Dartmouth College class of 1924, dropped out to work in lumber camps in the Pacific Northwest, flirted with the radical Wobbly movement, and finally returned to finish his degree. He'd earned a master's at Princeton in 1928, then a doctorate in art and archaeology. By the time the Princeton team was bound for Antioch, the thirty-one-year-old had served for two years on digs at the ancient Greek city of Corinth and was associate professor of archaeology at Wellesley College near Boston. Morey was high on him: "He was one of the best graduate students we ever had," he wrote Fisher, and was being groomed to succeed Fisher later on. "You will find Campbell an apt pupil, a mature person who is also able to handle workmen."

Then there was young Glanville Downey, a first-year grad student in classics, with several scholarly articles already to his credit. "He will be particularly interested in the Greek and Latin inscriptions and coins"—both crucial to dating finds—"but will understand that he must turn his hand to anything" asked of him. And C. K. Agle, the team's meticulous architectural draftsman, maker of maps and drawings, holder of a Princeton master's degree in architecture. Also bound for Antioch, Morey advised Fisher, would be a representative of the Musées Nationaux de France, as yet unnamed.

In the same letter, Morey noted that their budget was based on forty cents a day for unskilled labor—the men who dug, swept away dirt, carried it off, passed buckets up steps hewn into the walls of the deepening hollow belowground; that up to 250 men a day—this estimate proved low—would work on-site; that they'd probably be able to dump refuse right into the river; that he thought it best to rent rather than buy land until they better knew Antioch; that the dig's budget did not provide for living expenses, each man paying out of his own pocket, but that at the start it would probably be best to put them up in an Antioch hotel; that thanks to Bayard Dodge's "close acquaintance with M. Seyrig," the French antiquities director, himself a veteran of the French expedition to Syria of 1924 and 1925, "I feel sure that we shall have the amicable cooperation of the French throughout the dig."

Such long, fact-filled letters—maybe half a dozen of them each way by late February—were how Fisher staked out his authority on the excavations and Morey maintained overall control. On paper, at least, it made for an equable, mutually respectful arrangement. In later letters, Fisher prepared lists of books required by the dig's library—like O. M. Dalton's *Byzantine Art and Archaeology*, H. B. Walters's *History of Ancient Pottery*, and Harold Mattingly's *Coins of the Roman Empire*; they'd need a surveyor's drafting machine, a beam compass, an optical square, several Chesterton steel set squares, a range of watercolor pigments, sable brushes, and a roll of thirty-inch-wide Imperial tracing linen. "I am afraid," James Montgomery wrote Morey around this time, "that you will find Dr. Fisher rather requiring in his wants."

On January 6 of the new year, Morey wrote the High Commissariat of the French Republic in Beirut, which oversaw the Mandate, with a round of routine business: The terms of the concession required that he furnish the name of the general director of the excavation, namely Elderkin, which he now did. He had asked for permission to consign materials destined for the expedition to the care of the High Commissariat. He wanted to obtain aerial photos of Antioch and its environs. And he wished to report "that the expedition will be joined by M. Lassus from the French School at Damascus. . . . We are looking forward to making his acquaintance." In closing, Morey made some effort to express in English some of the flourishes even routine French correspondence required: "Hoping that you will accept, M. le Commissaire, the expression of my greatest good wishes for the coming year, and of my highest esteem, I am, very sincerely yours . . ."

On January 14, Morey wrote Étienne Michon, director of Greek and Roman antiquities at the Louvre, with a few samples of their new stationery. "Committee for the Excavation of Antioch and Its Vicinity," as it had been dubbed the year before, was arrayed across the top, the names of each subscribing institution just below. Off to the side, upsetting the visual balance in an oddly charming way, was a small sketch or design, the size of a postage stamp. It could seem like some generic, vaguely classical female figure, but this one was quite specific—the Tyche of Antioch. "Tyche," rhymes with psyche, was the ancient Greek goddess of good fortune. Each of the great cities of the ancient world had its own. Antioch's depicted a goddess rescuing a child from the waters of the Orontes, the river that flowed around and through it down to the shores of the Mediterranean.

Michon should accept his best wishes, Morey concluded his letter, along with his hope "that we will have a successful season under the protection of the Tyche of Antioch."

CHAPTER FOUR

Aboard *Excalibur*

On February 23, 1932, the SS *Excalibur* left New York from the American Export Lines terminal across the Hudson River in Jersey City, bound for the Near East. Home to the Princeton archaeological team for the duration of the voyage, it was set to arrive in Beirut on March 14.

Among transatlantic liners of the era, *Excalibur* is not a storied name. And seen from an ill-chosen angle, the 9,400-ton vessel, with its single smokestack, might have seemed homely. Inside, though, it was as luxurious as many a larger and more famous ship. It boasted superbly furnished staterooms, mostly with private baths. Eight neoclassical columns flanked the double-decked central court of its dining room. Its semicircular Smoke Room Bar, with its green leather-upholstered seating, was worthy of any fine men's club. Here for almost three weeks, eastward-bound the whole way, across the Atlantic to Gibraltar, then through the Mediterranean to Beirut, Elderkin, Campbell, and the others (Morey remained in Princeton) could compare notes and look ahead to the work awaiting them in Antioch.

Not only as scholars was the ancient city known to them. In the United States, twenty towns and cities, a university, and dozens of churches bore the name of Antioch. Those on the Princeton team raised in any of the

Christian denominations were likely to have encountered it in the New Testament's Acts of the Apostles, where it figures prominently; in Antioch, it records, Christians were first called Christians. The city was a cauldron of religious proselytizing. Its streets, its crowded warrens and spacious villas, its pagan temples, synagogues, and early churches served as stage set for the emergence of the new religion. As any reader of Acts could plainly see, Morey told readers of the *Princeton Alumni Weekly* on the eve of the excavations, Antioch was "more entitled to consideration as the cradle of Christianity than Jerusalem, for it was here that the new faith shook itself free from the shackles of Judaism, and was revealed by the genius of Paul as a doctrine of universal appeal."

That memorable first-century religious moment inevitably made for an ideal subject of art and popular literature. *Ben-Hur*, the spectacularly successful 1880 novel by Lew Wallace, a Union Civil War general, tells of a young Jewish prince smitten by the teachings of Jesus; it is set largely in Antioch, where its famous chariot race is enacted. Subtitled *A Tale of the Christ*, it was by some accounts the most read novel in America prior to *Gone with the Wind.* Decades before it was made into the Academy Award–winning 1959 film, the story had already become an icon of American popular culture, a version first appearing on Broadway in 1899, as a fifteen-minute short in 1907, and a full-length film in 1925.

A later novel, *Antioch Actress*, also set in Antioch, during the reign of the emperor Trajan in the first century CE, is subtitled *A Novel of Pagan against Christian.* The work of Jacob R. Perkins, the white-haired, pool-playing pastor of a Congregational church in Council Bluffs, Iowa, it tells the story of a beautiful young actress, Cynthia, a native of Antioch, who agrees to perform a savage mimicry of the local Christian community, against which she has a childhood grudge.

For both novels it was the moments of high drama from Christianity's early years that made for special interest, when the new religion was just one of many cults and sects competing for adherents among the city's Jews, Greeks, and Romans. The city's roiling vigor courses through both novels. In Reverend Perkins's, a public procession during the reign of Trajan exemplifies Antioch's seemingly infinite religious variety. There were

> the priests and priestesses of Cybele-Attis; of Atargatis-Hadad; of Isis-Osiris; there was the pontiff of Rome's masculine and military faith, Mithraism; and there was the popular Aphrodite-Apollo cult whose devotees outnumbered all the other sects put together—the most orgiastic of all the religions and the most dangerous to Caesar's soldiers. And there were the priests of lesser cults, each eager to bask in the favor of Caesar for a day. They passed us in their flowing robes, swaying rhythmically to the music of chanters, drummers, and cymbalists, a veritable tide of faiths, rival creeds in temporary fusion through the genius, power, and personality of Trajan.

Antioch's history went back to long before Trajan, long before Christ. When Alexander the Great was asked who should succeed him after his death, he is said to have replied, "the strongest." What followed were years of bloody conflict among four of his generals. One of them, Seleucus, wound up with Alexander's eastern empire, a territory reaching east from the shores of the Mediterranean, through Mesopotamia, flanking Arabia, and all the way to today's India. Seleucus named numerous towns and villages across his vast domain after his father, Antiochus; several still bear his name. Our Antioch, founded in 300 BCE, is normally called Antioch-on-the-Orontes. For most of the next three centuries it was the capital of the Seleucid Empire.

In 64 BCE, when the Roman general Pompey overthrew the last of the Seleucid kings, Antiochus XIII, Antioch was absorbed into the Roman Empire. Over the next six hundred years, it came under the dominion of a succession of Roman emperors, some of whom periodically took up residence there, as did governors of its province of Syria. Many of them showered Antioch with largesse, erecting ranges of high protective walls, theaters and baths, rebuilding after earthquakes, minting coins with their likenesses, waging war, managing plagues and recurrent eruptions of religious and civic disorder.

The emperor Constantine's conversion to Christianity in 312 CE set in motion vast changes in Antioch, as everywhere in the Mediterranean world. "In the early fourth century," Edward J. Watts has written in *The Final Pagan Generation*, it would have been "as easy to conceive of a Christian Roman Empire as it was to imagine a Roman imperial rail network." But Christian empire it became, if not all at once. Men and women brought up in the pagan world of the Greek and Roman gods confronted a new religion, the cult of Jesus, the destruction of old temples, and the building of Christian churches.

Recoiling from this revolution, the emperor Julian, great-nephew of Constantine, moved to Antioch in 361 and launched a reformation. At the imperial level, the influence of "Julian the Apostate" was short-lived, as he died a few years later, on a military campaign in Persia. But in Antioch, it remained true, the pagan gods were never simply eradicated from practice or memory. Even by the end of the fourth century, as Watts has written, Antioch "had tens of thousands of images of the gods publicly displayed, and . . . the streets regularly filled with processions and festivals honoring the traditional gods."

While the Princeton men en route to Antioch aboard the *Excalibur* possessed more than the usual interest and affinity for the city's history, none were proper historians. Downey was still a grad student. Elderkin, an art historian like Morey, was more attuned to the nuances of Hellenistic and Byzantine art than to the broad brushstrokes of Antioch history. Campbell was an archaeologist by trade, his two strong years of field experience served in Greece, not the Near East.

But even had they been more expert, they could not have boasted genuine intimacy with Antioch; few people anywhere could. The few who had traveled there faced the broad, irreconcilable gap between the magnificent city about which they'd read and the shattered remnants of it that lay before them; neither in Rome, nor in Constantinople, nor in Alexandria, was this gap so great. When French geographer Jacques Weulersse wrote of the Antioch he visited in the early 1930s, his tight focus was on *la ville actuelle*, the living city of his day. Though built along the same valley, in the shadow of the same range of low peaks, the Antioch of the 1930s had "nothing any longer in common with the mighty cities which preceded it there, from Seleucus to the Crusaders," and with which he cared not to trouble himself. The travel writer Henry Vollam Morton visited it around the same time to trace for modern readers the footsteps of St. Paul through the Near East; he too felt obliged to observe that Antioch's "beauty is no longer the splendour of temple and colonnade, and her gold is no longer that of wealth, but of sunshine lying over desolate hillsides." Old Antioch was invisible, inaccessible, all but lost.

When, in 1961, three decades after arriving in Antioch with the Princeton delegation, Glanville Downey published *A History of Antioch in Syria*, its very subtitle, *From Seleucus to the Arab Conquest*, might have foretold the irritation of some later readers: The Arab conquest dated to the seventh century CE, and with it, wrote Downey, "Antioch soon ceased to be a major city." Its history over the next 1,200 years had no place in his story. More recently, Andrea U. De Giorgi and A. Asa Ager pointed to this lapse. Their account, *Antioch: A History*, was offered as a "complete" one, giving those centuries, that tradition, their due.

But all that came later. In 1932, no single work of history could have left the Princeton team with anything like an intimate portrait of the city they were to excavate and explore. Instead, its past reached the modern mind primarily through a handful of memorable historical figures.

Best known was Libanius, orator, rhetorician, and teacher; had a newcomer to the story of Antioch heard of no one else among the Antiochenes, she'd have heard of Libanius, a native of the city, its most loyal and ardent defender. "During his teaching career," Edward J. Watts writes, "Libanius taught in his home, beside a pool in a bathhouse, alongside a temple, and in a room within Antioch's bouleuterion," or council house. He lived through most of the fourth century, hundreds of his formal "orations" coming down to us. None were more impassioned and articulate than No. 11, "The Antiochikos: In Praise of Antioch." "This I can say of my native city," he starts off, "that it is the fairest thing in the fairest land under heaven."

Antioch, he declares, has everything. "There is no lack of anything which, if present, would be an improvement. If you mention Dionysus, he revels in our midst; if Athena, the earth is luxuriant with her olives. So wine in plenty is exported to our neighbours, and a still greater quantity of olive oil is transported to all quarters in merchant ships." Even the seasons collude to bring beauty and pleasure to Antioch: "Each season remains within its own limits, and detaches for itself an equal portion of the year, and departs on the approach of its successor. . . . We alone enjoy a climate where the season, whichever it be, is pleasant, and the one to come no less so."

At one point Libanius describes a prominent feature of Antioch geography, the city's famous island, "made by the river dividing into two. . . . For most of its course, the river flows in a single channel, but here it splits, encircles the area and flows by it on either side." By 1932, this island was long gone, one of its encircling arcs filled in by sediment over the centuries, its original course uncertain. But through the eyes of Libanius we glimpse the island as it was, "encircled with an unbroken girdle of wall. From four arched vaults linked to one another in rectangular formation, as though from the navel, four pairs of colonnades extend to each part of the compass." Here, and elsewhere, his account is detailed and specific enough one half expects to know just what that first archaeological spadeful of dirt would reveal.

Libanius, as we have seen, was a pagan at a time when Christianity had become the state religion, and in this, his most famous oration, composed around 359 CE, he doesn't mention Christianity or even Antioch's recently dedicated Church of Constantine. Rather, writes one of his translators, he focuses resolutely "on the Greekness of the society and on the old religion with which that Greekness is inextricably linked." Some of his friends and pupils were Christian, Glanville would observe, and for them Libanius could feel respect, "but Christianity itself he regarded as a subversive and un-Hellenic force, and on the whole he ignored it."

One can't spend much time in Libanius's Antioch and not think of today's New York City; like a latter-day Jane Jacobs, he embraces many of a devoted urbanite's notions of the ideal city, discerning them in fourth-century Antioch. His is a city of welcomed immigrants. If you wished to know all the peoples of the world, he wrote, you could hardly do better than plant yourself in the Antioch market square and there

> scrape acquaintance with every city in the world, so numerous will be the people from all quarters with whom [you] will come into contact. . . . Foreigners love this land which they have preferred to their own, as if it were their own. . . . This immigration to our city began in the distant past and has never stopped, nor will it ever do so.

Libanius's Antioch was crowded, yes, but in that wonderful way New Yorkers, especially, honor and appreciate: "Here, the throng of pedestrians allows no empty patch to appear. . . . [A visitor might guess] that there was a festival being held outside every gate in the city, and that by some custom or another the city was pouring out to visit them."

Like New York, Antioch was ever metamorphosing. "There is always building going on in the city; some buildings are up to rooftop height, some half built, or with foundations just laid or else being excavated. Everywhere you can hear the workmen being told to hurry up. The vegetable gardens of yesterday are today built-up areas."

And while Antioch didn't have a Broadway-lit Great White Way, it was famous for its oil-fed street lighting. "We alone," he writes of his fellow Antiochenes, "have shaken ourselves free" of the tyranny of sleep. "Night here differs from day only by the kind of illumination. It is just the same in the workshops, where some busily ply their trade while others give themselves up to joyous merriment and song. Night belongs to Hephaestus and Aphrodite alike."

Libanius is so single-minded in his defense of Antioch, one is hesitant to place uncritical stock in his claims. Yet on the whole he has inspired respect and trust among historians. The same cannot be said of Ionnis Malalas, who lived in Antioch during the reigns of two sixth-century emperors, and suffers from condescension that can border on black humor. His account of Antioch—"a secular chronicle written by a pious layman," one historian called it—has been faulted for portraying some of the worst Roman emperors as benefactors and for interpreting events from the second century through the lens of the sixth. As Downey would write of him,

> The author appears to have had a poor knowledge of history, to have used his sources uncritically, and to have been credulous of material that he ought not to have accepted. He cites his sources in such a way as to give the impression that he has used them at first hand, whereas it is clear—often from the chronicler's own childish mistakes—that he has obtained his citations through intermediate sources.

Downey credits Malalas for a large and variegated inventory of sources, but sees him as "incapable of consistently judicious use of them." And when he does cite Malalas he sometimes apologizes for doing so in the next sentence or footnote.

And yet, in the end Downey does what every chronicler of Antioch had to do, if reluctantly—accept and welcome his contribution: "In spite of all these limitations, the work of Malalas remains one of the major sources for the history of Antioch."

A few weeks before the *Excalibur* sailed, Morey wrote Clarence Fisher that "the topographical indications which are coming out of the indices being prepared by Professor Kraeling and Mr. Stinespring and by Mr. Downey at Princeton, are beginning to be of sufficient importance so that I think they will determine the orientation of the main dig." "Topography" referred to where things were or were thought to be, what you'd see on the ground, raw material for any detailed map of the ancient city. And two years in the making, the topographical indices developed by the two Yale Divinity School scholars, together with Downey's separate study, promised clues to the whereabouts of Antioch's treasured monuments—buildings, baths, temples, and works of art once part of the physical fabric of the city and thus possibly still to be found there underground—ripe for the archaeological picking.

Back in the fall, before the Penn Museum withdrew from the excavations, Morey had written Fiske Kimball with an early draft of the Index: "I am sending you a copy of the results of Kraeling's work so far on the Index

Antiochenus, which he is compiling from the ecclesiastical and Arabic writers." It listed temples to Apollo, Demeter, Heracles, and Hermes; public baths going back to the emperors Julius Caesar, Diocletian, Hadrian, and Commodus; it cited arsenals, mints, villas, theaters, and libraries mentioned by the ancients; statues—of Isis of Memphis, Antiochus Epiphanes, Tiberius. Names and places fairly rolled down the page, each drawn from a reference in the literature, each a potential find. One page was given over to specific works of art, like ones celebrating the emperor Constantine or the goddess Athena; talismans against demons, bugs, and violent winds; a statue of a child; one of Amphion, a priest. In a few cases the historical sources knew or guessed at the locations of specific structures. In others the Index cited the emperors who had bestowed them on the city, thus linking them to particular periods and so, at least in principle, to their relative depth underground. There were public buildings to look for, like the Theater of Trajan, the Stoa of Rufinus, and the Hippodrome of Agrippa; sacred buildings in the city and its suburb Daphne; finally a few Christian churches, including the great Church of Constantine, thought built on Antioch's "Island" and destroyed in 587.

There it was, neatly typed, the centuries tumbling together—shards of Antioch's rich history. Morey had been reminding Kimball of the scholarly and aesthetic payoff Penn's support could yield. But Index Antiochenus did not begin as a sales tool. Rather, it was a resource to which the excavators could turn once in Antioch, a rough guide to what they might find and where they might find it. Now, three months later, aboard the *Excalibur*, it was in the hands of George Elderkin, along with other materials—pagan, Christian, Byzantine, and Arab—bearing on the ancient city.

The Princeton team included men of knowledge, intelligence, and experience. They were bent on making a fine job of it in Antioch, learning much, recovering artistic, scientific, and historical treasure. But inevitably, their work would be undercut by deep fissures in their geographical and historical knowledge. They'd reach Antioch with their Index Antiochenus safe with Elderkin. They knew their Libanius and Malalas. But altogether, it's fair to say, they arrived in the East with as much muddle and uncertainty as clarity.

Perhaps more even than they thought or could acknowledge.

PART II

East

CHAPTER FIVE

Points of Origin

Clarence Fisher, that curious and problematic figure, had been in Antioch for a month before the Princeton team even set sail. From the looks of it, he'd set right to work.

From Ramallah, the Palestinian town north of Jerusalem where he lived, the new field director of the Antioch excavations drove across the border, checking in with French authorities in Beirut. There, at the offices of the Department of Antiquities he had documents to fill out, revenue stamps to buy. The night of January 17, he arrived in Antioch by car, Adib Ishak, his Palestinian assistant, following behind in a recently purchased old truck, serviced with new piston rings, loaded up with surveying equipment, office furniture, and cameras. They headed up the spine of the Levant, more or less parallel to the coast but inland, toward Antioch. When they arrived, "it was moonlight and very cold and the streets were already deserted." On the outskirts of town, they stopped at the first hotel they could find and put in for the night.

Once in Antioch, Fisher had been advised in Beirut, he should meet the local representative of the French antiquities service, Claude Prost, which he did the next day in the office of the governor. "A most delightful fellow," Fisher pronounced him in his review of these early weeks in Antioch. Prost knew little English, but the two of them hit it right off.

Everyone seemed to hit it off with Monsieur Prost, a figure in and around Near East archaeology since the 1920s. Years back he'd converted to Islam and, during the Great War, was caught up in the Arab Revolt (enough to get a mention in Lawrence of Arabia's *Seven Pillars of Wisdom*). Linked to the French Institute of Near Eastern Archaeology, he was himself an archaeologist, though by dint of just what formal training is unclear; he did author at least one slim treatise, on ceramic surfaces in Islamic monuments. But, as would be said of him later, he "was not a *savant de cabinet*," a bookish sort eager to get back to his study, but possessed "a kind of instinctive taste, a certain charm," and seasoned archaeological instincts. He knew everybody. He spoke Arabic and Turkish. He knew Syria, knew Antioch. He had a "detailed knowledge of his province," British archaeologist Leonard Woolley would write of him in 1936 after his death in a car accident, "such as no other man possessed."

Soon Fisher was meeting with him regularly, acquainting him with Princeton's plans, sopping up his local knowledge. Prost, wrote Fisher, "has made a study of the topography of Antioch"—that is, where things from the ancient city were or might be—"and is sure of the locations of the main streets, gates and many of the principal buildings."

Or as sure as anyone else was—which, with modern Antioch having been wiped almost surgically clean of its past, wasn't much.

—

Antioch lay spread across a low plain along which flowed the river Orontes. To the east rose a line of mountains that up close could seem more daunting, more *present*, than they ever did in old pictures and maps. Upon this plain, set out on an urban grid pattern like many another Roman city, had once lived men and women in their hundreds of thousands.

In *Antioch Actress*, set in the time of the emperor Trajan, Reverend Perkins's vision of how Antioch looked to visitors was perhaps only an inspired guess, but maybe a pretty good one; Perkins was said to take seriously the research for his biblically themed novels.

We sighted the towers of Antioch two hours before sunset. There seemed to be a forest of them rising irregularly from massive walls that lifted from the south bank of the river to the foothills of a peak called Silpius. When we drew closer to the walls I caught my first glimpse of Antioch's notorious suburb, Daphne, an unwalled village in a wonderful grove of bay trees, with the Syrian Temple of Apollo at its center, like a great block of snow gleaming among the laurels and ferns.

An hour later we came to a great stone bridge that spanned the Orontes and led to the gate in the north wall. As we drove slowly across it I looked up the river and beheld the Palace rising from an oval-shaped island like an iceberg on the back of a monster turtle. The oldest part of it was as old as the first Seleucid kings, the newest as recent as the reign of Caesar Trajan.

Nothing remotely like this greeted the Princeton archaeological team when they arrived in Antioch in the early spring of 1932; gone utterly was the great metropolis of the ancient texts. Before them stood a sad little city, home to perhaps thirty-five thousand Turks and Arabs, presided over by their French masters. "Imagine London levelled to the ground, all the bricks and stones carted away, all roads obliterated, and a gipsy encampment between Tottenham Court Road and Charing Cross still calling itself 'London.'" That was how writer H. V. Morton pictured Antioch in the 1930s.

Of the other great ancient metropolises, Alexandria was still a bustling city. So was Constantinople, today's Istanbul. So, of course, was Rome. In each, the remains of spires, columns, amphitheaters, palaces, and temples could still be seen; you needed only a modest historical imagination to accompany the ancient accounts, because vestiges of the past—the Colosseum in Rome, say—stood before you. Any potential dig site was likely to push up against the pulsing life of a still-thriving city.

But the Antioch of the 1930s reflected little of its Greco-Roman past. It was a dusty Levantine town of stone walls, garlanded by Islamic minarets, a few ancient monuments up in the hills, nondescript heaps of

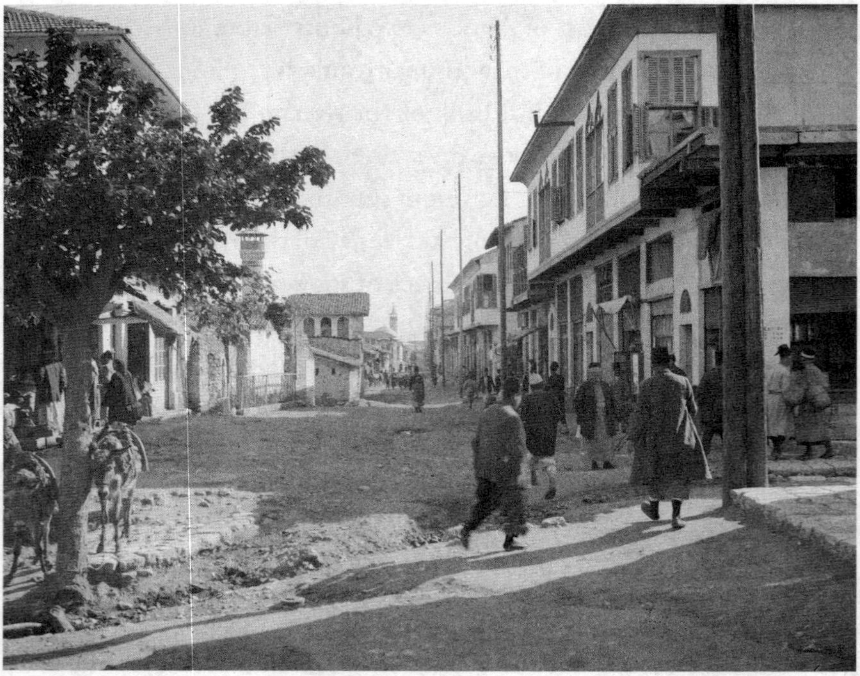

Antioch's main street, looking north, around the time the Princeton team arrived in town. At the ancient city's height, 1,500 years before, this same spot would have looked grander, bigger, busier.

rubble, coughing automobiles, unpaved streets. Electricity had reached its public buildings only a few months before the dig's start. Generally, better-off residents lived near the river or the commercial center, the poor and middle class to the east and on into the foothills. As for physical vestiges of the city's ancient splendor, virtually none remained. Two millennia of plagues, wars, sieges, and earthquakes had seen to that. Those, and thick deposits of silt.

This last, the product of waters coursing down from the adjacent hills, was a less obvious factor in the erasure of the old city, but just as significant. The heated baths of ancient Antioch, the cisterns and terra-cotta piping that served them, found early in the excavations, represented water marshaled and controlled. But peculiarities of local topography and meteorology meant that Antioch's waters often surged, flooded, destroyed. Periodic floods overwhelmed aqueducts and channels, sweeping down onto the plain the rocks, dirt, and dust of the centuries, silting up rivers and canals, burying the past.

To Antioch's east and south lay five hundred thousand square miles of Syrian desert, home to Bedouin tribesmen and their flocks, that in some places got less than an inch of rain yearly. But the desert didn't reach across the mountains to Antioch itself. If modern meteorological records don't too badly distort the record, the city's average annual rainfall came to twenty-six inches a year, about like London. But Antioch's rains came unevenly across the year—four or five months of summer drought, one or two months on either side of summer that could go either way, and a long winter often visited by torrential rains that roared down the mountains to the plain below.

Antioch sat on this low plain, the fertile agricultural country around it pushing right up to its urban fringes. But rising up beside it to the east was that line of mountains—Mt. Silpius, Mt. Staurin—not so high, really, about 1,600 feet, but steep, vitally present, from many an Antioch window seeming to loom just outside. So when the rains came, they dropped down off these mountains in great torrents, encountering little that might curb their force. The largest of them was the Parmenius—the "winter torrent," as Malalas called it—its bed formed along the line of confluence between the two mountains, the force of its flow nourished by both.

Certainly a pretty little story could be told of Antioch's climate and its waters; and Libanius told it—of the city's sweet waters, its baths and conduits and cisterns, of worthy attempts over the centuries to channel and control it. So much was true. But just as true were the winter torrents that scraped off mountainsides, burying the plain below beneath layers of rock and sediment, sometimes, later excavations revealed, thirty feet of it.

Finally, to the factors that conspired to erase physical evidence of Antioch's past must be added one more: If a temple, theater, or villa built from great stone blocks was leveled by, say, an earthquake, it might seem that its ruins, at least, would remain. But building anew often put to use old ruins. Libanius wrote: "As you dig the ground to lay foundations, everywhere you find traces of the past, and many people use the material they find instead of what they had intended to use." The many lime kilns found among the ruins testified to the efficiency with which blocks of limestone from ancient structures could be mined anew: Through fire and simple chemistry, the kilns transmuted them into mortar and cement for new construction—and so helped further efface the past.

Of course, archaeologists are used to potential discoveries lying invisible, underground. But in Antioch, more than at many ancient sites, you hardly knew where to *start* looking. It wasn't just that most of its great monuments and structures had been reduced to ruins; the ruins themselves were gone. And this was no matter of mere poetic nostalgia, for it led to the knottiest of practical, professional problems: Just where were you supposed to dig?

Imagine excavating Manhattan two thousand years from now, where surviving texts and old maps assert it had once been home to tall buildings, rail stations, tenements, museums, and concert halls, wonders of the twenty-first-century world. But then we get there and there's nothing to see. The street grid is gone. If ever there was an Empire State Building there is no evidence of it now. The very shorelines of the Hudson, Harlem, and East rivers have shifted or disappeared. We are left to start digging on a vacant, unmarked plain. We need starting points, points of origin, and we haven't got them.

"At Antioch," one of the excavators, Jean Lassus, would write, "one must remind oneself of the historical references one has read to be convinced again that a city here lies buried." Only the ancient city wall was there to prove it.

"God knows, no one really knows anything about ancient Antioch," wrote another of them, Robert Schirmer, a few weeks after his arrival. No one knew anything about "where it lay in reference to the modern town, etc. It's all guesswork."

The best map they had to go on was from Carl Ottfried Müller's 1837 study, based on ancient texts; but then again, he'd never set foot in Antioch.

Early in the dig, Clarence Fisher imagined how the dig might go: "It will take careful exploration to establish any definite point in the city plan, but when we have found one such central feature [such] as the Tetrapylon"—a structure of four ceremonial pillars used to mark the crossing of major roadways—"we can work from that in all directions and gradually establish the positions of buildings mentioned in classical and mediaeval records." That was the idea. But just now they had no tetrapylon, nor any other such point of origin.

"Our principal problem now is the selection of the best spot to commence the dig," Morey wrote the Louvre's Étienne Michon. "On this point, we have the advantage of the two years' work of Professor Kraeling and his assistant, Mr. Stinespring." Morey placed great stock in their efforts, crediting them, perhaps, a little more than was warranted. "Their opinion is that the most fruitful digging would be done to the south of the actual town, between it and the mountain with an extension to the west and east of the town."

That, as he said, was their opinion. But in early 1932, other opinions could be heard, none inspiring perfect confidence. When, on February 1, Fisher, after two weeks in Antioch, was ready to start digging on his own, Morey all but stopped him in his tracks, cabling his new field director:

> MAKE SOUNDINGS AT DISCRETION POSTPONING MAIN DIG ARRIVAL ELDERKIN WITH TOPOGRAPHICAL DATA FROM LITERARY SOURCES STOP.

Later, Morey asserted: The Kraeling indices "will determine the orientation of the main dig."

They did not.

—

Modern Antioch was a shabby little place, but some locals were well aware of its distant, vanished glory. Almost from the beginning, his Princeton colleagues not yet arrived, Fisher heard of buildings, churches, mosaics, walls, or other choice sites that might be worth assailing with a spade. Prost and the province's military governor, a Lieutenant Gondouly, advised Fisher that *sondages*, archaeological surveys, done too capriciously would be "fatal" to success: Once property owners realized what the Americans were after, land prices would soar, "and it would be difficult to either lease

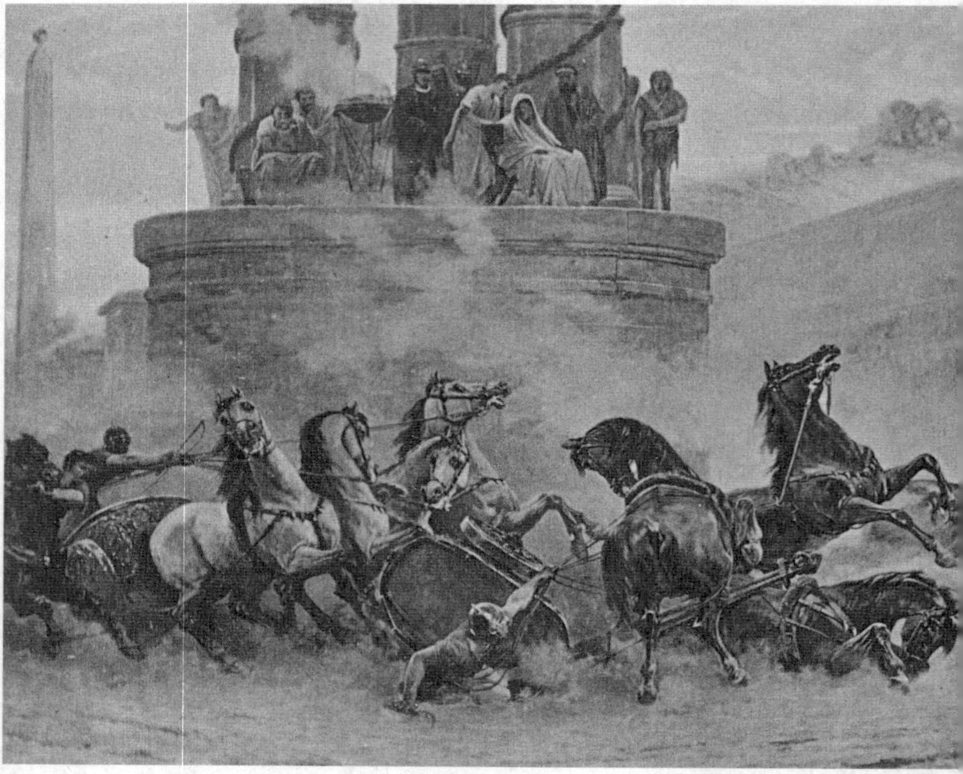

This image, from an 1881 painting, and similar scenes in the 1925 film of *Ben-Hur* based on the novel were supposed to depict the circus, racetrack, or hippodrome that Lew Wallace had in mind for his novel's great chariot scene, set in Antioch. Of course, no one knew what the hippodrome looked like. But in 1932, the expedition traced its location and dimensions well enough to estimate its capacity at about eighty thousand people.

or purchase land without resorting to government interference such as expropriation"; the French authorities could do much as they wished in Antioch, but they weren't looking for trouble. Keep your head down, Fisher was advised, settle on a favored spot, "then lease or buy it quietly through an intermediary."

One area Prost and Lieutenant Gondouly suggested to Fisher was a mile and a half north of the modern town, boasting a rare surface relic of the ancient city. Here were the bare bones of what everyone agreed was Antioch's hippodrome, a large, oblong "circus," in antiquity the site of public amusements, including chariot races.

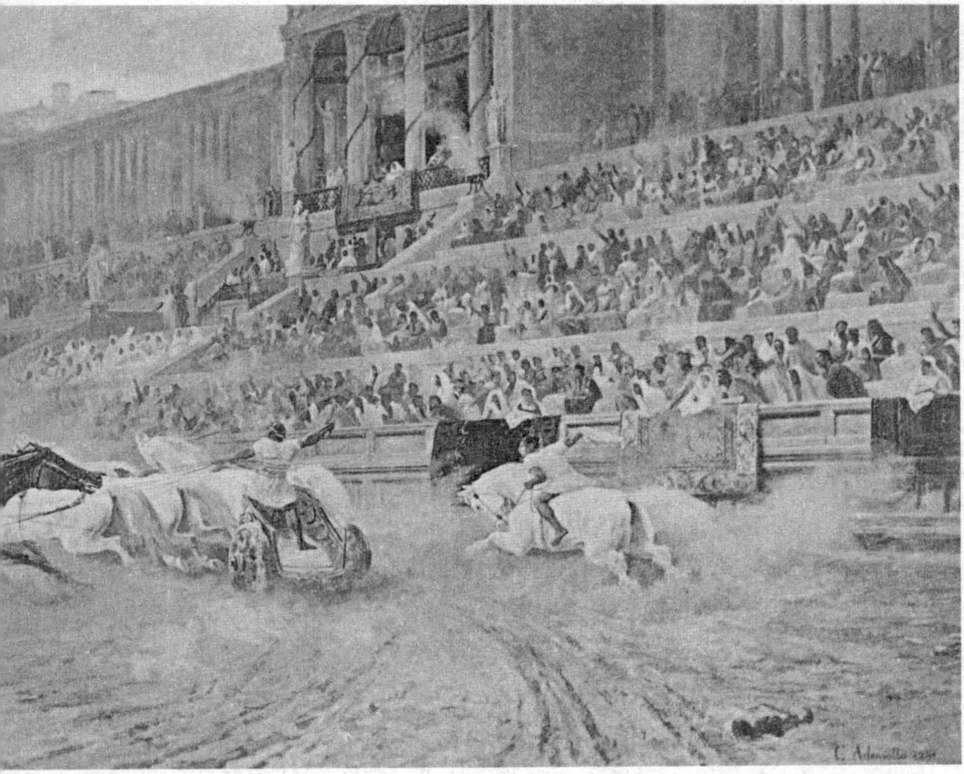

As pictured on book jackets and on the screen, *Ben-Hur*'s most iconic scene is the great chariot race between the Jewish prince Judah and his mortal enemy, Messala, their four-horse chariots whirling around the Antioch hippodrome to the cheers of thousands. The producers of the 1925 film, at one point billed as the most expensive ever made, erected a vast set in what would become downtown Los Angeles, near the intersection of Venice Boulevard and La Cienaga. Framed by banks of columns, palace cornices, and imperial eagles, Hollywood's hippodrome was modeled on the Circus Maximus in Rome; no one knew what Antioch's looked like.

But now, here, halfway around the world, stood the remains of the real thing. "Of this monumental structure," Sandy Campbell, by then Fisher's second-in-command, would comment, "are left only a number of the blocks of rubble concrete which supported the stairs leading up into the tiers of seats. The rubble concrete cores of the stairways exist only on the long east side of the Hippodrome and on the semicircular north side. Not a trace remains above ground of the great arches, galleries and tiers of seats."

As to the hippodrome's overall contours and dimensions, you could get a better idea from aerial photographs taken by the French than you could from the ground; the images revealed telltale traces of its long sides extending about five hundred meters north to south. Campbell figured it could have held eighty thousand spectators, about as many as a large football stadium today.

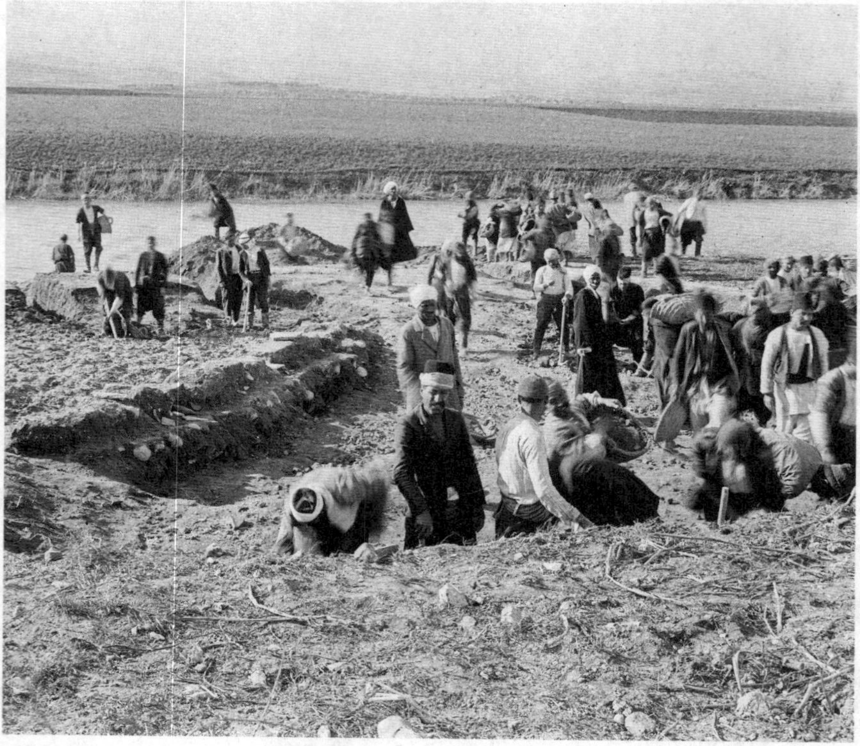

By the end of the first season, the excavators had mapped out the location of six ancient baths. All were located in or near "the Island," an area north of the city center on which the hippodrome was confirmed to exist and where a great palace was reckoned to be but never found. The first of the six, Bath A, was dug out along the banks of the Orontes, the river that flows in and through the city. (Among the men shown here may be seen two in turbans and long flowing cloaks who are probably *reises*, the specialized dig foremen Clarence Fisher brought in from Egypt.)

Those vestigial blocks of ruin visible aboveground weren't much, but they were something—fragments of real, incorruptible, physical evidence. And when, still a month before the arrival of his new Princeton colleagues, Fisher sought a site for the initial dig, his affable friend Monsieur Prost suggested one near these remains.

In his infamously late preliminary report back in November 1930, Fisher had suggested a site a little to the east, near where the road from Aleppo rolled into town, closer to the foot of Mt. Staurin. It was just an open expanse of field, but maybe ripe for spade and shovel, maybe best to begin there. But Prost championed the hippodrome site, a bit west, closer to the banks of the Orontes. And that's where the two of them met on the morning of January 19, 1932, to review the situation. There were no orchards here like those seen everywhere around Antioch, no small farms, no olive trees, just a few small hillocks that to an eager, maybe overeager, eye suggested masonry remains.

The surrounding area, Prost proposed, likely covered the ruins of the imperial palace, a potential prize of the dig often mentioned in Morey's early entreaties. Old maps and old writers, including Libanius, pictured it on an island, formed by the river Orontes flanking one side, a tributary or side channel of it the other. Nothing of this island remained—though as the Island, in uppercase, it would sometimes appear in expedition correspondence; the tributary had long since dried up or silted over. When Fisher and Prost inspected the area, they found potsherds and fragments. In the end, Fisher agreed to lease it for two years for $1,800—almost two-thirds of their total budget for land acquisition.

On February 21, Fisher joined Prost and Midhat Bey, a prominent landowner and local public official, for a more thorough reckoning of the parcel. The filled-in bed of the old river channel tracked inner fortifications ascribed to the emperor Justinian of the sixth century, Fisher concluded,

> and can be traced between a series of low hills, part of which are on our land. These hills I take to be the ruins of large towers along the palace wall, and we shall test these out early in the campaign. I feel sure that the land we have secured is a part at least of the island

and that we have a good chance of finding the whole plan of the imperial palace, a most promising opening for the dig.

I take to be . . . I feel sure . . . a good chance . . . a promising opening . . . There was science to digging in Antioch, and art, and local knowledge. And deep wells of scholarship. But as for artists and scientists alike, even the most gifted of them, it could often seem they were in the dark, with few or uncertain signposts, leaving them to guess, muddle along. So it was for Fisher and the others in the early months of the dig.

On February 29—the Princeton men were somewhere in the eastern Atlantic by now, perhaps approaching Gibraltar—Claude Prost came by to tell Fisher of, as he recorded it, "some fine mosaics which had been found in an orchard east of our area. . . . M. Prost thinks that this area is part of the finer residential district and that the floor recently found is part of a bath in a large mansion."

The "fine mosaics" to which Prost referred and "the floor recently found" were one and the same—floor mosaics. These and almost all the others found in Antioch were the floors of baths and villas, stepped on and scuffed like any other, not adornment for walls. A 1947 book by Italian art historian Doro Levi was titled *Antioch Mosaic Pavements*. He studied them as works of art. But pavements they still were. Many were too big for walls, could never be hung in a craft show or gallery. Think *room-sized*, think *wall-to-wall*.

On March 2, Fisher and Prost visited the plot of land harboring the mosaic. They found marble column bases, stone flooring, and two mosaic fragments, which the landowner had come upon while plowing his field. One sported a geometric motif with a chevron pattern executed in red, black, gray, and white tesserae, the small tiles that make up mosaics. Fisher agreed to rent the site for a test excavation, and to later lease it outright should it prove worthy. For now, they'd have to be gone by March 22; the tomatoes needed planting.

Word had gotten out: "During the day," noted Fisher, "several owners of land came in to offer their ground for excavation. . . . Owing to the hard times which prevail here this year, we can dig almost anywhere we wish by paying a comparatively small sum."

On March 3—we might reckon this the real beginning of the dig—Fisher began work "with 12 locals" to clear the road to a site near a masonry fragment that was "supposed to be a tower." By the end of the day, they'd gotten down about a meter, revealing a structure Fisher thought might be a cistern, or water tank. The next day they went deeper. They found some "water conduits," red and brown terra-cotta pipes laid end to end, one end smaller to fit the larger one of the next, the joints cemented to make them watertight. "The system is exactly like that used in modern drain tiles," Fisher observed. Someone commemorated the moment with a photo—fields in the background, hills rising behind them, a turbaned overseer in the foreground standing tall beside the new excavation, lengths of intact piping at his feet.

Cisterns and pipes might not rank as the primo finds you'd want to tout back in Princeton or Paris; it was as if, seeking a marble masterpiece, you found a cast-iron radiator from the sculptor's studio. Yet these, too, revealed the past, part of the material life of any Roman town. During that first season in Antioch, the excavators would uncover no fewer than six baths near the hippodrome (not all in use during the same epochs), varying in size and splendor, each with furnaces to heat water and deliver warm air through under-the-floor conduits known as hypocausts. "Every quarter of the city has a profusion of private baths which beggar description," Libanius boasted in the fourth century. Neighborhoods competed to host the best of them.

Fisher's days were becoming ones of thickening detail and mounting problems. On receiving their first week's pay, his workmen "grumbled a great deal at the wages," he wrote; in fact, he judged their work highly and resolved to raise their pay to as much as thirty-two piasters a day. A hundred piasters made a Syrian pound, which was worth about $1.15, making their pay close to the forty cents a day Morey had counted on.

Two months after his arrival in Antioch and thirty-seven pages into his dig diary, he wrote about the maps he'd obtained from the local authorities.

He planned to now superimpose on them a new, tighter grid of squares each representing two hundred meters on a side, "marked from west to east A, B, etc. and from north to south 1, 2, etc. Each of these is subdivided into four squares of 100 m. each," and so on.

By March 11, Fisher had eighty men, mostly Arabs, regularly reporting for work in the area near the river, home to what Fisher simply called a "large fragment of masonry," the area's only aboveground landmark. "We cannot employ a larger number until we secure more picks and hoes. When Adib goes to Beirut to meet the party he is to secure all these additional supplies."

By the "party," Fisher meant the men finally arriving from Princeton.

—

On Monday, March 14, George Elderkin and most of the rest of the Princeton contingent arrived in Beirut. There, as Elderkin wrote Morey, they "found the automobile and truck waiting for us." They went briskly through customs, the only item of the slightest interest to the inspectors being the mysterious-seeming Kraeling index, with its list of local sites and monuments. Late the next day they arrived in Antioch. "Soon after we were settled at the hotel, Dr. Fisher came in for supper and I had my first opportunity to get acquainted" with him.

In their potentially contending roles—Dr. Elderkin in overall charge, Fisher directing the dig—their relationship was perhaps never likely to end well. At first, with Elderkin and his Princeton colleague still busy settling in, Fisher seemed to take scant notice of the newcomers. His dig diary, however, does cite Elderkin's just-off-the-boat admonition that "this season must be one of richness in finds so that the subscribers at home may be kept interested." Just two weeks later, Elderkin would himself be burdened to report that so far there'd been no real finds, "rich" or otherwise.

Elderkin was not entirely at ease with the East and its ways. At one point, he wrote of how he eagerly awaited Claude Prost's return from Palestine: "I need his advice in my various negotiations with these crafty natives." At another, he described Turkish landowners with whom he dealt as "the most slippery eels in and about the Orontes." The Antiochenes all thought "we are hot after gold" and wanted their share. Even the mayor, "seeing a rusty iron nail come out of a tomb on his property, asked if it was gold." Why, the locals would sell their relatives for five piasters, Prost commiserated with him. Some of them, replied Elderkin, would be content with three.

In reports to Morey he dispatched on weekly flights to Marseilles, Elderkin told of an imbroglio with a Turkish landowner: Mr. Bereket's plot lay near a cemetery along the road to Aleppo from which he, Elderkin, hoped to excavate tombs. Prost assured him he could dig there, and soon Elderkin's body of laborers were eight feet down. But then Bereket said no, the Americans would have to pull out. A hundred Syrian pounds would buy his reconsideration. Prost suggested they offer ten; either that or simply grab the land, through state action. The Turkish community had to realize, Elderkin wrote Morey, that "we shall not argue with them over prices but that we shall resort to expropriation." The local landowners, he groused, had "no interest whatever in our mission," either for science's sake, or for that of the local economy.

Prost had begun expropriation proceedings against Bereket, Elderkin wrote back to Princeton on April 12. "Prost will make an object lesson of the affair," by seeing to it that "enemies of the old skinflint" wound up on the local committee charged with valuing his field. But then Elderkin began to hear disquieting rumors that this Bereket was a dangerous low-life, a real gangster. He was said to have done away with some who crossed him. "I hope I survive the negotiations."

In the end, West and East settled on thirty-two Syrian pounds as the price to keep digging.

—

On March 30, Fisher recorded that "Mr. Agle and Mr. Schirmer" were "taking levels"; this meant measuring the depth of a find or archaeological feature relative to a fixed datum point. C. K. Agle was the dig architect, draftsman, and mapmaker, among those who'd came over on the *Excalibur*. Schirmer, at Morey's behest, had the year before tried to round up financial support for the expedition—only to finally throw up his hands and admit defeat. Later he'd asked Morey if he might join the expedition himself, as photographer. The expedition couldn't afford its own photographer, Morey had advised Fisher; if they needed photos—which of course they would, thousands of them—they were on their own. So Schirmer's offer was too good to turn down: He was a young man of means, as Morey described him, and could pay his own way.

Schirmer had gotten a taste for archaeological fieldwork the previous summer when he'd accompanied Sandy Campbell on an excavation at Angers in France. He hadn't sailed on the *Excalibur* with the others, but instead reached Antioch on his own—by ship to Cherbourg, then Paris, Marseilles, four days on the puddle-jumping little planes of the era—all "vibration and rocking to the nth degree," he'd say of the ordeal, "penned in like a sardine, deafened by the motors, alarmed by all the alarming things planes can do—plus only about 4 hrs sleep per night." Then to Beirut, north to Aleppo, a large Syrian city in the middle of the desert, finally west toward the coast, and Antioch. Now he had arrived, ready to work, ready to look—and ready to tell his wife all he saw and thought, in dense, pages-long, cheerfully unhinged missives.

His letters to wife Mabel are those of a young lovebird—animated, sometimes charming, in their use of a kind of private baby language sometimes silly, thick with almost impenetrable thirties slang, rife with parodies and burlesques of the Near East's panoply of ethnic and religious groups. "Five or six languages" he found spoken in Aleppo, "all being jabbered (they do sound Semitic)—I mean of course like 'Sholom Aleicheim,' pure Hebrew noises—nothing Yiddish—all very guttural—full of clicking, choking gurgling sounds."

He tells of locals garbed in "absolute literal rags and tatters, filthy things worn by both sexes—such poverty and misery as you can't imagine—people and children with sores and scabs and bandages—like the worst neglected cats in Palermo.

"You see in real life every face you ever saw in a religious picture about Christ—I might admit that even I am impressed by the great dignity of these semitic faces, that is, the middle aged and old ones. They seem to have all the wisdom, suffering and pride of 5 or 6,000 years summed up in our day and age."

All this, it should be said, before even reaching Antioch on March 22, almost coincident with the rest of the party. When he did, he had nothing good to say about it. "The only decently paved street in town was barely wide enough to accommodate two cars.

> The rest of the town is a maze of little alleys which they call streets—these streets have no names—the houses have no numbers—there is not a single light of any kind in them at night. The "streets" are paved with rough, large cobbles—down the middle is an open gutter—about 3 feet wide—a rushing brook when it rains—at each side it is raised about 3 or 4 inches—but that is not a sidewalk—for the cars have to run on it to get through at all—it is simply a part of the street that is less filthy and muddy than the center.

As for those populating the wretched place, they were "about the lowest type imaginable—Arabs & plenty of Turks. . . . The town is unruly by nature—there are brawls and small riots among the natives from time to time." All this and more, asserted as statements of simple fact after three days in Antioch.

About the dig itself those three days were enough for him to form similarly vivid impressions. He appreciated immediately—or he had imbibed as much from Agle, Campbell, or others among those he called *les jeunes* of the dig—the unassailable charms of Claude Prost. Here, he averred, was "the nicest kind of a Frenchman—just dying to please, to help us in any way. Prost is smart, he has been scratching around, asking questions, finding out from the natives the old traditions, about where such and such a ruin stood 50, 100, or 200 years ago."

And yet Clarence Fisher had ignored Prost, couldn't find it in himself even to be polite! "He will not and has not since he has been here had anything to do whatsoever with Mons. Prost." This impression, of course, runs wholly counter to what Fisher's own diary entries from the previous two months plainly record—namely, that almost immediately upon arriving in Antioch, long before Schirmer's coming, Fisher had met Prost, seen his worth, made the rounds with him among the local authorities, and freely taken his advice.

In any case, Schirmer decided, "Elderkin has completely corrected that bad start—he got right in with Prost & they are great friends. Elderkin is shy and speaks vile French, but no matter. He & Prost are buddies." Of course, Elderkin could do nothing to undo "the horrible blunder Fisher made by spending all our money for land."

By Schirmer's lights, the whole expedition was, or should be, after "Greek stuff," meaning Hellenistic finds, from the Seleucid era, the 250 years or so from the city's founding after the death of Alexander to its absorption into the Empire. Any such treasures, it seemed obvious to him, would likely surface in the oldest part of Antioch, in its crowded little center of souks and administrative offices. Digging so far from there was a mistake, consigning the expedition to Roman materials that he, Schirmer, deemed worthless.

He was not alone to think that Greek and Hellenistic finds counted, whereas Roman did not. "After two weeks of excavation," Elderkin wrote Morey on March 19, "nothing but late Roman work has been brought to light." The Seleucids had founded Antioch, and it was their stamp on the early city that they coveted; the Romans were Johnny-come-latelies—or, in the words of Agatha Christie, wife of Near East archaeologist Max Mallowan, then on a dig in Mesopotamia, and from whom we'll hear more later—"hopelessly modern, children of yesterday."

Schirmer had other faults to find with Fisher. He hadn't bothered to bargain for the land, just gone along with an offer made to him. He'd blown yet more money on needless equipment and supplies—"dozens of ledgers, record books, he had thousands of cards and forms printed, the most complicated things you could imagine"; these, of course, served Fisher's tested system for recording finds. Likewise, draftsman's supplies. "He got tons of them—drawing tools so rare and little used that Agle, our architect, has never seen them in any N.Y. or university drawing room."

Not surprisingly, Schirmer's sketch of Fisher himself was severe:

> He is a short little man—gray hair—looks near 60—mustache covers his mouth—but it seems to me that his mouth is slanted to one side—probably a stroke—he has other signs of paralysis—very jerky movements—speech very indistinct and blurred—he never looks you in the eye—he never talks at the dinner table in general conversation—just will mumble things in an undertone to the man next to him—as a matter of fact, he avoids talking at all generally—he never gets together with Elderkin.

So bleak was the impression Fisher made on him that it spilled over to archaeology as a whole. The field, he wrote Mabel,

> attracted all the worst psychological misfits, all the introverts, defective personalities who happen to have good intellects & a classical education. I often wonder why it fascinates *me* so—whether there's something wrong with my makeup. I am so conscious [in Antioch] of being a healthy normal animal among a lot of suppressed *odd* birds (not Sandy, that goes without saying—he's real & human).

And abruptly, there, within the span of a single sentence, Schirmer was slip-sliding into how Sandy sorely missed his cognac. Elderkin, it seems, frowned on booze. But at least, Mr. Schirmer crowed to Mrs. Schirmer, by a "masterly exhibition of tact, diplomacy," and timing, he had at last succeeded in opening meals to wine and beer. Elderkin was softening. For their drive to Alexandretta, the next day, Elderkin had proposed to take along a flask, "to warm us up."

It seems to have occurred to Schirmer around now that his letters home might just possibly be deemed indiscreet. On March 30, he addressed a picture postcard of Antioch to Mabel.

> Keep all that dope about the blunders, quarrels, dissensions and general bumbliness *strictly confidential*. Impress on mother, sister & Gus that it must *not* get back to Princeton. . . . I fear this dig may

> end in a fiasco, a complete flop from a scholarly & every point of view & do lots of harm to Princeton's reputation. Elderkin's career is at stake and he has *lots* of enemies.

Think what you will of Schirmer's excesses, he expressed himself with energy and spirit. And, refreshingly, he was just as free to retract his opinions and overturn his biases as to assert them—and would, in the next few days, do just that.

—

By March 30, the dig was focused on a small bath by the Orontes, later known as Bath A, where they methodically dug, discovering rooms, exploring its water-supply system. A little to the south, the hippodrome, whose ruins and Prost's assurances had first attracted their archaeological gaze, now, it seemed, had a cousin: Later referred to as the new circus, or the Byzantine stadium, or Hippodrome B, it was in Fisher's diary at first simply as "a great mass of masonry." But as they dug, it emerged as a long south wall, which just kept on keeping on. Into an orchard it went, then seemed to turn back on itself the other way, at last revealing its true shape and contour—a second hippodrome, displaced a little and at right angles to the first.

Around this time, too, a fragment of masonry spotted peeking out from a clump of bushes half a kilometer east of Bath A spurred a separate exploratory dig. And even by the next day, Fisher was saying "the work at the new area is proving more interesting than any other except the long wall" they were still trying to trace. This new area seemed to include another bath complex linked to a villa. Soon, when Fisher referred to "the main dig," he meant this one, the original bath beside the Orontes becoming "the river bath."

By April 12, they had worked through the upper reaches of the "new area" to a level twelve to fifteen feet down, where they cleaned a section of floor to reveal a mosaic. It had "an elaborate floral scroll border in tiny tesserae and well blended colors," Fisher wrote. This border, in turn, framed a panel that, dirt scraped away, revealed a "nude figure seated on a stool, with a dog beside it." The top third of the mosaic had been disfigured by a later wall, built over and crushing that part of it; but the rest was intact, and of superb quality. Fisher guessed it went back to about 100 CE. "So far as I can at present judge, it is one of the finest pieces ever discovered in the East."

The mosaic showed Aphrodite, the Roman Venus, goddess of love, seated beside her mortal lover, Adonis, male beauty personified, and his dog. Adonis is about to set out on the fateful hunt in which a wild boar gores and kills him. "Boldness is dangerous," Venus, in Ovid's telling, had warned him:

> *Never provoke*
> *Quarry that nature's armed, lest your renown*
> *Should cost me dear. Not youth, not beauty, nor*
> *Charms that move Venus's heart can ever move*
> *Lions or bristly boars or eyes or minds*
> *Of savage beasts.*
> . . .
> *But his bold heart rebuffed her warning words.*

It was a pity they'd lost that one broad swath of mosaic imagery, but what remained was stunning. "I should say they used 10 or 12 shades of stones," Schirmer guessed, "giving the most delicate nuances in the flesh of the man's nude figure." The excavators had found a few mosaics earlier, but of only middling quality. Nothing like this.

The room accommodating the mosaic, about sixteen feet by twenty-four, was a dining room, a traditional Roman triclinium by the looks of it, in a house south of the hippodrome that from then on was simply called the Roman Villa. Aphrodite and Adonis was just one of its five mosaics, all contained within a stubby upside-down T that comprised about two-thirds the room's overall area.

Entering from the south, you'd face a row of three mosaics receding back from you. The large, dominant one was the Drinking Contest of Herakles and Dionysus, as it's known today. "One of the common Bacchanalian scenes," Fisher called it:

> Within the deep shadow of a cave, a female, nude to the waist, reclined on a green and purple covering. Her left arm rests on a pillow and in her right she holds up a drinking cup which she has drained and is tilting to one side. In the left hand she holds a long staff decorated with green leaves at the tip and hung with ribbons. Behind her is seated a garlanded main figure of the picture, a heavily built man with short beard.

Two much smaller mosaics, depicting traditional dancing figures, a maenad and a satyr, flanked it. The fully draped maenad on the right plays a tambourine. "The colors of her robe," Fisher records, "are a delicate yellow and deep blue, reminding one of the rich colors of Maxfield Parrish."

The rest of the room was given over to an unprepossessing sea of trapezoids—a purely geometric pattern not apt to compete with the figural mosaics. Indeed, obscured as it was by the three couches (from which "triclinium" takes its name) normally placed over it, you'd mostly never see it. From those couches at the north end of the room—now viewing the T right side up—guests could look out over two other mosaic panels, together making the "post" of the T. Both were large, almost square, and bordered by fabulous intricacies of winding grapevines set on a black ground. One of them, out in front, was the damaged Aphrodite and Adonis. Farther up the post, at the very center of the composition, was a complex figural vista, with seated and standing figures, five of them, traces of greenery, various pikes, staffs, and spears, which the excavators couldn't right away identify.

In his late preliminary report from 1930, Fisher had explained how, when happening on an important find still in the ground, his practice was to take on much of its cleaning himself: The regular laborers would be reassigned other tasks, while that of cleaning the new treasure became his own job and that of a few dependable colleagues. Clarence Fisher was a man of habits, systems, methods. He had his ways, his "best practices," refined over the years. And now in April 1932, a dozen feet of earth and rock cut through to reach the mosaics, still partially encrusted in dirt, the job was handed over, wrote Fisher, to "the members of the expedition." With small knives and brushes they scraped and whisked away the dirt of the centuries, "disclosing the tesserae below."

The next day, he and Sandy Campbell were working on one of the panels, the central one, the one with the five seated and standing figures, the pikes, staffs, and spears, when, to Campbell's eye, the image before them rose up out of the dirt and dust, the darkness of the ages, and revealed itself: The mosaic before them, Campbell suggested to Fisher, depicted the Judgment of Paris.

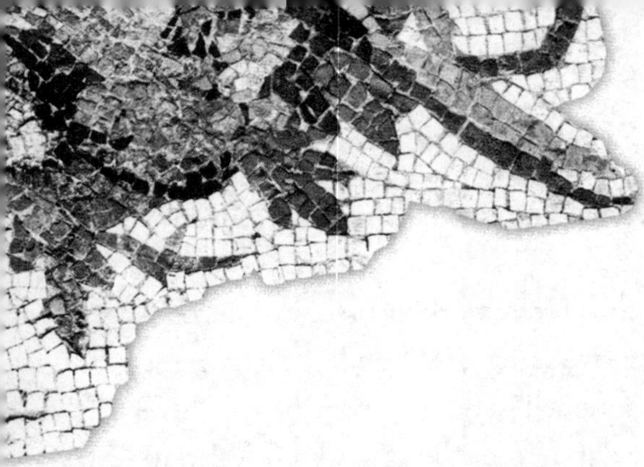

CHAPTER SIX

The Judgment of Paris

It is one of the most famous myths of antiquity, going back to the Greeks, intimately linked to the *Iliad* itself: A young prince, Paris, son of King Priam of Troy, is asked to judge which of three goddesses is most beautiful. Hera, wife of Zeus? Athena, goddess of wisdom? Or Aphrodite, goddess of love? Into their presence Paris is led by Hermes, Zeus's messenger. All three try to win him over with promises, respectively, of eternal greatness, military valor, or the love of the world's most beautiful woman. Paris chooses Aphrodite, who bestows on him Helen, a Spartan woman. But Helen belongs to another, the Greek warrior Menelaus. Determined to return her to her rightful husband, the Greeks, under Menelaus's brother, Agamemnon, lay siege to Troy. We know the rest—the surrender of Briseis, the rage of Achilles, the death of Patroclus, the embassy of Priam, and the myriad other scenes and stories bestowed on Western civilization by the *Iliad*.

This beauty contest of goddesses and Paris's fateful choice is among the most iconic scenes in the whole mythic history of the West. And long before discovery of our mosaic in the ruins of the Roman Villa, later "Atrium House," it had appeared elsewhere, everywhere, for millennia—in sixth-century BCE vase paintings, a fresco from the House of Jupiter in Pompeii, paintings by Rubens and Botticelli, and later in novels and operas.

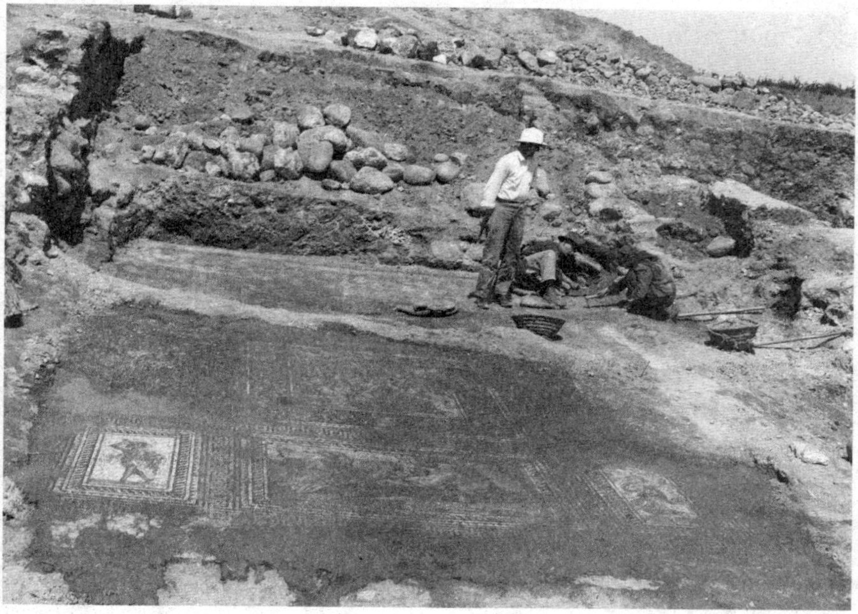

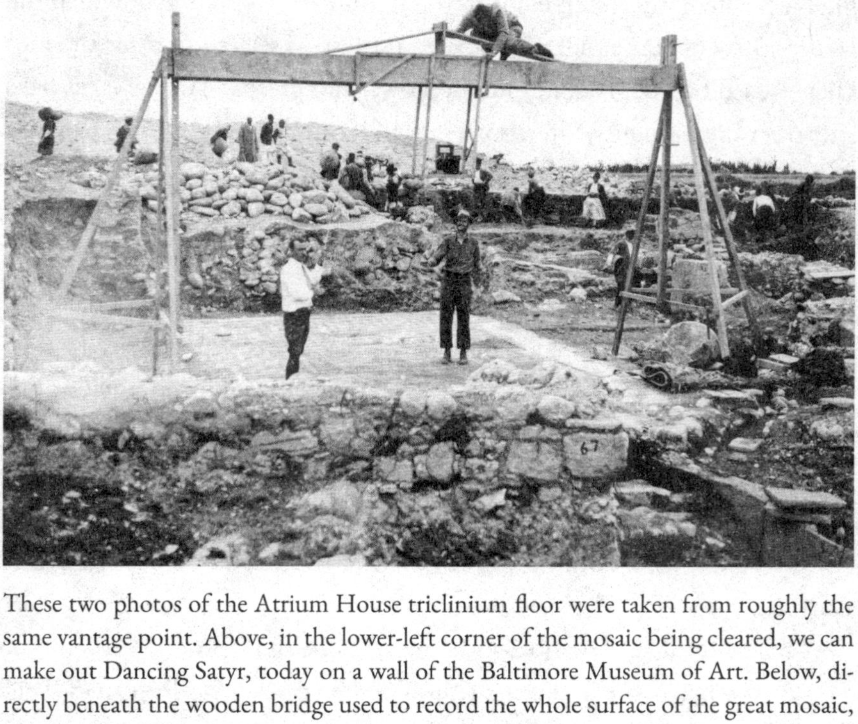

These two photos of the Atrium House triclinium floor were taken from roughly the same vantage point. Above, in the lower-left corner of the mosaic being cleared, we can make out Dancing Satyr, today on a wall of the Baltimore Museum of Art. Below, directly beneath the wooden bridge used to record the whole surface of the great mosaic, are photographer Robert Schirmer and, in white shirt, architect C. K. Agle.

Here, though, in this work of no artist known by name, it was not flaking wall paint or fading ink that told its story, but a hundred thousand or so discrete tiles of stone and colored glass, cut, selected, fitted, and laid down one by one.

By any standard, the mosaic was superbly executed. To depict in mosaics the sweep and play of soft garments and, especially, human faces demanded detail—exceedingly small tesserae set down at high density. The geometric border areas of the Atrium House mosaics were rendered at about two hundred tiles per square decimeter, a "standard" area about that of a cell phone screen. But the faces of the five human figures in the Judgment sometimes got five hundred or more. Mere arithmetic, and thus no fit measure of artistic excellence? Certainly, high tile density was not enough, yet was necessary to depict elusive color and contour, so the viewer could feel the image's movement. "The modelling of the bodies and drapery is wonderfully done," wrote Fisher, "the tiny tesserae being placed to emphasize the contours and shadows," the flesh tints "admirable and lifelike." There was much color to the Atrium House mosaics, which the color palette of stone tiles was hardly up to; so at select locations the mosaicists used bits of glass, in blues, yellows, and greens. "All the faces have a distinct individuality," he wrote, "and Hermes especially has a naughty twinkle in his eye."

—

In the Atrium House mosaics, the Princeton team had made a crucial find. And not just in archaeological or art-historical terms, but practically: The early weeks of the first season had left the French uncertain about continuing their support; but an understanding that the Judgment of Paris would go to the Louvre changed all that. "What valuation do the experts give for it?" Jean David-Weill, a curator and collector high in the French art world, asked a colleague, according to Jean Lassus, the French representative at Antioch.

"Four hundred fifty thousand francs," came the reply.

"And what is the amount of the French contribution?" David-Weill asked next, turning to the director of the Louvre.

"Two hundred fifty thousand francs."

Well, then, he pronounced, "The excavation of Antioch will continue."

Like first word of a gold strike, recovery of the Judgment of Paris and the other Atrium House mosaics hinted at untold riches to come. They were not just works of art, the mosaics, but assets, articles of currency. They assuaged French doubt and pride. They raised the Princeton excavations in the eyes of the world and in those of the excavators themselves. On April 27, Morey wrote Elderkin, "We are all very excited."

—

Excited, that is, about "the mosaic with five panels and twelve figures." But what—precisely, please—was the mosaic they'd found? Were all its individual panels and neighboring geometric borders properly viewed, studied, appreciated, and understood as elements of a single composition? Were they a single work of art? Or were they five distinct mosaics that, without a backward glance, could be split off from one another? "I hope," Morey wrote Elderkin of the mosaic as a whole, "that this will prove something that can be removed, and possibly divided for the benefit of the subscribing museums." Yet there was something troubling about the idea: "I have to rely on your judgment and tact in presenting this idea to M. Seyrig," the French antiquities director in Syria.

Back in Antioch, the potential delicacy of the issue was not lost on Elderkin. Writing to Morey on May 12, he reported that Henri Seyrig had dropped by a few days before and pronounced the mosaic, in Elderkin's words, "the best so far discovered in Syria. Yesterday, the French high commissioner came with a veritable retinue to see it." Schirmer and Agle were just then busy photographing it, all of it, section by section, from an overhead wooden bridge of Agle's design. At night it was guarded by workmen.

Elderkin had said nothing to Seyrig or Prost about breaking it up. "I did entertain secretly the hope" that it could be, he confessed to Morey, "but it would do violence to a work of art because three of the mosaics form what might be called a Bacchic trilogy"; its broader effect would be lost. Then, too, its division "would nullify the border pattern of the whole mosaic." Seyrig, he suspected, had "never entertained the idea that the mosaic would leave Syria," figuring it bound, rather, for a new archaeological museum in Antioch. Seyrig might wish to keep the subscribing museums happy, but Elderkin doubted whether he could bring himself to cut up the mosaic.

He later reported to Morey on his conversation with Prost, who "very definitely informed me that all objects awarded Syria in the distribution [to come] would be the property of the Sandjak of Alexandretta," the province comprising Antioch, "and would remain here. So that settles the matter," which of course it didn't.

A week later, the Atrium House mosaic began to be cut up into sections, ten of them. In the end, four American museums and the Louvre came away with pieces of it. What had once made for a single spectacular impression on any who stood within its aesthetic force field would now be seen as individual works of art, visitors to the museums exhibiting them perhaps not even aware of their original context.

The Louvre's representative, Jean Lassus, not yet twenty-nine, didn't much like what happened to the mosaic, but mostly kept his mouth shut. "Have we the right to split up a pavement, [just] because it is composed of independent panels each within its own frame?" he'd ask in an essay written many years later. In the end, "the mosaic loses its unity." True, the original composition might remain known, thanks to color drawings and photographs. Still, "I have always, for my part, suffered—silently—from these divisions, which seemed to me mutilations."

—

On April 16, Robert Schirmer began another long letter to his wife, one he'd work on intermittently over the next few days. Maybe he was lonely. Maybe he simply had too much to say and needed an ear. Maybe he was a little full of himself. But when he was finally ready to ship off this one missive, it would consume, as later transcribed, eleven typewritten pages of dense single-spaced text. "It will cost a fortune in airmail stamps," he wrote.

A month on-site, and Schirmer still indulged his many headlong judgments and opinions. If it came to it, "I could run the dig there," he told Mabel. "Well, as a matter of fact, I could. Of course, I still have my overwhelming enthusiasm and self-confidence, but *sérieusement*, I think I could run any of the digs around here. That is, at least as well if not much better" than it currently was.

Just the previous summer he'd been initiated into archaeological work by Sandy Campbell, whom he, like pretty much everyone else, admired. But here in Antioch, he complained, things were done in such a "haphazard, trust-to-luck manner." According to him, Sandy had been advised they didn't need careful stratigraphic records: "Just dig and hope to hell you find something and as for the rest of it write a lot of hypothetical bullshit and get your architect to draw it up with plenty of imagination." As for himself, "I am itching to get my hands on something small, concrete, and tangible like a tomb or chapel and see it done right. I would make my observations privately and show them to Sandy because E[lderkin] and Prof F[isher] don't seem to care."

Elderkin had by now slipped in his estimation. Maybe he was a fine "book scholar," Schirmer felt, but he lacked practical field experience. "His ebullient temperament is unsuited to running a big expedition. . . . I only feel sorry for the man. He's up on the crest of the wave, with the wildest schemes and hopes—then the bubble is pierced and he's a flat tire." First, and for weeks, "it was tombs, tombs, Greek tombs. E somehow hoped to find perfect ones, untouched, right at the surface—just by digging anywhere (a crazy idea), now it's mosaics. For we have found a *gorgeous* mosaic—the first and only work of art and real value so far."

Like everyone else, Schirmer was enchanted by the Atrium House mosaic. It, or part of it, would soon be bound for Paris. But how, he wondered out loud to Mabel, would they get it there? How take it up in the first place? He outlined the steps for her. First, you'd construct a wooden bridge to straddle the mosaic, still lying in the ground, and photographically record its entire face, section by section; this they were already doing. Then you'd affix layers of cloth, glue, and plaster of Paris to the front side of the mosaic and let it thoroughly dry, making for a thick, rigid, protective cake. At this point, you cut the mosaic into manageable pieces, maybe five feet on a side. Only then could you go back and slice each piece off its original

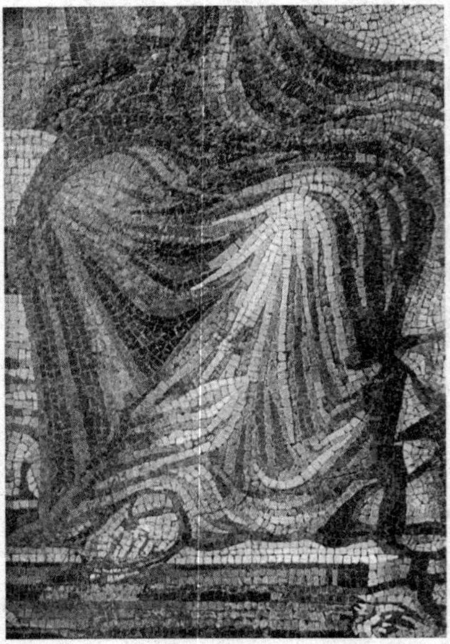

Simple stone tiles, in the hands of a master mosaicist, convey the fine drapery and sweep of the goddess Aphrodite's dress.

base, lift it by crane, and drop it into a prepared wooden frame full of wet concrete ready to receive it. Later, with boiling water, you'd remove the paper and cloth covering, leaving the mosaic ready to wash, scrub, store, and later ship.

"It is easily worth $10,000," Schirmer guessed, probably referring only to Aphrodite and Adonis, not the whole room of Atrium House panels. They'd need two more such finds, of course, for the French, Baltimore, and Worcester museums. "If so they would have been more than repaid for their [first] year's gifts even if we don't find any other works of art. So you can see why E has now raised the cry of mosaics! Lots of mosaics!! You know it's just blind luck that we got this one and you can't expect to guess where other good ones will be."

—

By the time of his next letter home, on April 27, perhaps infected by the goodwill billowing up from the mosaic finds, Schirmer had changed his tune about much he'd seen earlier, his judgments more measured and reflective:

> The business of living intimately with other strange people isn't easy. Out here, it's like being married to 5 new people. We are so much together—24 hours a day—personalities are bound to scratch, rub up, irritate. Good old Sandy and I get on swell, but even we have little flare-ups—absolutely of no importance—but with the others there are frictions at times—usually about the

> work—there is an undercurrent of grumbling, fussing, finding fault and criticizing.

And yet, "for a group of 6 people living an unnatural, uncomfortable, strained life, we get on very well out here—all 6 are really good and very nice at heart. *Les jeunes* are swell and we have lots of fun, laughter and good times."

And now Schirmer was no longer so critical of Fisher. He still saw him as "inclined to be theoretic, doctrinaire, arbitrary, i.e. adopt a priori reasoning and force all the facts to fit it." But what he wrote next to Mabel must seem his most astonishing about-face of all:

> And Doc Fisher turned out to be the grandest old guy—a real sense of humor. . . . We've had to change our opinion about his technique of archaeology, too. It isn't wrong as we thought! It's merely different from what they use in Greece [where Schirmer had worked with Campbell] because conditions out here are different.

Fisher, he reported, "is very, very fond of me. Sandy tells me. And I like him, too—he's been 'growing on me' ever since a week or so after I arrived." One day they drove to Aleppo to buy photographic supplies. "We talked about everything under the sun and came back 'buddies.' His stammering is terrible, and he is very sensitive, but those are not things against him." It astonished Schirmer "how every one of us has completely changed around about Doc and see what a brilliant archaeologist he is & at the same time what a fine, loveable personality he is."

Everyone, that is, save Elderkin. Their enmity, ever threatening to erupt, had "been suppressed—it's like a volcano—if it ever lets go there will be a terrible explosion and several will leave."

In his time in Antioch, Schirmer had taken 250 photos, he wrote Mabel on May 8, plus some motion pictures, and as part of the expedition he'd

> done every imaginable kind of work: helped with the surveying, relieved E and others in taking charge of trenches for a morning or afternoon, helped catalogue, worked cleaning coins, helped in

> French interpreting, frequently driven one of the cars . . . , dug delicate objects of trenches in important spots—God knows what all—from 7 am breakfast till 10 or 11 pm bed.

For all his voiced frustrations and showboating, he'd contributed much and come away with much.

—

By mid-May, almost ninety typed pages into Fisher's diary, the dig had spilled out over three distinct sites, employing 420 local men. "About sixty men under *reis* Ali, who was transferred from the dig at the Atrium House for this purpose, were started in at the old Bath A area," Fisher recorded.

At Bath C, the head *reis* had two hundred men under him. "Far too many for the best results," he thought. "We should have more *reises*, and these must be from outside, as the locals will not and do not obey men whom they have known all their lives as one of themselves. We have tried this, to help in keeping the line of basket men moving, and not a single local has handled the gangs successfully."

Fisher went on, piling detail on detail. A mosaic floor he judged to be from about 450–500 CE disappointed him. "The colors are very soft but the laying out of the detail is not well done." An old repair with marble fragments had been "very carelessly put in."

A large bronze bowl with fluted sides and wide scalloped rim was found in Atrium House.

Meanwhile, with one of the team, Glanville Downey, busy in Daphne, "we had to engage a local young man, named Reynolds, to clean coins and keep this part of the work up to date."

So it was, as the dig neared the end of its first season, three months or so in, that any broad patterns or principles that might be gleaned from the mosaics lay obscured in muddles of dirt, dust, mud, men, and machine. Most everyone from Princeton by now looked forward to going home.

Earlier that month, Schirmer imagined his wife, hurtling toward him from America to their reunion in Paris on the speedy *Île de France*, "all excited, eekish and disorganized!" He'd had enough of the dig. He was "so fed up with the gadge bumbly business—not bored—but disgusted with the inefficiency and with all the conflicts of authority, petty pride, criticism—just general dissatisfaction." The rift between Elderkin and Fisher persisted. No yelling and screaming, exactly, "but under it all . . . the most violent disagreements, pulling in opposite directions, etc. . . . Doc Fisher has been on the point of quitting several times." Or so he'd learned from Campbell, who, in Schirmer's telling, wanted out himself, but couldn't leave; he needed his paycheck.

"All five of us unanimously swear never to come again if E does. . . . What a god-damned horse's ass of a fool, namby pamby, scatterbrained prudish hypocritical *obstinate* tactless, ignorant son of a bitch Elderkin is."

A little later, Elderkin advised Claude Prost that the physical fruit of the first year's campaign was not ready (or else too thin) to be divided up just yet. Most of it was in storage in Antioch, a few finds of exceptional value consigned to the basement of the Banque de Syrie; among these were the mosaics from Atrium House, distributed among ten crates.

Elderkin began his "First General Report on the Excavations at Antioch on the Orontes" this way:

> It is a singular and lamentable fact that thirteen weeks of excavation at Antioch brought to light very little sculpture and very few inscriptions. That in ancient times there was such deficiency is unbelievable. The later authors cite many works of sculpture. The disappearance of plastic [sculpted] and epigraphical monuments is to be explained in part by the limekiln which did its work so thoroughly in the excavated area that pieces of marble of large size rarely turned up. . . . So far at Antioch no statue or relief in marble has been found completely preserved or half preserved in our excavations. Even the fragments that survive can be counted for each category on the fingers of one hand.

For sculpture as for inscriptions, the finds were "few, fragmentary, and late," by which he presumably meant late Roman.

One didn't have to read deeply into Elderkin's report to see the first year's dig as unsettlingly close to a failure. They'd gathered some three thousand coins and almost eight hundred other objects, fragments, pots, chunks of shattered sculpture, hands and feet broken off. But little that much mattered—little of great beauty, of historical significance, of special interest to museums, of happy mystery or surprise. Elderkin's account of a trial dig he had himself begun behind the French army barracks was dark with disappointment: It "yielded nothing but two meagre and miserable terrace walls. . . . Not a single object of significance was discovered."

A dig, Elderkin reminded Morey, "is a gambler's game."

The only real bright spot of 1932 were the mosaics from Atrium House.

—

Later that year, before the reprise of the dig set for the following spring, Morey resolved to see that the enmities of the first year didn't leach into the second. On their return to the States, Morey interviewed the men individually. For Rob Garrett he prepared a cogent, clear-eyed study of what he'd learned. Maybe Fisher could be read as "lazy and suspicious," as Elderkin claimed. But he was supremely competent, his reports meticulous, and, once they got to know him, he inspired the staff's confidence. Nothing like that could be said of Elderkin. "Campbell, who is a man, I think, of very fine character, told me rather reluctantly in answer to a direct question that he would not return to Antioch in 1933 under Elderkin." And the rest of the team, Morey confided to Worcester's Francis Taylor a few days later, felt the same. Schirmer's reading of the antipathy to Elderkin was on the mark.

So when plans were made for the second year's excavations, Elderkin was out altogether; as a sop he was named general editor of publications. Fisher would be back as field director, Campbell as his lieutenant.

—

The first season closed out in June 1932. The second was to begin the following April. But in between, months before the Princeton team was due back in Antioch, an orchard outside Daphne, a few miles south of Antioch, near a spring known as Ain-Djamous, in a village called Yakto, yielded a mosaic like no other.

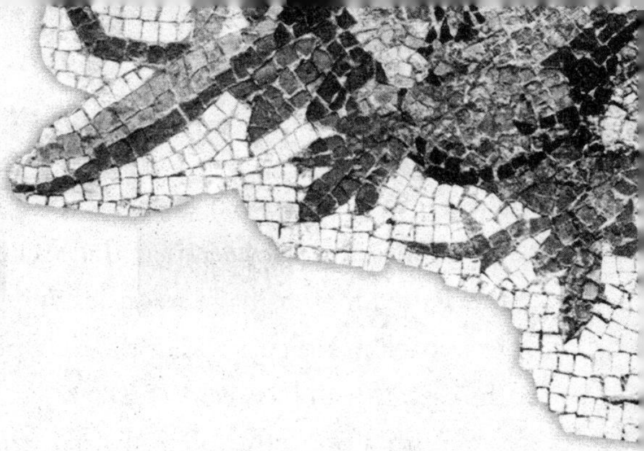

CHAPTER SEVEN

By the Side of the Road in Ain-Djamous

In the place where the mosaic turned up, Jean Lassus would write later,

> the first hills rise up from the bed of the Orontes. Rather than drop down abruptly as in Antioch itself, the mountain, swathed in pleasing vegetation, rolls along in easy undulation. Everywhere arise streams, running in rivulets. On its slopes, cultivated land is set off in terraces often bordered by stone walls. Sometimes, a road runs alongside it. . . . It was beside one of these roads that the mosaic was discovered.

A land surveyor had noticed it, through an errant breach in a stone wall, peeking up from the ground a few feet below the level of the road.

Almost from the moment it was found, everyone seemed to realize this mosaic was different, and important. The land surveyor wrote the Service des Antiquités about it, and soon Claude Prost was at the site, in the village known as Yakto. Fisher advised Morey of Prost's appraisal, that it was "one of the finest documents for topography found anywhere," one promising an illuminating glimpse of Antioch as it was 1,500 years earlier. "It should show you what we may expect to find at Antioch and should cheer up the Committee." In September, the French began a preliminary excavation, but halted it after just a week, leaving it for the Princeton team once they were back in the spring. For the time being, Seyrig left the Yakto mosaic in the care of Jean Lassus.

With a pocketful of credentials from French educational institutions and several scholarly papers already to his credit, young Lassus was already an expert in early Christian and Byzantine art. He'd been in Syria two years, based in Damascus, when Seyrig tapped him to represent France in Antioch. The day he showed up, Clarence Fisher pronounced him "very agreeable. He had been delayed in [Aleppo] with a heavy cold, and had left his wife and two-year-old son there." As a married man, Lassus would not share the house in town that quartered the Princeton men, but would rent one apart for himself and his family. Over the next eight years he would earn the respect of all and contribute hugely to the expedition—but always at some slight Gallic remove from the Americans.

The Yakto mosaic, whose excavation Lassus would oversee during the 1933 campaign, was almost square, twenty-four feet on a side. A single Greek word, inscribed in tesserae, flanks the bejeweled woman who commands its center medallion: *Megalopsychia*. She is surrounded by hunting scenes, of wild lions, leopards, and bulls, speared and stabbed by named mythological hunters, including Actaeon—who, Ovid tells us, was changed into a stag and attacked by his own hounds after he spied the goddess Artemis bathing. From the four corners of the composition, a symmetrical array of trees jut into this tableau of refined slaughter.

As for *megalopsychia* itself, this was a moral sensibility honored and coveted in the Greco-Roman world, especially among its elite. It meant something like "magnanimity," "generosity," or "greatness of soul," but fairly begged for interpretation: To Aristotle, according to Glanville Downey, the young Princeton historian who would make Antioch the center of his life's work, *megalopsychia* made a man both "worthy of great things" and acutely aware of his worth. Here, it may have been toasting the mosaic's generous patron; or perhaps spoke of the huntsman's bravery in subduing dangerous beasts; or else of his equanimity, his imperturbable self-control, in doing so. Then again, perhaps any ambiguities were best left unresolved, the mosaic's few words and rich imagery a spur to personal reflection or high-minded conversation.

In a year-end letter to Étienne Michon of the Louvre, Mr. Morey reviewed the find, noted its title, its bejeweled woman, its hunting scenes, and its mythological figures, only to acknowledge: "Up to here, without doubt, nothing new." That is, many mosaics were uncovered at Antioch and elsewhere in the Roman East with similar themes and subject matter; and were likewise framed by borders with intricate geometric patterns, like guilloches and dentils, familiar enough to get their own names.

The Yakto mosaic had a border, too. Indeed, it was its border that made for all the stir.

Out beyond the hunting scene and a thin, intermediate belt of "looped guilloches," it was like nothing seen elsewhere in Antioch or, for that matter, anywhere else. For proceeding around the mosaic on all four sides was a kind of cartoon, with little in common with the rest of the mosaic in content, style, or execution.

This border, or what was left of it—its east side was broken up and incomplete, the north missing entirely, only the south and west sides more or less intact—was a band of images, originally about a foot and a half high and nearly a hundred feet long, rendered in tesserae of brick red, black, beige, and white. While showing no extraordinary finesse, it did exude a kind of folksy charm, its imagery drawn not from mythology but from the world out of which it, the mosaic itself, had come: veiled women, men on horseback, two men throwing dice, the Island in the middle of the Orontes, a stadium, the Church of Constantine—a day in the life of Antioch, circa late fifth century, many of the little pictures with identifying captions, in Greek, all set in tesserae. These occupied the outward-most perimeter like a cartoon strip, each image flowing into the next, a gallery of snapshots, lively scenes, the rudiments of stories, work to be done, life unrolling before your eyes. No one knew what Antioch looked like back then? Well, the Yakto mosaic helped you imagine it. And not as it was at some uncertain moment in the shadowy past, but from within a narrow range of years after 450 CE: "We have been able to identify four or five of

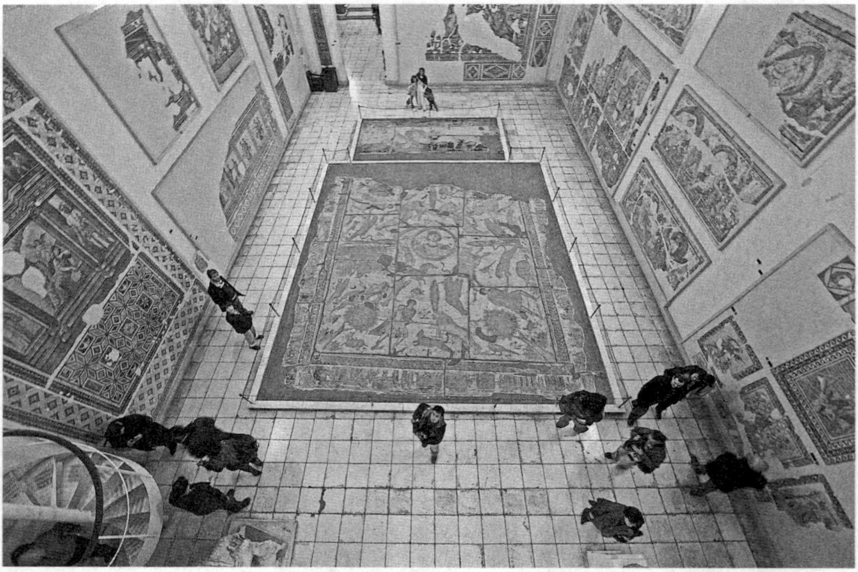

This 2008 photo shows the Yakto mosaic, its topographical border on three sides of it, in a gallery of the old Antakya Archaeological Museum.

the buildings which appear in the border," Morey wrote Fisher. And one, duly labeled, was the villa of Ardeburius, a notable local official, his life well attested in place and time.

One might see in the Yakto border only a collection of random images, with no definite order or direction, as Doro Levi, a devoted student of the Antioch mosaics, would later suggest. But more often, in the near-century since the Yakto border came to light, the inclination has been to see in it cinematic movement: The border can seem like it has something to say, that it wants to direct you, take you by the hand, and show you around Antioch and environs, especially Daphne, its renowned suburb.

But were the sites depicted (together with those lost, from the mutilated sides of the border) arrayed as you might encounter them in life? Did they accurately represent Antioch and Daphne? And if they were really supposed to launch you on a tour, where would you start? And which way, left or right, clockwise or counterclockwise around the Monopoly board, were you supposed to go?

Yakto was mystery and puzzle, one with too few clues, too many missing pieces. Its first student, Lassus, confessed later that on first contact with Yakto, constrained by time, "I took some chances . . . , made mistakes." Later, he more methodically went through the surviving border images, numbering them from *1* to *56*. From these, he conceived a tour starting from the lush, ever-flowing springs of Daphne into the city, past a bath, then the Olympic stadium, a succession of workshops, three private houses, outdoor merchants displaying their wares, and so on.

Glanville Downey would later conceive a tour much like Lassus's, except in reverse, beginning in Antioch, ending at the famous Daphne springs. For him, "the scenes in the mosaic begin in the left-hand corner as one enters the room and succeed each other in order from left to right around the room." This, to him, seemed more natural than Lassus's in which the scenes unrolled from right to left, opposite to the reading of Greek.

Maybe, Downey proposed, Libanius had inspired the tour in his fourth-century ode to Antioch, where he imagines a visit to Daphne:

> As soon as the gates are left behind, one is struck by the variety of gardens on the left-hand side, of places of entertainment, the abundance of fountains, villas hidden among the trees, with rooms overlooking the treetops—a spot fit for Aphrodite and her archer son. As one proceeds, on either side of the road can be seen innumerable vineyards, lovely villas, rose gardens, plantations of every kind and streets. One's gaze is attracted first to one side, then to another, and amid such pleasures, one will reach Daphne the peerless. . . . The radiance which fills his eyes causes the spectator to turn his gaze to view the temple of Apollo or that of Zeus, the Olympic stadium, a perfectly delightful theater, a thick high mass of cypresses, with shady paths.

However the Yakto border was best read, it seemed to address the core problem of *where things were* in Antioch and Daphne, which had all along bedeviled the Princeton excavators. "It can readily be understood," Morey wrote in the *Bulletin of the Worcester Art Museum* in 1933, "how welcome this find will be to the student whose task is to reconstruct the topography of the city and its suburb, aside from the intrinsic interest of this curious conceit of the fifth century A.D."

But caution was due. In 2020, for example, a French scholar, Catherine Saliou, of Paris's École Pratique des Hautes Études, looked back once more at Yakto, pointing up uncertainties of interpretation. Was the border an itinerary? A road map? Maybe so, maybe not. What did strike her with irrefutable force was how the border testified to Antioch's dynamism. It depicted a vital city, a place rich in life and interest, a fifth-century metropolis. Maybe it offered no true map, but in the scenes and settings it selected as worth the viewer's attention, it showed how Antiochenes viewed their city. It revealed "a city in motion, not only by showing a cityscape alive with people on the move but also in serving up a snapshot of an urban place in the process of change."

In the late 1950s, a young MIT-trained architect, Kevin Lynch, interviewed residents of Los Angeles, Boston, and Jersey City about the streets, buildings, and monuments of their city; what notable locations—what paths, nodes, districts, and landmarks, to use Lynch's new vocabulary—bubbled up in their awareness? In Boston, for example, they included familiar spots like the Boston Common, Scollay Square, and South Station. In his book *The Image of the City*, Lynch depicted the fruit of his interviews in rudimentary, unscaled maps and simple sketches. The Yakto border comes down to us in this spirit—a depiction of Antioch and Daphne that, in memorably recognizable places, scenes, and monuments, adds up to a collective sense of the city by the people who lived there. The iconic blue cover of Lynch's classic book, with its rude stick-figure urban scene, could have come straight from the Yakto border.

The Yakto border exemplified Antioch's promise of future discovery. For Downey it would rank as "one of the most precious documents of ancient life ever recovered by archaeologists." The whole mosaic would go first to a new Antioch museum, planned as a showcase for the excavations (to be presided over by Claude Prost), there to dominate most of a large room. After 2014, it would go to the magnificent new Hatay Archaeology Museum. Like the Judgment of Paris, it was one of the earliest and brightest stars in Antioch's mosaic firmament, remaining so even in the wake of future finds.

—

In Antioch, Clarence Fisher was boss of the dig and on his shoulders lay the burdens of decision. His field diary for the second season was shot through with tasks, preoccupations, worries. From a local landowner, they needed to gain access to another part of his property. They needed to cut a trench from the hippodrome across an adjacent field to the old Roman temple a few hundred yards east; they had to deal with sudden downpours that flooded dig sites, and transform an excavated bath beside the river into a dump site. Each day, gangs of laborers, under the direction of one or more Egyptian foremen, the *reises*, were shuffled off to suit the goals and directives of the excavation, going where they were sent, doing what they were told.

Film clips from early in the excavations—seventeen minutes of damaged black-and-white footage survive—show lines of men scurrying along dirt paths, down sandy slopes, and up steps cut into the side of the excavation, with spades, pitchforks, and trowels, but mostly wicker baskets, scooping up dirt, and clambering back up to the surface to unload their meager loads into the dump. Basket by basket, as obscuring dirt is swept away, they leave walls, pots, coins, vases, and mosaics open to collection and review. Each payday, they cluster in tight clutches of a hundred or more, sitting or squatting around the expedition paymaster, waiting to hear their names called. When they do, they run up to him and his cash box, where they receive a few coins of their own.

On April 18, 1933, Fisher, Lassus, and Sandy Campbell went up to Yakto to inspect the ruins of the villa there. "Every room has either a marble floor or mosaics," most of them well preserved, wrote Fisher. "The whole villa cannot be laid bare, because of large olive trees which the owners wish to have left." Ultimately, some of the trees had to be removed. According to Fisher, the owners were well taken care of, reimbursed practically on "their own terms"—yet now dared complain. "The agreement is, however, in writing and they have no excuse."

On April 24, Fisher heard from Lassus in Yakto that "one of the head locals" had insulted him, demanding more money and urging the workmen to walk off the job. After lunch, Campbell gathered up the head *reis* and went to the office of the governor, Lieutenant Gondouly. "The man again persuaded the workmen to leave and was making additional threats when the two police which Gondouly promised to send arrived." He was taken away. "He should never be employed again," decreed Fisher.

A little after this, Mr. Morey arrived in Antioch with his wife, Sara, on his first trip to the excavations, for a week of meetings, dinners, and discussions. On May 6, the Moreys hosted Gondouly, Claude Prost, Colonel Paul Jacquot, the district's chief political officer, along with the Princeton crew, Lassus, and his wife. "It was a very happy gathering, quite informal."

Late that month, Sandy Campbell visited the office of a Beirut shipping firm, Debbas, to arrange for shipment of five cases of mosaics, each weighing some 1,500 kilograms, to the States. Some days later, he was presented with an estimate for trucking them to Beirut, and for wharf dues, crane use for loading them aboard ship, export duties, lighterage fees, and other costs of shipping big, heavy, awkward things across great oceans.

Campbell wrote Debbas a few days later: "I wish to impress upon [you] that the trucks you send for this trip must be in first class mechanical condition so that there will be no breakdowns on route, and that the entire shipment must be made with greatest care and safety possible." He wrote Morey, apparently to reassure him about how the mosaics were to be loaded aboard ship: The shipper's representative "promised to stow the cargo in number 3 hold under the bridge," and to have ship's officers personally oversee the slings and winches required.

It was minutiae. It was endless. It was necessary.

—

At some point that spring, expedition staff gathered in the courtyard of the excavation headquarters for a kind of class photo: three graduate students, Fisher in jacket and tie, the other senior men tieless, in crisp white shirts. Lassus, taller than the others, in the back row with a big expansive smile, dark hair combed back and parted in the middle, arms crossed in front of his chest, looking well satisfied. His wife in the front row in a white dress and white caftan-like chapeau; their son, in shorts and sandals, beside her. Schirmer was gone, so was Downey, and of course Elderkin.

The photographer included one further compositional element: On the floor between Mme Lassus and their son sat a headless but otherwise largely intact marble sculpture, about a foot and a half high, retrieved from Yakto. It depicted a seated boy or young man coiling his left foot around his body, struggling to extract a thorn.

During the second year's campaign, work on the hippodrome continued, and a new bath, Bath D, was found northwest of it. The year-end report offered a statistical breakdown. A 4,800-square-meter area had been excavated around Bath D, which yielded 147 coins, 7 mosaics, and 40 other objects. At Yakto, under Lassus, a gang of fifty laborers had excavated 2,500 cubic meters of earth, finding 173 coins and 9 mosaics. All told for the second campaign, 31 mosaics had been lifted, along with almost 13,000 cubic meters of dirt and 409 "objects."

One was the small marble of the boy with the thorn in his foot, today occupying a glass case in the Baltimore Museum of Art. I came upon it—or really "him," as he seemed to me—one day in the museum's Antioch Court. Viewing a mosaic with any special interest leaves you periodically stepping in closer, individual tiles full in view; then stepping back, the tesserae magically slipping into their larger design. At one point, inching back, I sensed I had gone too far, was about to bump into something, and turned to see the headless boy in the glass case, the Thorn Puller of Yakto.

CHAPTER EIGHT

Daphne and Apollo

Not the least significance of the Yakto mosaic was where it was found. Most of the first season had played out on the Island, two miles north of the sadly diminished twentieth-century city. Now, though, the new discovery helped shift attention to Daphne, the legendary suburb that encompassed Yakto.

The ancient myth of Daphne—daughter of a Spartan king, chaste nymph, virgin huntress—reaches us today through Ovid's *Metamorphoses*: To the god Apollo she is beautiful beyond compare. He catches sight of her from afar, runs after her, she flees—in Ovid's telling, "he sped by hope and she by fear." Terrified, she cries out to the river god, Peneus: "If mystic power / Dwells in your waters, change me and destroy / My baleful beauty that has pleased too well."

Apollo reaches her, reaches *for* her. And at his first unwanted touch, Daphne's soft, lustrous body changes:

Her tender bosom
Was wrapped in thin smooth bark, her slender arms
Were changed to branches and her hair to leaves;
Her feet but now so swift were anchored fast

In numb stiff roots, her face and head became
The crown of a green tree.

Apollo's lust subsides, but his love only grows, the laurel tree itself, its leaves and blossoms, evermore the object of his devotion.

Today—or so it was before the February 2022 earthquake—a small museum across the river from the old center of Antakya displays a life-sized sculpture of that fraught moment: Apollo grasping, Daphne straining to elude his grasp, the two figures rendered in ghostly white. It is not an entirely successful work. It is a far cry from, say, Bernini's astonishing seventeenth-century sculptural depiction at the Galleria Borghese in Rome. Certainly, something in that moment of erotic desire roused, denied, and transfigured would seize the imagination of generations of (male) artists. And some afterglow of it would cling to Daphne, the place, helping make it, like the virgin huntress herself, an object of desire

"Chief among the glories of Daphne, indeed of the whole world," declared Libanius in his buoyant way, were its springs, which erupted from the sides of the hills on which it was built and coursed in tinkling rivulets and bubbling falls down its slopes. Three of these springs lay just below the Daphne plateau, with others scattered across adjacent hills. The slopes they watered and left shaded and green made living there delightful, as did Daphne's groves of laurel and the breezes that billowed up the valley of the Orontes from the sea.

Seeing Daphne, wrote Libanius, a visitor was apt to "leap up with a start, clap his hands and congratulate himself upon the sights and almost take wing in his pleasure," lost to "shady paths, harmonious bird song, a gentle breeze, and odors sweeter than incense. . . ." So enthralled was Libanius that he was prepared to dismiss the traditional account of the Judgment of Paris, supposed to have taken place on the sacred mountain, Mt. Ida, in Crete. No, said he, it was Daphne: "When the three goddesses began to quarrel about their beauty, it was here that they came to bathe for the judgment."

Even by the 1930s, around the time the Princetonians arrived, Daphne exerted a hold. In his 1936 book, *In the Steps of St. Paul*, H. V. Morton wrote of being offered a hotel "room overlooking the great vale where Daphne . . . prayed for aid and was turned into a laurel tree.

> There was no sound but the rush of water falling from rock-pool to rock-pool. I could see the dark clumps of laurels which still grow in the once sacred grove. . . . When it was dark I would open my windows and see a red fire pricking the night in the hills below, and hear, rising in the stillness, a little endless rune played on a flute, as if someone in the laurels of Daphne were mourning for a lost world.

So brightly did Daphne glow in ancient writings that sometimes Antioch was mentioned in relation to it, rather than the other way around. But Daphne was no real city. Efforts to reconstruct its overall plan have revealed nothing like the familiar grid pattern of Antioch and most other cities of the Roman world. Rather, Daphne was all villas and gardens, set down irregularly across its slopes, situated on terraces a few hundred feet above the valley below, just high enough up to confer a sense of restful remove. If Antioch could be likened to Paris, a Victorian *Dictionary of Greek and Roman Geography* asserted, Daphne was its Versailles.

There in ancient Daphne was enacted the age-old story, played out today in places like Vail, the Hudson Valley, or Lake Como: People of means choose beautiful natural settings in which to live, or those ennobled by history and legend, or both. There they build fine homes, delighted to show off their wealth, their taste, or their deep, personal intimacy with a glorious past. In the early centuries of our era, one way to do so was to commission, plan, design, and make the magnificent mosaics that, beginning in 1932, the Princeton team found all over Daphne.

Even before setting out on *Excalibur*, it had not escaped the notice of the Princeton team that Daphne might contribute much. The Kraeling index made specific references to likely finds there, including a Temple of Hecate bestowed by the emperor Diocletian and a Church of St. Babylas. Even in the earliest days of the dig, soon after arriving in Antioch from Ramallah in 1932, Clarence Fisher arranged to be driven out to Daphne for a tour. There, "we looked at the slight remains of a Byzantine church and also discussed the probable location of the Temple of Jupiter [the Greek Apollo]. . . . M. Prost said that the whole Daphne area is full of very fine tombs and [that] some excellent things had been found there by natives."

The coming years would see the discovery of countless villas and the recovery of their mosaics. "The cemeteries of Antioch, the numberless villas which fringed it, the remains of its beautiful suburb of Daphne," Rufus Morey wrote at the end of the second season, "all await the spade." Daphne, especially, monopolized their attention.

Jean Lassus would recall a moment from a few years later when Sandy Campbell, by then field director, dropped by to see him in his office. He looked worried. "Sandy was a good person to work for," one of the Princeton team, Donald Wilber, would recall, good-natured and easygoing. But not so much today. The whole expedition, Campbell reminded Lassus, rested on the financial support of their contributors—the American museums and the Louvre, who looked to Antioch for the big pot of finds they'd been all but promised. But by this time, into the fourth year of the dig, *sondages*, or test excavations, conducted in Antioch itself were yielding little. Atrium House and its riches from the Island were old news. They would need to work new sites, said Campbell now. Especially in Daphne. And especially its mosaics. He'd asked expedition secretary Adib Ishak, with his knack for dredging up news, gossip, and leads, to inquire among the Alawite Arabs of Daphne. Ishak came back certain that, beneath Daphne's olive trees and orchards, lay a mother lode of luxurious villas. Mosaics, time-consuming and expensive to make, fed on wealth, and Daphne was all wealth.

"Which of you two," Ishak asked in Lassus's telling of the story, "will run the dig?" *What a question!* thought Lassus. If Campbell, they'd go after third-century mosaics rich in mythological subjects. If he himself, he'd seek more recent pavements, say from the fifth century, the eve of the Byzantine era that so fascinated him, with great decorative panels, animals, hunt scenes.

In the end, Campbell chose to preside over Daphne himself. Ishak was delegated to lease a plot from a landowner, Soleiman Hindié, who had come upon a mosaic while digging a well on his property. That led to discovery

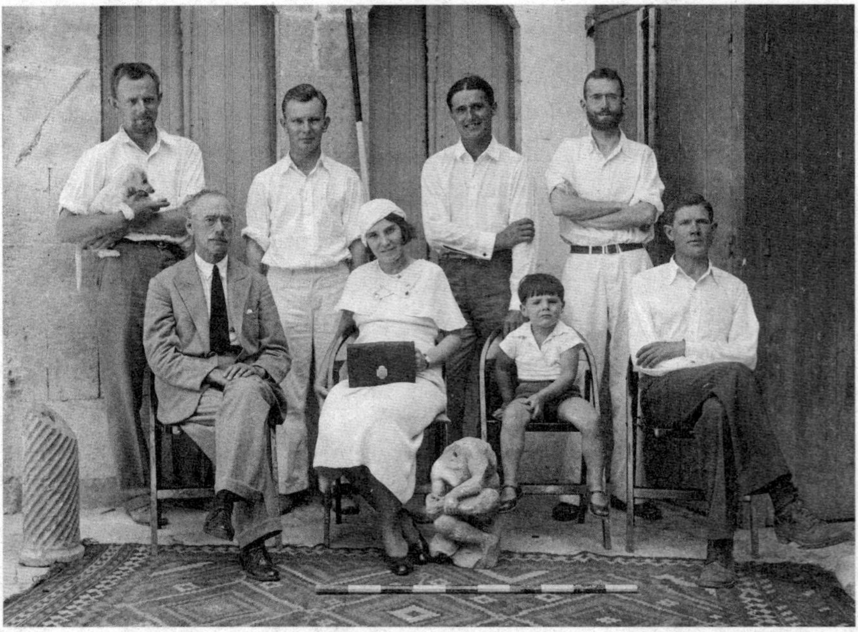

This "class picture" of some of the 1933 team shows Clarence Fisher in the first row, along with Mme Lassus, her son, and William "Sandy" Campbell. Jean Lassus in the second row stands third from the left. In front, the Thorn Puller of Yakto.

of the ruins of a villa fairly stocked with mosaics, including the Boat of Psyches—the one in which, as Lassus painted the fanciful vision, Eros, god of love, "flies off on a chariot pulled by goddesses with butterfly wings."

For Lassus, the meeting with Campbell was pivotal for the Antioch excavation: For one thing, word of the riches of the House of the Boat of Psyches got back to Princeton, moving an American philanthropist to put up another thousand dollars, enough to employ a hundred workers for three weeks. "The mission was bailed out," Lassus would recall, much as it had been three years earlier by the Judgment of Paris.

The sites Fisher had excavated during the first season were, as we've seen, mostly public or semipublic places. Those from Daphne were more often from fine villas, which, elite fashion seemed to dictate, simply *had* to be graced by mosaics, sometimes in almost every room. So they'd chip away and sweep aside the layers of obstructing dirt from a room in the House of the Green Carpet, say, or the House of the Mysteries of Isis, photograph the mosaic where it lay, freshly bare in the scarred, disordered soil, slice it into sections, fragments, and chunks, lift it up, and store it in the expedition headquarters or the basement of the Banque de Syrie.

The Princeton team would extract from Daphne some of its most magnificent mosaic finds. One, set on what resembled a theatrical stage, shows human figures representing Fruit, Field, and Vine—this last a sorry-looking fellow, bedraggled, belly hanging out, half-drunk.

A mosaic from the House of the Man of Letters, with its gently irregular placement of tesserae representing lobster, scallop, snail, and other marine species, suggested a view through clear, rippling water.

A hunt mosaic, a veritable tapestry of hunters and wild animals, was larger even than the one lying within the borders of the Yakto mosaic.

Then there was the small female figure, labeled *Ktisis*, from a Daphne villa the excavators named the House of Earth and the Seasons, set within a broad field of complex geometries.

And another rendering of Daphne and Apollo, again less inspired than Bernini's—hands and arms clunky, Apollo's lust less stirring, Daphne's terror less visible.

And a series of smaller mosaic panels under the theme *Philia,* which showed pairings of predator and prey from the animal kingdom, like lion and oxen, but here, in these images, friends.

The Princeton excavators came upon new discoveries themselves but, just as often, were alerted to them by local farmers and landowners. As Campbell noted in 1934, the expedition made it a practice to respond to these alerts, because

> our continual presence there, we hoped, would have the effect of preventing the peasants from destroying the mosaics they happen upon, [giving] . . . no notification to the antiquities service nor to us. One may consider it the rule that barring the intervention of such authorities, a mosaic found is a mosaic lost.

That is, its very existence and revealed location placed it in jeopardy. So if only as a protective measure, Campbell ordered *sondages,* those small test digs, at these sites, any mosaics found noted on their maps for fuller exploration later.

A big archaeological dig extending over several years, like Antioch's, could be seen as a succession of "campaigns." As in a military campaign, you marshaled resources, human and material, fashioned a strategy, responded to threats or opportunities that might come up. The first Antioch campaign had been confined largely to the Island. But by the fourth year, as mosaics spilled from one excavated villa after another, Daphne was no longer a distracting second front to the main action on the Island; it was the new front line. "The work at Daphne," wrote Morey in a May 1935 issue of the art journal *Parnassus*, was yielding panels "with almost embarrassing frequency, and with an extraordinary consistency of good quality."

From now to expedition's end, the unrelenting tide of mosaics never let one's gaze leave Daphne for long.

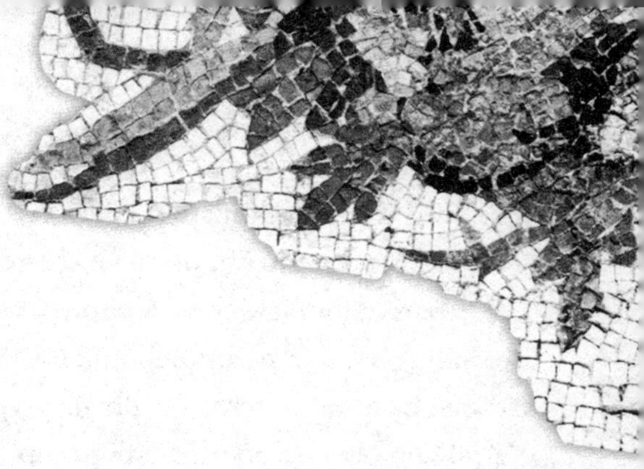

CHAPTER NINE

La Fouille de Mosaïques

By any ordinary measure, it would be hard to reckon the mosaic fecundity of Daphne and Antioch as anything but an archaeological and institutional success story. Reports from Princeton and articles in popular magazines certainly said as much. So did Mr. Morey's own articles and book—which, for all their substance and genteel air, sometimes bore a whiff of promotion. So did many among the visitors who came to view the mosaics. Later, some would assess the Princeton expedition more critically, but in the end one had to acknowledge that the expedition did come back with all those mosaics and that they were ardently coveted by museums in the States; why, they looked like they *belonged* in museums. They were big, colorful, and showy. In their formidable stony presence—many of them almost wholly uncorrupted by their many centuries underground—they rewarded close viewing. And through all the years of the excavation, they kept coming.

A professional mosaicist, William Gad Gabriel, an Egyptian Copt, was named head of a specialist mosaic crew. This team took on the tricky job of cutting up large mosaics into smaller pieces, settling them into thick, heavy, concrete-and-steel-backed parcels, extracting them from the ground, and delivering them to sites of secure storage. From there they could be shipped to their ultimate destination, whether by truck across town to a new Antioch museum or down the road to Beirut to be loaded aboard a ship bound for New York. A photo from the Princeton archives shows Gad standing beside Barbari Mahmud Isa, among the most respected of the half dozen or so *reises*, ceremonially removing the cloth and paper facing from a mosaic. At one point, Gad's group was working through one mosaic a day; the figure touted for the third season was 126 mosaics in 126 days. It was as if some breath of the early industrial efficiency experts had settled on Antioch.

The Princeton team grew used to new mosaics being brought to their attention every time a plow scratched a farmer's field. By the third season at Antioch—which played out in two parts, the spring season under Campbell, a second in the fall under Lassus—mosaics were no longer just one among many welcome products of the dig; they had become *the* product. Think of modern industrial agriculture, where a rich and diverse landscape of mixed crops gives way to a single, profitable one—cotton, say, or corn—a monoculture.

Indeed, with the dig a kind of production line, was there a risk that the speed and efficiency with which the mosaic crew was enjoined to work might subvert the excavation's loftier ends? "Most—if not all—pavements," Andrea De Giorgi, professor of archaeology at Florida State University, would lament in his study *Ancient Antioch* many years later, "were lifted without adequate consideration and description of their original physical and cultural settings, let alone of the surrounding topography." It was one thing to retrieve an object from the ground—any grave robber or looter could do that. It was quite another to come back with the detailed stratigraphic evidence—what, and how much, lay above the mosaic, what below—that made archaeology something like a science.

The way Jean Lassus framed it later, Campbell's 1935 visit to his office had triggered twinges of regret about the excavation. He saw many of the large mosaics broken up, their unity obliterated, pieces of them distributed hither and thither, tesserae at the borders of cut-up sections lost entirely or else gathered up for use in later restorations. But more, it seemed to him, the Antioch *fouille*, or dig, had now become "*une fouille de mosaïques*," a dig for mosaics—ancient, interesting, and beautiful, yes, but maybe obscuring some of the expedition's original objectives. The dig was no longer one in search of Antioch in all its aesthetic and cultural richness, but now only, it could seem, of its mosaics.

Lassus would recall these doubts from a distance of almost half a century. He may have gotten some details wrong. He may have overlooked nuance or spoken with at least some slight deficit of tact. Still, it seems plain, the fortuitous early finds from Atrium House, the bottomless bounty of Daphne, and then the keen interest in the mosaics from other American museums had deflected the dig. Lassus wanted more from Antioch than mosaics. And what he especially wanted—what everyone had wanted all along—was to know what ancient Antioch looked like.

—

Even some years into the dig, the confident and assertive map you might assume they'd been able to make of old Antioch by now, showing this great temple or that proud monument, palace, or crossroads, still did not exist. The excavators did know where a few of the ancient baths stood. They had numerous maps from the distant and recent past—Muller's from 1839, Le Camus's from 1890, Paul Jacquot's from 1931. And they had delicious clues from the Yakto mosaic border. But all these were just that—clues, suggestions, guesses. After all, even maps of familiar, recently surveyed places can prove surprisingly difficult to make sense of. Differing choice of scale and extent, of what to feature, what to exclude, where to zoom in close, where to pull back, the very idea of the map, can leave you unsure of what you're looking at. All the more so with Antioch's, from different epochs in its two millennia past. Malalas's insouciantly irregular "history" and the milder distortions of Libanius offered plenty of room for, say, a novelist's imagination. But not the certainty and precision needed to draw a decent map.

In his report on the 1934 fall campaign Lassus took up the frustrating "topographical" problem once more. It was he who'd lamented that in Antioch an archaeologist needed historical accounts in hand to believe a great city had once stood beneath his feet; there was just so little to go on. Even now, a few years into the excavations, the broad plan of the city eluded him and the others. And this ignorance, of course, looped back to the hugely practical question, *Where to dig?*

"The obvious impulse," he wrote, reviewing strategies, was to do as Fisher had done—dig "outside the congested alleys of the modern town," on the Island. That had yielded the hippodrome and "profitable exploration in its immediate vicinity," including the baths, the first round of mosaics from Bath A, and, especially, Atrium House; Lassus was giving Fisher his due. But then again, Fisher "had been lucky"; in 1932, the groundwater level had been unusually low, allowing him to reach some pre-Roman remains without being much troubled by water-swollen trenches—a happy break not repeated since.

A second strategy relied on "accidental discoveries," chance finds delivered on a silver platter, as at Yakto. But wasn't it a little unbecoming to make "discoveries" that way? To rely on dumb luck and the natural acquisitiveness of the locals? Ought you turn your back on your training, on science itself, and just run off to wherever the local landowners point you, gather a crew of laborers, and start digging?

Lassus didn't put it as baldly as that. But he did seem to snub this approach in calling for a third way, "more systematic without doubt, but more difficult of execution," one that he had selected for the fall 1934 campaign over which he presided: The ancient sources, historical records, early maps, and even aerial photographs taken by the French authorities had convinced him that they needed, first of all, a more accurate map of the ancient city. In particular, it seemed to Lassus, they needed to precisely chart Antioch's main street, which, hugging the base of the adjacent line of mountains, seemed to correspond to, or overlay, a street much heralded in antiquity.

Beneficiary of the resources lavished on it by a succession of emperors, grandly colonnaded for miles, lined with shops and houses, this thoroughfare ran straight up through the city to the northeast, becoming the road to Aleppo. Down the other way, to the southwest, it continued toward and

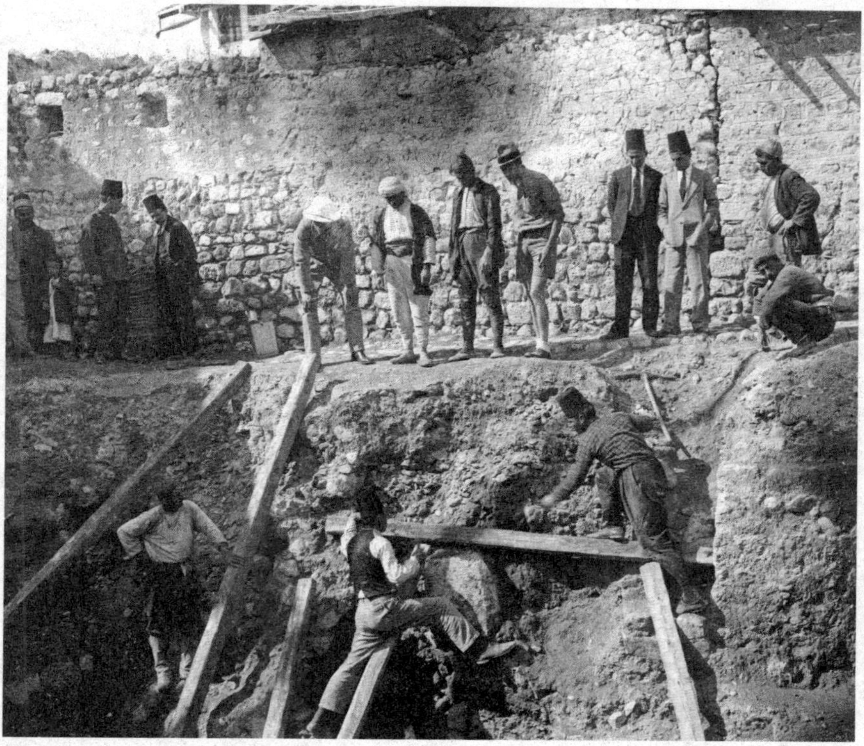

The city's "main street" in ancient times shot up from the south of the city, traced a line along the base of the mountains to its east, and then up through the north of the city toward Aleppo. What came to be called "the Main Street dig," presided over by Jean Lassus, was a series of digs at nine locations along its length. The original street had been largely buried in rock and sediment; gaining access to its remains meant going down deep, thirty or forty feet below the modern street. Here, workmen place shoring timbers in position at one of the nine sites.

through the south gate to Daphne. "The roadway was open to the sky," Glanville Downey would later write of it,

> but since it ran north and south it was shaded during part of the day, and it caught the breeze which blew up the Orontes Valley in the summer. It was full of the most varied traffic. Travelers on horseback or in carriages drawn by mules; donkeys heavily loaded with burdens of all kinds, singly or in strings, led by drivers armed with sticks; two-wheeled carts carrying building materials; porters

> bearing heavy loads—every kind of activity could be seen in this thoroughfare and the side streets which opened from it. . . . Women hurried on errands, their children trailing behind them. Boys walked to school, chaperoned by slaves carrying their books and wax writing tables secured in leather straps. High officials and army officers passed on horseback, their harness and uniforms glittering.

This street, if Lassus was right, would be the essential point of origin, or, better, *line* of origin—the long, central axis of the city—needed to grasp how ancient Antioch was put together, a vital help to tracking down other landmarks thus far resistant to discovery.

He had not favored Fisher's original dig strategy, and Fisher was, those first two years, field director, and his boss. But Lassus represented the Louvre and France, so Fisher evidently felt obliged to appease him: "To respond to my concerns," wrote Lassus, Fisher assigned him to oversee a small *sondage* in a crowded part of the old city, a site made briefly available by civic improvements planned for the area. Lassus's trench cut across the inner court of an abandoned soap factory, beside a mosque, and across the street on which Lassus pinned his hopes. Later, in a fall 1934 dig, with Fisher gone and Campbell now field director, Lassus launched in earnest what became the yearslong "Main Street Dig," a series of nine coordinated excavations stretched out along its length that would occupy him for the rest of his time in Antioch. Later, they would lead to a great oversized volume, fifth in the series of Princeton University Press books devoted to Antioch, *Les Portiques d'Antioche.*

Along the way, Lassus found pots and sculptures and even a few mosaics, including a fragment of a pretty, sixth-century one, rich in its geometry. He may have deemed these incidental to his larger aim, a reliable map of the ancient city. But he couldn't help but acknowledge the sheer clout of the mosaics: "The collection of mosaics now in the store room," he wrote at the end of the 1934 season, "has an amazing effect on the visitors," including such established archaeologists as Albright, Seyrig, Jean Sauvaget, and the Egyptologist Sir Flinders Petrie. All had "expressed their admiration so strongly," he conceded with a nod to his misgivings about the dig's mosaic-centeredness, "that I am obliged to be worried of the value of my own opinion."

Lassus appreciated the scholarly and aesthetic value of the mosaics as much as anyone. But just now it was their real-world value to which he referred: "It looks very easy now to find money from museums," he wrote in a telling aside. "It will be necessary, therefore, to find mosaics for museums."

Quid pro quo.

CHAPTER TEN

Divvying Up the Spoils

In late summer 1934, a few days before the handover from spring work overseen by Campbell to the fall work directed by Lassus, preparations were made for transferring mosaics that, since 1932 and 1933, had been stored in the basement of the local bank. Twenty-three mosaics had been unearthed in the dig's first year, including the Judgment of Paris and ten other Atrium House finds; thirty-one in the second, including the big hunt mosaic from the Yakto villa with its topographical border. "The hay in the store room has been removed, the walls repaired, plastered and whitewashed, and the floors smoothed," wrote Campbell in his official diary. "The room is completely ready for the transport of the mosaics from the Bank Store Room."

During the 1934 season, the Princeton excavators recovered 868 coins, 860 miscellaneous objects, and 67 mosaics.

Then, during the 1935 season, they found 1,774 coins, 1,073 objects, and 118 mosaics, some of them room-sized, too big to come out of the ground in one piece.

But what was supposed to happen to these finds? Where were they bound? Who would get them?

The coming "division" would furnish answers.

During these years, the English mystery writer Agatha Christie was married to a British archaeologist, Max Mallowan, whom she often accompanied on digs in the Near East. At sites in Mesopotamia, across the Syrian Desert from Antioch, she helped in the dig's daily work. And occasionally she turned her literary talents away from murder on the Orient Express to the pleasures and peculiarities of archaeology. Her little book *Come, Tell Me How You Live* was published after the war, in 1946, but as its introduction says, "in both spirit and content it belongs to the thirties." Christie ably conveys the rhythms of the dig, culled from five seasons on-site, among an exotic cast of sheiks, customs officials, colonels, ferrymen, and laborers.

At the conclusion of each season's work came, in Christie's words, "the burning moment of 'The Division.'" The year's finds were to be divided between Syria and the British Museum. A French official would choose between two caches of presumably equal value and interest. "The real agony lies in making the two collections," Christie writes: Which amulets, pots, beads, black obsidian, or otherwise ambiguous "cult objects" would go where? "You are bound to lose certain things you want desperately. Very well, then you must balance them on the other side." Christie, her husband, and others would all weigh in over a frenetic couple of days. But then, finally,

> all is over! The Division has taken place. M. and Madame Dunand have examined, handled, reflected. We have stood looking on in the usual agony. It takes M. Dunand about an hour to make up his mind. Then he flings a hand out in a quick Gallic gesture.
>
> "*Eh bien*, I will take this one."
>
> True to human nature, whichever half is chosen, we immediately wish it had been the other.

So it was in Mesopotamia in the 1930s. And while the mechanics, details, and rules of the game differed, some such "division-of-finds" was always part of the life of digs in the Near East, involving Syria or another host country, France or Britain, and the excavators themselves. The other word for a division was "partage," from the French *partager*, "to share." The work, money, and trouble that had gone into finding precious objects were, for the moment, history. Now a few hours or a few days settled who got how much of what. It was a charged moment in the life of the excavation that left room for wheedling and wrangling. For each interested party, sunny visions of gain warred with bleak fears of loss. Even the otherwise high-minded could slip into Machiavellian scheming.

In early 1933, for example, after the discovery of the Yakto mosaic, Morey saw a chance to improve prospects for the American side. Étienne Michon of the Louvre had written him that he, Michon, thought the Yakto mosaic, with its one-of-a-kind topographical border, "would be of especial interest to the state of Syria." Well, Morey figured, acceding to that might make an opening for the Franco-American side: It "would make more likely a division of finds" that would leave "the fine mosaic discovered last season" from Atrium House in the hands of the excavators. And since from those panels the Judgment of Paris was destined, as already agreed, for the Louvre, the rest of them—"the symposium panel, and the two dancing figures considered together as a lot, and the damaged panel with the fine border"—well, then, those would go to the Americans. At the most recent meeting of the Committee, it had been thought best to avoid too premature a division of finds. But now, as Morey's departure for Europe on February 8 neared, he wrote Baltimore's Robert Garrett that, while in Antioch, perhaps he would "bring up the question" after all—"inasmuch as it looks as if we"—the Americans—"might get [the other panels from] the fine mosaic out of it." Which, in fact, they did.

Syria, the Louvre, and the American museums had agreed on set percentages. But agreements and percentages granted no exemption from the "agony" Agatha Christie saw as inherent in divisions. Set percentages of *what*, exactly? How could numbers translate into physical objects, and suit the particular interests of the subscribing institutions and their directors? How balance a fourth-century mosaic with a stunning work of sculpture, or a rare inscription? How measure beauty? Start weighing and quantifying and soon you were caught in a mire of the incommensurable—not apples and oranges, but apples and end tables.

The divisions raised all sorts of issues. At the end of a letter to Campbell reviewing the just-completed fall campaign of 1934, Jean Lassus wrote that he needed to know the date of the upcoming division, for it represented to him a deadline: Removal of the mosaics from the storeroom meant "the end of the possibility of studying" them up close. Once they were gone, the archaeologists would be reduced to the mean, insufficient expedient of black-and-white photographs. "Mosaics, you know it from the Yakto finds," he wrote, "cannot be studied by photographs. All the work for their publication must be made here. . . . That Fisher's mosaic went away is, even for us"—the French, the otherwise delighted recipients of the Judgment of Paris—"a great difficulty."

With the mosaics, then, "division" went beyond what Agatha Christie had seen in Mesopotamia. It meant more than a game of high-stakes dealing for the best of them. It meant hindrance to their study. It meant physical dismemberment. It meant potentially incalculable loss.

In late 1934, at a meeting of the Committee held at his house in Princeton, Morey reported to the rest of them Henri Seyrig's suggestion that Morey himself make the division for 1933 and 1934. Once the Committee had approved it, Seyrig would choose Syria's share. But that was only the beginning. The tentative division would be submitted to field director Campbell for suggested revisions; then to Michon at the Louvre, "after which it will be submitted to the American subscribers for final approval." Then back to Seyrig.

As should be plain by now, there was no one set way to manage the divisions, no recipe, no rule book. And what rules there were changed, were renegotiated, all across the years of the dig. Whatever the mechanics, every division was inherently fraught, hewing to no simple formula. Always, though, there was some sort of dry listing in the end—all the aesthetic force of the original art, its color, vibrancy, and meaning, transmuted into numbers, letters, and a few bare words of description: A mosaic, defined as "a830-M108, Panels A and B," of Narcissus, from the second century CE,

10′ 7″ x 12′ 0″, to the Baltimore Museum of Art. A "reclining Herakles," of the fourth century, 5524-M93, to Princeton. Three fourth-century circular medallions from the Constantinian Villa, panels V, Y, and W, to Worcester.

The Judgment of Paris did go to the Louvre, getting there in good order in November 1936. Other fine mosaics from Atrium House went to Baltimore and Worcester. The Yakto mosaic, with its topographical border, today reaches across a broad expanse of floor in the Hatay Archaeology Museum in Antakya, Türkiye. Today, no patron could guess the high-stake negotiations that led each of these stunning mosaics to their final resting place.

—

In its administration and funding, the Antioch expedition was a Franco-American affair. But expedition personnel were notably diverse. The *reises* were Egyptian. The administrative secretary of the dig, of course, was Adib Ishak, a Palestinian. The laborers were mostly Arabs; that first year, most of the Princeton staff took time to study Arabic. Apostolos Athanassiou, the gifted draftsman, was Turkish. The head of the mosaics crew, William Gad Gabriel, was an Egyptian Copt. It was a time of much casual racism, and people were routinely classified by their ethnicity. Athanassiou's wife, Victoria, one of the object recorders, was said to be "Italian, born in Constantinople, and combines admirably the better qualities of the Latin in the Levant." In his summary of the 1936 campaign, field director Campbell headed one page "Native Members of Staff," listing William Gad and Ishak among others. He gave no reasons for the separate record, except to say that "listing in this manner will avoid hurting feelings; at any rate that is the aim." Ethnic divisions, then, were never invisible, perhaps heightened by the poisonous racial obsessions leaching out of Nazi Germany. But even before Hitler's rise to power, it took only a few months in Antioch in 1932 for Elderkin to pick up on the "strong antagonism between Palestinians and Syrians."

Even the French and the Americans did not always see eye to eye. Lassus and Campbell mostly did. But it was by no means certain by 1935 that the French concession would be renewed. Campbell wrote Morey that while Seyrig, representing French interests in Syria, did want to renew, he wasn't sure about the Louvre. Seyrig "seemed disgusted by the attitude of the Louvre toward our mosaics." Meanwhile, Lassus at one point became so sure the Americans would bow out altogether that Campbell, in a letter to Morey on May 15, 1936, pictured him as ready to work under solely French auspices and "already selecting his own staff."

When he'd first tried to secure support for the Antioch venture, Morey had encountered real mistrust of the French among his colleagues. Now, working together, mutual suspicion had not entirely disappeared. Back in 1932, on first reporting for duty in Antioch and meeting with Clarence Fisher, Lassus had suggested that France was not obliged to share the finds according to any set formula. This was news to the Americans. To stem a potential insurrection, Seyrig had to go back and explain that no, "neither concession nor law specifies fifty-fifty division, but usage confirms it. . . . Believe you have no concern."

Thoroughly capable, fluent in English, but otherwise a Frenchman out of central casting, an immaculate dresser, Henri Seyrig was one smooth customer. He made himself useful to the Americans but, perhaps inevitably, was not always so forthright with them. At one point he tried to convince them, without success, to leave formal publication of the mosaics to the seasoned Swiss archaeologist and art historian Marguerite van Berchem, instead of to editors at Princeton. Writing to van Berchem on May 13, 1936, just before the big division set for July, he confided something of what he thought of the Americans: "What they have written about the Judgment of Paris mosaic and on that of Yakto is so bad; their inability, not only to resolve problems but even to notice them, is so obvious that I don't see much good" in their doing it themselves. Relations between the Americans and the French remained mostly cordial; but the two expedition partners were never entirely of like mind.

Then again, neither were the Americans themselves. Writing from Baltimore at the beginning of the second year, Rob Garrett advised Morey that he and Worcester's Francis Taylor were fine with leaving the distribution of the mosaics in his, Morey's, hands. But such deference could not last forever, and soon Baltimore and Worcester were speaking up for themselves. After meeting with Morey in May 1935, Taylor set down for him the terms of what he deemed a "satisfactory arrangement" on the divisions. He'd hoped to postpone any division until the end of the first five years of the concession. But that, he realized, wouldn't sit well with Baltimore, which "came out rather badly in the [previous] division." So he accepted terms Morey laid out to him, with one condition: His "trustees feel that it is only fair and right that we should have first choice next year"; and Garrett, on behalf of Baltimore, had agreed.

But Taylor wasn't finished caviling about the hand dealt Worcester: "The Trustees have instructed me to protest formally . . . against the rapacious attitude of the Louvre in this proposed division. . . . The great majority of the best objects have been earmarked by the Louvre, the next best for Baltimore and the rather sad left-overs for Worcester," which he represented as scarcely worth the cost of shipping them across the Atlantic. If the excavations went beyond the initial five years, the Americans should go it alone, without the Louvre; they'd have to discuss this when they met, as then planned, the following March in Antioch. In the meantime, they'd need to get across to the French and the Syrians that the American subscribers "are becoming a little restive. . . . I can see no advantage to handling the situation any longer with kid gloves. The time has come for a little polite but plain speaking."

A few days later, Garrett "happened to drop in" on Mr. Morey in Princeton, as he put it in a letter to Taylor on May 14, finding him "a good deal upset by your letter," and moving Garrett to offer a little fatherly advice. Taylor's "plain speaking" would not do:

> Because in this matter we are dealing with foreigners I think we could not handle this in the way you suggest. The representatives of the Louvre and Syria are Frenchmen and one has to be very diplomatic with them, especially in view of the fact that they are the real ones in authority. We must not approach them in the direct rough and tumble manner more or less characteristic of American businessmen.

A certain coarseness did sometimes creep into the vernacular of the dig. The stakes were high, the "sides" sometimes at odds. At one point early on, George Elderkin wrote Morey that Prost had asked him "what you wished to do with reference to partition of the spoil." And later, in a talk in Baltimore, Morey anticipated that an upcoming "division of the spoils" might spur some real horse-trading among the contending museum representatives. Of course, it would all be fair enough: Finds would be "divided into first class, medium and inferior pieces, and an effort will be made to see that each party gets a choice."

—

By the late 1930s, political uncertainty had begun to complicate and corrode the Antioch excavations. The armistice ending the Great War in 1918 had settled nothing. Toxic nationalism was rampant. Europe was uneasy, hurtling toward new hostilities. Hitler came to power in Germany in 1933, denounced the Versailles Treaty in early 1935, won back the Saar industrial region from France a month later, and that same year proclaimed the Nuremberg Laws, which legitimized the persecution of Jews, already a fact of German life. "A catastrophe has befallen us with regard to land," Campbell wrote Morey that April. "It seems that the French government is going to settle Antioch and its vicinity with Jewish refugees from the Saar"; the first three hundred families were due in a month. If the rumor proved true, it would boost the price of land, including land on which the expedition might wish to dig.

Meanwhile, Syrian nationalists were challenging the legitimacy of the French Mandate. Bayard Dodge, asked by the Committee "to take any measures deemed necessary" to protect the mosaics and other expedition property should the political situation worsen, wrote Morey with his reading of the situation: Antioch, it seemed to him, was safer than ever. The Turks, Brits, and French seemed to be cooperating better. Moreover, "the European powers have unusually large military forces at this end of the Mediterranean so that the native populations have no idea of making trouble at the moment." Still, if events got out of hand, "we can take some action to assure the safety of the mosaics." He hoped Morey would visit in the spring, "as the mosaics make a splendid display"; and hoped, too, that the upcoming division, then set for March, would be "pleasant and fair."

Campbell and Morey were not wholly reassured by this sunny appraisal. A few days later, at Morey's behest, Campbell wrote William Gad Gabriel, head of the mosaics crew, with "a letter of thanks and praise for your good work of the past season." He asked Gad to remain in Antioch after December 1, at full salary, "to be ready to help pack and ship the mosaics in case there is danger to them from a war in Syria." Gad was to take direction from a group of three that included Dodge:

> What I want you to do if they tell you to move them is to call your men and make boxes and straw mattresses for the mosaics and have your men load them on trucks for Beirut. I know that you will do these things in your careful way and I trust the matter to your hands. . . . May God grant that no war comes to Syria and that we shall meet in peace and health in March,

for the following season at Antioch.

War didn't come to Syria in March 1936. Nor, for that matter, in July, when many of the key figures in the excavations converged on Antioch for the division-of-finds, the first in several years. It was an opportunity for some of them to meet for the first time. There was business to conduct, agreements to hammer out, but also a chance to relax in a congenial setting, as at luncheons in the sun-dappled courtyard of the excavation headquarters.

All seemed to realize it was an auspicious moment in the life of the expedition, coming as it did at the end of its fifth season, near the end of the French concession, and prompting some little ceremony. In one of many group photos taken that summer, Lassus, Adib Ishak, Richard Stillwell, a Princeton archaeologist visiting the dig, and some of the others stood gathered in an expedition storeroom beside local dignitaries, a dozen or more of them, in fine beards and mustaches, long robes and varieties of Near Eastern headwear. One of them was Suleiman Hindié, whose Daphne property had yielded the Boat of Psyches. In the front row, squeezed in among them, in dark suit and tie, arms folded across his chest, looking his usual mildly forbidding self, was Mr. Morey, a few days off the boat that had delivered him to Beirut.

In another photo, the Westerners got together for a dressy dinner in the headquarters courtyard, a dozen of them or so crowded around the table, with linen tablecloth, flowers, bowls of potage, seeming to let down their hair. There was Campbell, Seyrig, looking dapper as ever in his light suit, across the table from his wife, Miette, along with her Olympic sailor friend and fellow adventurer, Ella Maillart. There, too, was the unlikely American duo who had helped make the excavation possible, Rob Garrett from Baltimore and, down the table's long axis from Morey, Francis Taylor from Worcester. The photograph recording the moment appears damaged, part of the original negative apparently double-exposed. Yet by some strange aesthetic alchemy the blemish contributes to the energy of the scene, the broad smiles and ebullience among several of them, the clash of mismatched images and a peculiar ghostlike blurring lending a sense of vivacity, of palpable bonhomie, to the moment.

In the end, the Americans and their French counterparts, including Jean Charbonneaux of the École du Louvre, didn't entirely resolve the division of objects collected since 1933. They did agree to press forward with the concession for another six years and extend its scope to Antioch's ancient Mediterranean port, Seleucia, founded a few years before Antioch itself. The previous spring, British archaeologist Leonard Woolley had led a productive dig there for the British Museum. "It was Woolley's arrival in our territory," Campbell wrote Francis Taylor on December 11, 1936, "that made me so anxious to have the Committee extend its concession to include Seleucia." The prospects there were "promising." Also promising, he assured Taylor, might be a renewed dig on the Antioch Island, site of the first important finds in 1932. Up to now, they had been thwarted by a Turkish landowner determined to recoup his gambling losses and demanding an exorbitant price for his land. He was a big shot around town, and the Mandatory government preferred not to irritate him by expropriating his land. But then, reported Campbell, the problem vanished when he was murdered and his property passed on to more agreeable successors.

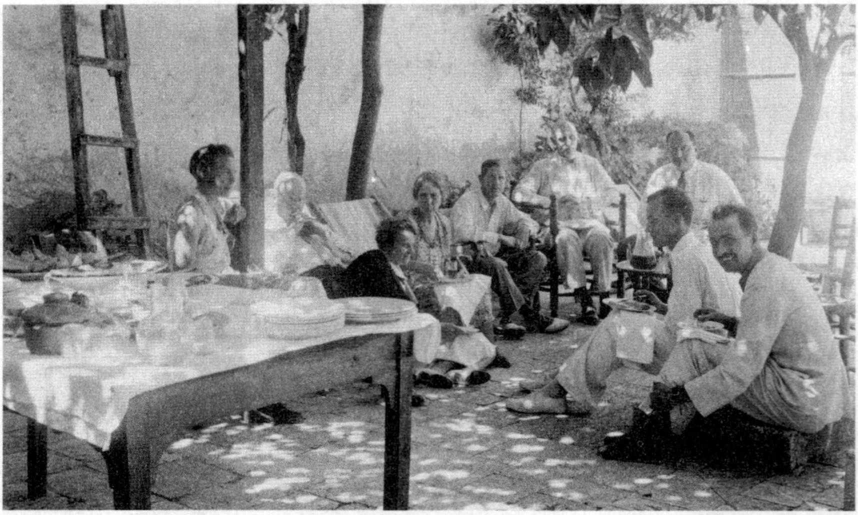

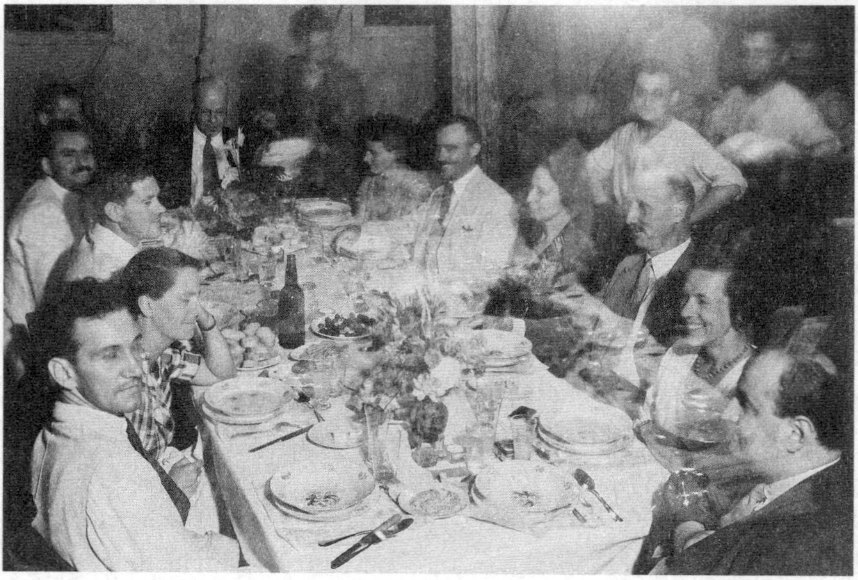

In July 1936, several of the expedition's key figures converged on Antioch to divide mosaic and other finds, reestablish personal ties, and take a social breather after five seasons of excavation. The courtyard photo shows Robert Garrett and Francis Taylor seated at the far end of the courtyard, just to Sandy Campbell's left as he leans forward in his chair. At far left, Charles Rufus Morey, chin in hand, sits beside author and journalist Ella Maillart, wife of Henri Seyrig, the French antiquities director. The dinner party photo (with ghostlike images of unknown origin) seems more formal, linen and flowers gracing the table. It shows Taylor, closest to us on the right, and Garrett two places down. Natty Henri Seyrig, smiling broadly, sits toward the far end of the table, Rufus Morey at its head.

CHAPTER ELEVEN

Buffet Supper

In the years after 1936, and with the renewal of the concession, the Antioch expedition opened a new chapter. It had some institutional maturity by now, more of a public presence. "New Theater Discovered in Daphne," "New Mosaics Bound for Baltimore," read headlines back in the States. The Committee had originally settled on a policy of no new subscribers. But in late October 1937, Morey reported that, at an "informal meeting" at Worcester in February, it had been rescinded. New money materialized. Even as Baltimore and Worcester planned to withdraw their financial support after their promised six years, others stepped in. The Institute for Advanced Study, located in Princeton near the university but independent, contributed. So did the American Philosophical Society. So, finally, did Harvard University.

This last subscriber was a center for Byzantine studies occupying a Washington, D.C., mansion known as Dumbarton Oaks, soon to become affiliated with Harvard; its wealthy owners, Robert Woods Bliss and his wife, Mildred, old friends of Morey, threw in their support for the excavation. Back in 1931, it would be said, Harvard had "missed the train" by turning down Morey's invitation to help support Antioch. But now, five years later, it was on board.

Each spring the Princeton contingent arrived from America, Barbari Mahmud Isa and the other *reises* from Egypt, and Arab workers from in and around Antioch. After 1932, Campbell was a steady presence as director, except for one semester when Wellesley couldn't release him from his professorial duties. The other constant was Lassus, who, despite the personal angst of his fruitless attempts to line up a faculty slot in France, served during most of these years as assistant director. Apostolos Athanassiou was engineer and his wife, Victoria, assistant recorder. And, of course, there was Adib Ishak, who managed everything, was never fazed, and wrote long, fact-filled reports for Campbell, Morey, and Lassus: "Acute, energetic, and an excellent negotiator who knows the proper Oriental approach to any delicate undertaking," wrote Dick Stillwell after a visit to the dig in the summer of 1936. Meanwhile, Sandy Campbell now had a second son; when Glanville Downey wrote to congratulate him he suggested the boy's middle name be Libanius, Malalas, or Seleucus.

Most expedition members lived in what Stillwell, seeing it for the first time in 1936, would describe as a "picturesque native house situated in the Turkish residential quarter of the town," with two-story wings surrounding a large, stone-paved court shaded by lemon and bitter orange trees, and trellises bedecked with vines. Some rooms had wood-paneled walls, "gaily painted with scenes and sprays of foliage." Seven minutes away on foot, by Stillwell's reckoning, were the Stores, the former British cavalry barracks, facing the Aleppo Road, affording substantial room for open-air storage. It was flanked by long sheds for working and additional storage. Its two-story gatehouse contained a drafting room, photographer's room, and quarters for some of the native staff.

Among those active in the campaigns of 1937 and 1938 were Frederick Waagé, recorder of finds, a young Cornell University archaeologist, veteran of a major dig in Greece. With him was his wife of two years, Dorothy, assistant recorder, a graduate of Kalamazoo College, in Michigan. New on the job and eager to share her experiences, she wrote long letters home to her parents in Kalamazoo about the life of the dig. In one, she wrote of trying to teach the kitchen staff "that a dish towel is something for dishes only, that a dish pan is not to be used for toilet purposes, that

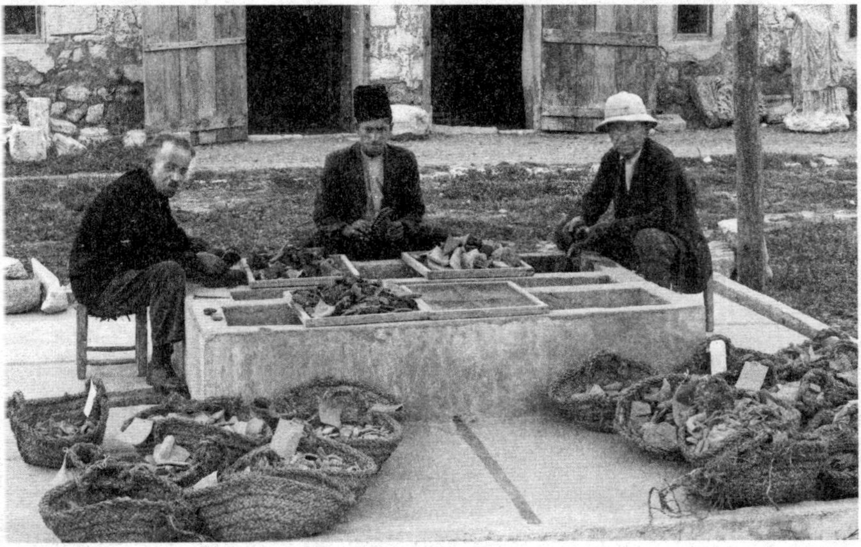

The baskets in the foreground, full of sherds—bits of pottery—need to be sorted, evaluated for their worth, and washed—all part of the everyday haul of the expedition. The expedition headquarters building stands behind these men at work.

the drinking water which is all boiled before we use it must not be filtered through any old rag."

In Dorothy Waagé's letters, the necessary order and routine of a dig, often overshadowed by the occasional Great Find, got their due: Each evening, twenty-five or thirty baskets would be delivered to her and Mrs. Athanassiou, each full of potsherds, bits of marble sculpture, coins, maybe the occasional bronze tool. First, their contents were washed, then placed on screens to drain and dry, then sorted. Dorothy wrote appreciatively of her husband, Fred, who could "go over a basket of broken pottery in a very few minutes, give the date of manufacturer of most of the pieces and so date the building or the level of civilization being excavated." The finds were sorted by a kind of archaeological triage—pieces worth fully cataloguing, those worth keeping for reference, and those deemed worthless. She and Mrs. Athanassiou marked those in the first group with date and place of find, entered them in a running inventory, and made out a card, with description for each. Every object was photographed, its picture pasted on a card, cards filed by category. Even those classed as worthless weren't: Sherds from Antioch, gathered in thick cardboard trays at Princeton today, are sometimes loaned out to colleges and museums to give students a hands-on taste for antiquity—innocuous bits of ceramic, some as small as an American quarter coin, some a couple of inches across, blue, celadon, or honey-hued; one with a suggestion of leopard spots, another with dark brown lines forming a fingerlike projection. Any of them could have been part of a much-loved pot, plate, or planter shattered in an earthquake, or by a moment's inattention.

Coins minted at Antioch from the earliest days of the Seleucid kings and all through the city's tenure as capital of a Roman province normally bore the profile of the emperor—Augustus, the Empire's founder, Nero the fabled fiddler, Julian the apostate. Those recovered during the dig were mostly of bronze and other low-value metals, not silver or gold. But, as Mrs. Waagé wrote, they were "one of the most important pieces of evidence in dating the objects found and so tracing the history of a people." An emperor's known reign might help fix a date for, say, a mosaic found just above or beneath the coins.

Waagé was still new to the arduous work, but she made it her own. Fifteen years later she'd publish a detailed, much-respected catalogue of some fourteen thousand coins excavated from Antioch.

—

After the summer divisions meeting of 1936 and into 1937 and 1938, things chugged along at Antioch, almost too well. The expedition had reached a stage where Dick Stillwell, who often seemed to see with new eyes, could wonder whether the excavations had become, if it were possible, *too* efficient, too focused on "the amount of cubic metres of earth dug up." In early 1937, Jean Lassus complained that the previous July's partage had consigned 110 mosaics to an unfinished Antioch museum unready to receive them, that they took up precious storage space and left little room for "the next round" of mosaic discoveries.

By now, the mosaics were famous in archaeological circles, drawing scads of visitors to the site—enough, by early 1937, to become a nuisance: So many were the French, German, English, and Americans among them,

Dorothy Waagé wrote her parents, and "such a distraction from work, that beginning tomorrow they are to be barred . . . except for two hours each afternoon."

Yet how reasonably expect them to stay away? The mosaics were a treat, offering an experience beyond anything they could get from books or research articles. Ancient visitors to a late antique villa, after all, savored mosaics close-up, in all their color, beneath their very feet. From that near perch to the black-and-white photos taken by Schirmer or expedition photographer Fadil Nasser Saba, squeezed into postcard-sized images on poorly printed paper stock, was a long way down. Visitors to the Antioch stores, on the other hand, witnessed the originals, in all their color, vibrancy, and sheer *presence*—women at a funerary banquet, peacocks in their plumage, playful Erotes, mystifying geometries. True, the larger mosaics were often cut into panels to get them out of the ground in the first place. And seeing them just piled into the storage rooms, leaning against walls, or laid out on the floor lost something, too. Still, it was the real thing, the original art, only recently extracted from the earth, still bearing the ghostly imprint of the hands that made them.

At a Committee meeting held at his house in Princeton on October 22, 1937, Mr. Morey read into the record a letter from Michael Rostovtzeff, a towering figure in the study of Greek and Roman history who had fled his native Russia at the time of the Revolution, wound up at Yale, played a key role in the important dig at Dura-Europos, and had recently stopped in Antioch to see the mosaics.

> I must tell you again how much I admired the mosaics of Antioch. I went there in a somewhat skeptical mood but after I saw the mosaics I changed my mind completely and I regard this set of monuments as one of the most important additions to ancient art in general and ancient painting in particular.

The haul for the 1937 season was seventy-five mosaic panels found, lifted, and cemented for storage; fifteen found but left in place; eighty-nine ready for the next division in 1938. One hundred eighty digging days, the work of 2,159 men. And 625 visitors to the mosaics collection. All through the later years of the excavation, the mosaics kept coming, the numbers piling up, the luster of the Antioch Mosaics—it's time now, I think, to endow them with uppercase rank—growing.

Early publication, word of mouth, and the appearance of a few of them in America excited curiosity and interest. Even by 1935, and accelerating across the next few years, the mosaics had become known among American museums beyond the original subscribers. Museums in St. Louis and Toronto wanted to buy some. Baltimore's Robert Garrett reported interest from Herbert Eustis Winlock, director of the Met in New York. Francis Taylor told of inquiries from the University Museum in Philadelphia and from the Yale School of Art. The mosaics were attractive, and they *attracted*. For the time being, however, "it was moved that no sales be made without the unanimous consent of the subscribers."

First to get such consent, two years later, seems to have been the Honolulu Academy of Arts in Hawaii, not then an American state. The mosaic panel it hoped to purchase, dated to the late fifth century or early sixth, was almost exactly square, nine and a half feet on a side. It depicted a maned lion in profile, the muscles of its tawny hide modeled in yellow-brown tesserae or, in the shadows, mauves and reds. It showed a leopard in pursuit of an ostrich, a tigress leaping onto the back of an antelope.

Among mosaics coming out of Antioch, several feature a hunting theme, the one lying within the topographical border of the Yakto mosaic not the least of them. The Honolulu Hunt, as it became known, was found in a room in the same Daphne villa as the much larger Worcester Hunt, and assigned to Princeton in the 1936 division. At the October 1937 meeting of the Committee came word that the Honolulu Academy had offered $4,000 for it. Make it $5,000 and it's yours, the Committee replied. Honolulu agreed; the young museum's new director, archaeologist Edgar C. Schenck, was a Princeton grad, class of 1931, who in 1933 had briefly served with the expedition team himself. Morey forwarded the check, credited to the Antioch expedition, to George Wintringer, Princeton's comptroller, "for the neat little sum of $5000"; may we imagine Morey rubbing his hands with glee?

By April 1938, a Honolulu newspaper reported, the mosaic was in its new home:

> Persons viewing the Academy galleries on a certain day last week must have wondered at the curious scene that confronted them—the placing in permanent position of this 5th century work of art. . . . It required fifteen men working over five hours (with additional help when the slab became too unwieldy) to move the mosaic into the early art room where it will be on display permanently.

This mosaic was apparently the first the Honolulu Academy had ever exhibited. Director Schenck, writing in the museum's *Bulletin*, felt moved to explain just what a mosaic was; that the word itself was unrelated to the Hebrew, as in "Mosaic Law," but went back to the Greek root for "museum"; that "the tiny bits of material which form the pattern are called *tesserae*." A mosaic was a little like a Hawaiian feather cloak, he observed, which was made of tiny feathers intricately arranged to form a pattern. As for "the exact meaning of the mosaic or the purpose of the villa" in which it was found, he couldn't say. Maybe the villa was actually a hunting lodge, the Honolulu mosaic and its sister in Worcester devoted to simple "pleasure without symbolical intention," as Morey's friend Erwin Panofsky had suggested.

"Our mosaic," Schenck concluded with what sounds like warm institutional proprietorship, "belongs to the period when East met West on the shores of the Mediterranean—many years before Europe was aware of the existence of Hawaii."

At the 1936 meetings it had been decided to broaden the dig's dominion to Seleucia Pieria, fifteen miles down the Orontes from Antioch; though once a port, two thousand years of sedimentation had left it inland. When it and Antioch were founded, Seleucia had for a time been the more significant of the two; now, awaiting the excavator's spade, it held rich archaeological promise.

"New Explorations Allowed in Syria," a headline appeared back in America, the accompanying article quoting Mr. Morey at length. Seleucia was

> the site of the famous tunnel, through the lower spur of Musa Dagh, which was cut by the Roman soldiery in the first and second centuries A.D. to form an outlet for a mountain torrent that otherwise would have flooded the town of Seleucia. In this tunnel the Roman legions have left inscriptions recording their labor.

The Tunnel of Titus, they call it now, named for the Roman emperor who advanced the great project. Tourists walk its rubbly way today.

As with almost every decision made by the Committee, the turn to Seleucia put the redoubtable Adib Ishak to work: "Last Wednesday," he wrote Campbell on May 21, he'd visited Seleucia—known in French as Soueidie, or in Turkish as Samandağ—where he'd "arranged for repairs of the road by the city gate." Local officials accompanied him, promising to start work the next day. Then, with Lassus, Fred Waagé, Apostolos Athanassiou, and their wives, Ishak had surveyed the area, looking into living quarters for them all.

As he protested to Campbell, Lassus was not eager to extend the dig to Seleucia that summer. The mosquitoes were horrendous. Seleucia was down near where the Orontes spilled into the sea. People working there the previous year had come down "terribly sick from malaria." Tents for the staff wouldn't do. They'd never be able to build a properly screened house in time. And the local peasants' houses nearest the dig were too dirty and too small. One local landowner, otherwise eager to rent out a house, had confided to Mme Lassus his frank astonishment that they'd picked "the hardest and most unhealthy moment of the year" to dig.

On page three of this same letter, abruptly done with Seleucia, Lassus slipped into a lighter key—no transition, no prelude, no preamble: "I am able to tell you," he announced with a ripple of fanfare, "what was the menu of a comfortable Antiochenian meal" in ancient times. This he proceeded to set out on the typed page, meticulously centered, like a menu from a French restaurant:

Soft-boiled eggs

Artichauts [artichokes]

Pork's feet with tomato sauce

Big fish and salad

Boiled ham with pimiento sauce

Roasted chicken

Turkey

Pudding

White and red wine *Pain à discrétion*

No coffee nor liquors

"Not so bad, anyway," he added—which, coming from a Frenchman, must rank as high praise.

The source of this charming if unsolicited knowledge? A few days before, a second- or third-century villa in Daphne had yielded a fresh mosaic find: Its outer border of regularly spaced diamond blocks was pretty much intact. Otherwise, there were frustrating losses, but enough was left that the excavators could make sense of it: A circular emblema depicted Ganymede, a Trojan prince of Greek myth whom Zeus, as an eagle, had spirited up to Mount Olympus to serve as his cupbearer. Set out around this panel, in a horseshoe-shaped array, were disposed a medley of dishes laid out on silver plates, the source of Lassus's menu. It took about two hundred tesserae to depict the pig's foot, seventy-five for each of the soft-boiled eggs.

Whoever wrote the minutes of the Committee's next meeting was equally taken by the image, which included two flasks of wine, three loaves of bread, and a "large three-layer cake with a thick icing." These dishes seemed quite ready to eat. Normally, dishes for a Roman dinner were brought out in a set order to which the mosaic seemed at least roughly to conform. On the other hand there was an all-at-onceness to the tableau; we imagine our guests at their languorous ease, free to select what they wish, in any order, buffet-style.

The villa in which this mosaic was found became known as the House of the Buffet Supper.

—

Antioch and Daphne recorded no slackening of finds in 1937 and 1938. The turn to Seleucia, only briefly delayed, bore fruit. The sale to the Honolulu museum represented a profitable new direction. The logistical problem—all those eager visitors getting in the way of the dig's work—could likewise be seen as a metric of success. Soon, though, the measured progress of the dig up to now would be disrupted by larger forces that the excavators had no power to arrest.

CHAPTER TWELVE

Omphalos

Work had to be stopped, Campbell wrote early in 1938, due to flooding. Later, as he reported to Morey, he heard there'd been "42 days of continuous rain but this may be an exaggeration. At any rate, it looks like a wet year."

A wet year it was, one that anyone there for any part of it would not soon forget. "The rain continued," Campbell recorded on April 16. "We tried to excavate but had to give it up."

In May, the Worcester Art Museum's associate curator of decorative arts, Louisa Dresser, arrived in Antioch to identify objects she hoped to bring back to Massachusetts. She was there just a week, but a memorable one. She saw a new archaeological museum going up in Antioch. She witnessed street battles between Turks and Arabs. And she saw the "torrential rains [that] caused mountain streams to run wild and sent the Orontes River over its banks." At one point, she stopped with Lassus and Campbell, along with one of the *reises* and Fadil Saba, for a photo of themselves gathered on the slope of a hill near the town of Narlidja, bundled up in rain gear like kids, cheerfully drenched.

"It rained steadily all night, with occasional downpours that increased to a cloudburst just before dawn," Campbell wrote on May 4 in the expedition log. "The street on which the [expedition's] house is located was a rushing torrent, knee-deep as far as the carpenter shops, where the depth was half way up the hips; all the shops were flooded."

The waters poured off the mountains and into the city. The Parmenius, which carried runoff down through the gorge between the adjacent mountains and into the city, wildly overflowed, leaving large areas of Antioch underwater. Fields and orchids in the valley flatness were reduced to lakes.

For Dorothy Waagé, as she wrote home to her parents, the flood was

> the event which loomed largest in our lives during the past two weeks. . . . In one night it sent rocks crashing down the mountain side to break houses and kill a few people; the river rose over the fields; the streets were over ankle deep in mud; roads were washed out. It was a major disaster.

This was all quite dramatic, of course, as extreme weather is. It halted the work of the dig. It took lives. But it also proved *interesting* to the archaeologists: "If this terrible storm has thus considerably frustrated our work," Lassus wrote, it had also granted them front-row seats on "one of those disasters of which the history of Antioch is so full, and which has brought about such major changes in the very geography of the site."

He, Dresser, and Fadil hiked up the slope of Mt. Staurin to photograph the flooded valley. The idea was to gain, if possible, a clearer idea of the shape of the original Island and the old river channels that had marked its borders; they knew where the Island was, but not its limits and extent. Maybe, somehow, the flood would clarify things. It did not. Their reconnaissance failed. The flooding didn't reveal; it obliterated.

Later, after the waters receded, Lassus went back and tried to review the damage inflicted though fresh eyes. He wrote of the "veritable river of stones" the flooded Parmenius had dislodged. "Across a length of several hundred meters it has dumped a bed of material which in places reached almost 1.8 meters thick, to judge by the narrow space left free above the doors" of some houses. Several people had died in their sleep. Some children, trying to flee, had been carried along in the street by the current of stones. The water swept all before it, scouring the mountain slopes, washing sand, dirt, and stone down onto the Antioch plain.

This wasn't news, exactly. Lassus knew that layers of sediment, the product of ancient flooding, lay over large parts of the ancient city, helping disguise its contours, mask its key sites, streets, and monuments. But now, in the spring of 1938, the excavators could see up close, in a way beyond mere knowing, just how Antioch had become so irremediably lost. Not earthquakes to reflexively blame this time, nor Pompeian volcanoes, nor overrunning armies. A single spate of storms across six weeks of 1938 told the story: The force of flowing water, ruthlessly overwhelming its channels and constraints, layering the mountain onto the plain, had effaced the old city. If in the ruins of some ancient structure they found only a few foundational walls, as Lassus summed up the lesson, "it is not necessary to believe it the result of human destruction."

Establishing the shape of ancient Antioch had devolved upon Lassus more than the others. By his particular bent of intellect, and maybe, too, as the only Frenchman, he had marked off terrain a little to the side of his mosaics-charmed colleagues. The first dig conducted under his auspices, near the Habib al-Najjar mosque in the middle of the city, had brought him, six meters down, to what he suspected was the original Roman road. Thanks to this modest success, he'd write later, "I found myself specialized," the great topographic problem somehow become his own.

What he wanted—what they all wanted, really, but what the mosaics had sidetracked them from—were solid archaeological facts, not vague contentions from the ancients or inspired guesswork, but physical finds in rubble and stone, at specific locations, so many yards underground, tucked below this stratum, above that one, here, not there. Such detail in hand, they'd better be able to locate the palaces, gateways, theaters, major streets, and stadia that from even before their arrival in Antioch had been their object. A proper map of Antioch had been all but written into the aims of the expedition. Now it had become Lassus's own mission.

An affinity for order, uniformity, and best practice influenced the design of Roman cities, similar architectural and planning features reliably recurring across the Empire. One element was a generally north–south street, the *cardo*, intersecting an east–west street, the *documens*, with the city's forum, its government and commercial center, nearby. Antioch's origins went all the way back to the Seleucid kings, but a succession of emperors had presided over it long enough, since 64 BCE, to make it truly Roman. The coins they struck and the urban structures they built reflected the largesse of each emperor in turn. As historian Andrea De Giorgi wrote, "No emperor shied away from leaving his mark on Antioch."

One of them was Valens, who reigned from 364 to 378. Otherwise undistinguished among the pantheon of Roman emperors, he did bestow on Antioch one notably grand urban complex—a new forum, much attested to in the literature and on every expedition wish list. The Forum figured in numerous maps coming down from earlier generations—as well as one drafted by the Princeton excavators themselves. This map shows with reassuring clarity the several important civic structures thought to make it up, including a basilica and a temple; the Forum virtually straddling Lassus's "Main Street"; the Parmenius, dropping down off the mountain. Yet it could undercut one's confidence by its very title: "Forum of Valens, Antioch: Restoration from Literary Evidence." Not physical evidence.

From the U.S. on March 1, 1937, Campbell wrote Lassus of the coming season's work, in particular about what the Committee thought might be his best shot at finding the Forum of Valens. He included a map that laid out a prospective spot at which to begin digging, adding:

> I hope you will understand that these suggestions are not intended by us to tell you where to dig. They are rather to give you the benefit of research at Princeton so that you can culminate your work on the Main Street by finding the Forum of Valens. . . . We are all watching hopefully for you to find the Forum, because then the real excavation of Antioch will begin.

Campbell was trying to defer to Lassus's sensitivities, but apparently didn't defer enough. Lassus wrote back, in English, "Are you sure it is extremely fair to change my program even by simple suggestions, without asking before for my advice? Perhaps I had some ideas about how to [find?] the Forum of Valens which would have been useful." He would do as requested, of course, but "may I ask for a more detailed account of the reason which make you choose that place" in which to dig?

To use a word more of our time than his, Lassus felt disrespected. At a meeting early the following year, the Committee chalked it up to a simple "misunderstanding"—that of Lassus, who had read the Committee's "recommendations" as an order. Later, the Committee would bend over backward to acknowledge Lassus's arduous struggle to make physical sense of ancient Antioch—in particular, its "Main Street," mentions of which appeared in all the ancient literature, its Forum of Valens, and its omphalos.

Omphalos is Greek for "navel," referring in this context to sacred stone artifacts found at the centers of ancient cities, like Delphi, and so presumably marking their earliest physical sites. Its location in Antioch was thought to correspond to a particular crossing of the great colonnaded Main Street. From some point along its length, near this omphalos, a ceremonial transverse street was thought to shoot off across the city to the Island, with its palace, hippodrome, and baths. Somewhere near the omphalos, too, would stand the Forum of Valens. All these named places likely lay at the base of the deep gorge, between the mountains Silpius and Staurin to the east, down which waters in flood became the Parmenius, whose destructive power Lassus witnessed in 1938.

Around these particulars the old maps, written accounts, and informed guesses of the expedition team all seemed to coalesce. Indeed—thinking roughly now—it could seem that the Forum, the omphalos, and the point at which the Parmenius coursed down from the mountain gorge across the colonnaded street and into the city all occupied the self-same spot on the map.

But how big is a *spot*? In modern New York City, Times Square, the Theater District, the Port Authority, Penn Station, and Madison Square Garden might all be imagined as inhabiting a single defined piece of Manhattan real estate. Down on the street, of course, they are each distinct entities, city blocks apart. But recalled only indistinctly, or from up in space, they could be thought to merge into a single fuzzy spot on the map of the city. A similar blurriness bedeviled the Princeton excavators. Even four or five years into the excavations, they had little to show by way of archaeological corroboration in mortar, marble, or stone for just how the Forum of Valens fit into Antioch. It was the detailed arrangement of the site, not merely its approximate location, that they sought.

In the end, Lassus was able to define the Forum in relation to yet another notable feature of Antioch geography: He would describe "an axial rupture" between the southern reaches of the colonnaded street and the northern, one abruptly veering off at an angle of about five degrees from the other. As historian Peter Brown has written, the street was "like a scar line drawn from one end to the other of the huddled modern city." It went as straight as you'd like for several miles along the base of the adjoining hills, only then to suddenly diverge—not much, but enough to notice. You could make out faint vestiges of the swerve in aerial photos the French took in the early 1930s, or in today's Google maps of the city.

Later, to listen to Glanville Downey, this gentlest of junctions was quite the aesthetic triumph, a statue of the emperor Tiberius once marking the spot: "As one walked along the avenue toward the center of the city, from either direction, one's view came to rest" there, granting "a more pleasing effect than a straight, unending row of colonnades disappearing into the distance." Where the two met, the point where one diverged slightly from the other, was the omphalos, about fifty meters south of where the Parmenius crossed the colonnaded street. It was no public plaza that stood there, Lassus found, but a bridge, which permitted the mountain torrent to flow beneath it; atop an arched stone vault going back to the second century BCE, the Valens Forum had been built, neatly propped up above even heavy floods.

Early in 1938, field director Campbell recapped his friend and colleague's success this way:

> M. Lassus uncovered the top of a large arched construction which subsequent excavation revealed as one of a pair of tunnel vaults

> that formed the Hellenistic Main Street bridge over the stream Parmenius. This was a discovery of major importance for the reconstruction of the plan of Antioch,

to a degree redeeming hopes originally held for the expedition.

Not every last uncertainty and imprecision had been erased. Still, Lassus's Main Street dig, his pursuit of the omphalos and the Forum of Valens, conducted across almost the whole span of the excavation, ranks as one of only a few elements of the dig to challenge its fixation on mosaics. Years later, as an old man, Lassus returned to Princeton to sort through the maps, drawings, photos, texts, and other material left from the thirties and finish a book devoted to this work.

Maybe, an errant thought intrudes, this was what they should have been doing all along? Think hard enough, pursue enough leads, dig in enough places, dig deep enough, push ahead with enough patience, and you might someday know where you were in old Antioch.

CHAPTER THIRTEEN

Out of Antioch

It was 1937, 1938, and 1939, and the world was troubled. The political situation across Europe and the Levant alike seethed with wayward and dangerous energy. Twenty years after the Treaty of Sèvres had dismembered the Ottoman Empire and all but ceded Syria to France, Syrians hankered for dissolution of the Mandate and their independence; Antioch's streets periodically shook to noisy expressions of their bitterness and pride. Meanwhile, France fretted over Turkey, across the Syrian border to the north. In the Great War, Turkey had fought beside the Germans and the other Central Powers, their defeat leading to the breakup of the Ottoman Empire. Now, in any new war, Turkey might again side with Germany—a rearmed, belligerent, National Socialist Germany.

Turkey's leader, Mustafa Kemal Atatürk, founder of the secular state that followed the Ottoman Empire's fall, saw the Sanjak of Alexandretta, which included Antioch, the fertile agricultural country around it, and the coastal harbor of Alexandretta, as properly Turkish; he called it Hatay, in homage to the ancient Hittites, whom he saw as its progenitors. "A land that has been Turkish for four thousand years," Atatürk told a delegation from Antioch in 1921, "cannot live a prisoner in the hands of the enemy." But for now, his Hatay remained in French hands.

In November 1937, a League of Nations–brokered agreement left the Sanjak of Alexandretta "distinct but not separated" from Syria diplomatically, while linked to both France and Turkey militarily. This was the first step in Antioch's geopolitical transformation.

In September 1938, the Sanjak of Alexandretta became the Republic of Hatay, under joint French and Turkish military control. It lasted less than a year. In June 1939, after a fiercely contested referendum, the Hatay legislature voted to extinguish itself and become part of Turkey. In July 1939, Turkey established Hatay as its sixty-fourth province; Antioch was now known as Antakya.

These years of political instability pressed hard against the excavations.

—

Antioch's rich ethnic, cultural, and religious mix across its history has been often noted, and extolled, the city seen as exemplar or paradigm for the creative energies kindled by diversity. According to the 1936 census, the 220,000 inhabitants of the Sanjak included 62,000 Alawite Arabs, 22,000 Sunni Arabs, 18,000 Greeks and other Christians, 24,000 Armenians, 9,000 Circassians, Jews, and Kurds, along with 86,000 ethnic Turks; they were the single largest group in the Sanjak, though nowhere near a majority.

While at times in its long history Antioch's various groups got along well, this was not one of them. The Sanjak was a cauldron of ethnic mistrust and division. "The Turks own the lands. The Arabs cultivate it on shares," Dorothy Waagé wrote a little sharply, if not inaccurately, to her parents. During these years, as Philip S. Khoury reviewed them in *Syria and the French Mandate*, you could tell apart three broad political/ethnic blocs by their *hats*: Kemalist Turks wore Western clothes, "in particular a melon-colored sports jacket and Western cloth hats." Certain Arab youth brigades adopted the *sidara*, a foldable cap popularized by the late king Faysal. Turkish and Alawite notables, Armenians, and Greek Orthodox Christians mostly wore the fez.

"We have had a rather unusual week here," Dorothy Waagė wrote her parents on June 6, 1937, from Antioch, one marked by noisy rival demonstrations by Turks and Arabs. At one point, "when an Arab sang one song out on the middle of the bridge, that started a riot, soldiers were called, a machine gun was stationed at the bridge, the Expedition's workmen on one dig fled, shops were all closed up. . . . The first sign of a revolution," she went on, by now, it seems, a seasoned political observer, "is the closing of the shops. Each shop has in front of it an iron door, like the top of a roll-top desk: these doors are let down with a great banging and padlocked."

A week later, things were quieter. "The revolution is over now," she wrote her parents. "The shops are open, and life back to normal. I hope that it stays that way." It didn't.

A loss of French say-so in Antioch didn't *need* to mean trouble for the American expedition, but well might. For it likely meant the abrogation of the generous French policy on archaeological divisions and its replacement by a stern Turkish one, which decreed that no antiquities leave the country, period. All through the late 1930s, as Campbell, Lassus, and the others oversaw the digs, attended to the mosaics, pottery, and sculpture they yielded, and catalogued their finds, Antioch and the Sanjak seethed. Weighing in on the situation in early 1938, Paul Alling, of the State Department, posted to Beirut, insisted "that the possibility of Turkish occupation or control of the Sanjak is remote"; besides, the French were presumably there to protect American interests. Wallace Murray, chief of the State Department's Division of Near Eastern Affairs, wrote Rufus Morey a little later that "we have received no information which would lead us to believe that American archaeological interests in the Sanjak are in any way jeopardized."

None of this stopped Morey from worrying. On the other hand, he didn't see a Turkish seizure of Antioch and a shutting down of the excavation as inevitable. Rather, things were, and would remain, confused. No one knew what was to happen in Europe, or in Antioch. Uncertainty hung over the Sanjak. Expedition minutes, reports, and correspondence were studded with uneasy references to "the political situation." Any reported negotiation, civic disturbance, news report, rumor, threat, troop movement, or act of political bluster could spur frantic concern; or else thoughtless dismissal.

"There is an uncertainty about everything we do here this year," Mrs. Waagé wrote home on March 23, 1938, "and a kind of undercurrent of sadness, for the international situation is so bad that it looks as if we might not finish the year, or if we do, we may not come back again for another season." Frenchmen she'd met were "convinced that there will be war," and soon. If so, she and husband, Fred, would head "straight home"; they'd already mapped out their travel options—either west across the Atlantic, or east to the Philippines and across the Pacific to the American West Coast.

In her next letter, she wrote of the upcoming plebiscite. Fifty representatives of the League of Nations were on hand to supervise it. But "over a thousand Turks" had been "imported" to vote for Turkey: "These men, fairly well dressed in European clothes, wander around the town all day with nothing to do, and have a kind of ominous appearance. . . . Turkish landowners are forcing their Arab peasants to vote for Turkey." France, meanwhile, had brought in "a whole brigade of Moroccan soldiers" ready to fight "at the slightest sign of violence from either party."

From his perch at the American University of Beirut, Bayard Dodge wrote Morey on May 16 that Henri Seyrig was "more anxious than ever to have valuable articles removed from the Antioch district before there can be danger of a new move on the part of the Turks." Seyrig suspected that, to maintain Black Sea access in case of war with Germany, the British and French had made "some secret deal with the Turks" that would leave them with the Sanjak.

In early May, according to an unsigned, but notably specific account in the Princeton archives, "the Turks opened fire on Dort-A-yaz, the 'alaouite' quarter of Antioch," wounding one person. A company of soldiers under a Lieutenant Mihran rushed in to establish order. "As the column headed for the spot, coming out onto the principal avenue of Antioch, it was greeted by fire from 30 mausers [German rifles]." Two soldiers fell dead. A policeman and a night watchman were wounded. Mihran and his men retreated, firing back to cover their retreat. "Some minutes after, the whole city was in a turmoil."

In a June 1 letter, Dorothy Waagé reviewed for her parents the increasingly fraught situation. As a force for order, the French and their Moroccan troops were impotent. "Whenever a man is hurt or killed the soldiers all come running and take out their three little armored cars and skoot around for a few minutes, and then retire. . . .

"Now, suddenly, everything has changed. The French commander has been told that Turkey is to control the assembly, whatever the outcome of the voting. Orders came from France. All fair play is off. The Sanjak is essentially Turkey's."

Meanwhile, the civil disturbances reduced the available labor force; Campbell opted to limit excavation to areas near the field headquarters. By June 6, the political situation seemed so grave that an emergency division was held. Expedition staff were sent to Beirut, together with antiquities to be left in the care of Dodge at the American University. Campbell cabled Morey:

> EMERGENCY EXISTS SANJAK UNDER MARTIAL LAW
>
> STAFF AND PROPERTY SAFE

That evening, in a hurried letter to Morey forwarded through Seyrig in Beirut, Campbell dished up the unnerving news in brief headlines, writing of a "coup that is to be pulled off at any moment by which the Turkish army will occupy the Sanjak and make it part of Turkey. This is straight dope and no rumor. [The news came] with cataclysmic suddenness and took all best-informed civil servants and functionaries here by surprise." Local officials had instructed the temporary American consul to order American citizens out of Antioch or else "remain on their own responsibility." Two other archaeological expeditions had already packed up and left.

"Our next job is to get the stuff out," Campbell wrote Morey. He meant the mosaics and other finds the recent division had allotted to the Princeton expedition. While the French commander of Moroccan troops acted as a figurehead administrator, the "real governor is [a] Turk named Dr. Abdul Rahman Melek," who'd assured Campbell that Ankara would honor the terms of the original French concession.

"Hold down American press to best of your ability since unfavorable or sensational accounts there may jeopardize our concession."

Despite the worry and urgency, Campbell managed to end the letter on a high note. "Certain amount of panic in town & all that goes with a situation of this kind—refugees, bawling around, pot shots, etc. but no real stuff yet. . . . Lassus splendid in action, Palestinians & Egyptians [among expedition staff] admirable—all standing by & working hard."

The next day, June 7, Morey cabled René Dussaud: "You will understand our concern . . . and our hopes for continuation of French influence when I point out that Turkish control would probably mean the application of the Turkish antiquity law." And that would mean "the collapse of our expedition." The American museums could hardly be expected to contribute "unrewarded by any acquisition from the division."

None of this could have been news to Dussaud, who wrote Morey that at the root of the deteriorating situation were "mainly racial disputes. . . . We are getting in Syria a repercussion of the Austrian incident," likening Turkey's grab for the Sanjak to the Anschluss, Nazi Germany's fateful takeover of Austria in March. Exploiting the European mess, Turkey had made it known what it would take to "ally herself on the side of the Western powers." Sure enough, Britain ponied up a big loan. "And we," wrote Dussaud, meaning France—"have had to give up the Sanjak. At this double price a general war has been avoided—at least for the coming months."

Earlier in June under a dateline of "Antioch, Hatay [*sic!*]," Campbell sent Morey a handwritten accounting of the mosaics bound for Beirut. It looked like this, except that it reached across three sheets of quadrille-ruled paper:

2511	12-F	5528-M97, Panel A (St. Babylas)
2505	"	5525-M94, Panel B
2506	"	5525-M94, Panel C

Campbell noted that the team was "taking every precaution to avoid giving the impression to the new Turkish governor that we are evacuating valuable antiquities." He went on to tell of "minor murders and gangster beatings," closing up shop for the year, protecting what could be protected, and preparing for the following season's campaign, if there was to be one. Adib Ishak "will remain here to look after our interests and the property that remains; he stands well with the local Turks." Antioch wasn't Turkey's, yet. French troops could still be seen around town. But the Turks were now the real force.

On June 25, Turkish officers visited the expedition's field headquarters, making clear they wanted it for themselves—or rather, that they wanted it *back*: Before the Great War, when Antioch was still Ottoman, it had been the barracks of the Sixteenth Esquadrille of the Turkish army. "You may well imagine," Campbell wrote Morey, "how glad we were that the Committee's share of the division was in Bayrouth." The mosaics were safe at the American University, "in the old College Hall, which is fireproof and has iron bars on the windows."

"The Turkish army is coming into the Sanjak any day now," Waagé had written her parents a few days earlier from Beirut, to which she and her husband had fled.

On July 5, columns of crisply uniformed Turkish troops marched across the bridge over the Orontes into the center of Antioch. Soon the Turks had taken most of the government jobs and a new Hatay parliament had been installed.

The big question was whether the new government would honor the old agreements under the Mandate. Of course, that had *always* been the issue. But now it was no longer hypothetical. What *might* happen *had* happened. The French were gone. A new government, a new country, was in place. Could the excavations continue? Would Campbell & Co. be able to keep the mosaics and the other "spoils"? Not long before, Calvin McEwan, field director for a nearby Oriental Institute dig, had fairly begged the new authorities for one particular object from its site. But despite recommendations from Seyrig and other French officials, he'd been turned down. This was ominous. Hatay was nominally independent, its own small state, but seemed to follow Turkey's harsh, intransigent line.

—

Back in October Morey had cabled Walter Wright, a scholar of Turkish history and language, president of the American College in Istanbul, and a Princeton grad, asking about the Turkish stance on divisions. Antioch wasn't part of Turkey, not yet, anyway. Just how strong, Morey wondered, was Turkey's gravitational pull on Hatay?

Well, Wright replied, on paper "no one in government service here is willing to admit the possibility that any decision affecting the new Hatay State can be made in Turkey." This was the "correct" stance, and they were sticking to it. As for future negotiations, Morey would do well to stress the purely contractual nature of any division-of-finds; to point out that they already had a deal, contracted years earlier with France, and that it had only to be left in place and implemented. This, he advised, was Morey's best course. Because were he to leave the safe setting of the legalities, he would find that

> the attitude of mind throughout this part of the world of the local inhabitants of all classes is that such a division as you have had always results to the advantage of the foreigner, that priceless relics of the past are lost for the National Museums, and that the local boys are always hoodwinked by skillful, subtle, and well-informed European or American archaeologists.

Was this how it really was *in that part of the world*? Morey and his colleagues might have wondered. The divisions left half of everything to Syria, as set out in the concession. The Americans and the French earned their half by running the excavation. Their expertise, initiative, ambition, and money yielded the mosaics, sculpture, inscriptions, and all the rest. How could the Turks or anyone else be troubled by that?

And yet there it was: Wright was attesting to deep-seated distrust. Local boys *hoodwinked*?! By privileged, *subtle* foreigners? It may or may not have been the majority opinion of Western archaeology, but Wright had his finger on something.

Two months later, Adib Ishak replied to an invitation from Ely E. Palmer, the new American consul general in Beirut, to help him understand the new Hatay. In a dense, four-page, single-spaced letter, Ishak reported that in its new parliament a Turk had stood up to say that archaeological expeditions in Hatay across the years had cheated them; that the foreigners had "taken all the beautiful and worthwhile antiquities"; that the French had "stolen" much; that supposedly on-the-square divisions had left an "inferior quality of objects" for the Antioch museum. And French rapaciousness, observed another member of parliament, had grown only worse since the death of Claude Prost in 1936.

Morey could not have been entirely surprised by such accusations. He, after all, was among those who spoke, easily and reflexively, of the "spoils" and "loot" to be gleaned from Antioch. And neither he nor his Princeton friends seemed in the least awkward or shy about picturing the French stance on archaeological divisions as "unusually generous."

Over the next century this split between East and West would sharpen. Greece, Egypt, North Africa, the Near East, and other once-colonized areas that had given up antiquities to Western museums would push for their return; some objects were returned. Directors of large museums of international standing, like the British Museum and the Met in New York, would be called on to defend long-standing practices, as well as their physical holdings. The ill feeling Walter Wright had described to Morey, and that Adib Ishak reported to the consul general, hinted at hardening views and museum policy shifts yet to come.

—

"December is upon us; the end of the season has come." Agatha Christie was marking the end of her fifth dig in Syria beside her archaeologist husband; this was probably around 1938.

> Perhaps because it is autumn and we are used to spring, perhaps because already rumors and warnings of European unrest are in

> the air, there has been a touch of sadness. There is the feeling, this time, that we may not come back.

So it was, too, during the last year before the war, among the Antioch excavators.

The Antioch dig was conceived in the late 1920s, a time of prosperity and postwar hopes. In the early 1930s, as he groped for the money needed for the dig, Morey had run hard into the Depression. But somehow, he had built those $6,000 contributions into an excavation that kept spewing out finds across a span of eight years. Now, in the late 1930s, nationalism ran amok. The Nazis demanded Lebensraum, the Italian Fascists a restoration of Roman glory, the Syrians their country back from the French, the Turks a corner of the Levant they had decided was theirs and always had been. You didn't need a crystal ball to see where this was going.

At a meeting of the Committee held at the Morgan Library in New York on February 18, 1939, Mr. Morey told of archaeologists with the Oriental Institute recently refused a division by the Hatay government—one more strike against a return to Antioch. The next agenda item was "Alternative Sites," which raised the question, *If no longer Antioch, then where?* Across the 1930s, an archaeological team of some standing had been built, with a record of real success, and the resources to keep them at work. So now, if nationalism and war were to close down Antioch, perhaps those resources might be applied elsewhere. Was this notion too brusquely hardheaded and opportunistic? Or simply sensible? One way or the other, Morey's agenda item seemed to say, they would find a way to dig. Writers write, surgeons operate, archaeologists dig.

Morey reported on an invitation from A. H. S. "Peter" Megaw, director of antiquities in Cyprus, to excavate there. About the size of the American territory of Puerto Rico, the British-ruled island lay in a corner of the eastern Mediterranean just opposite the mouth of the Orontes, pointing almost straight toward Antioch one hundred miles away. Like most Mediterranean places, it had harbored civilization for thousands of years and had a rich and variegated cultural heritage. Of two sites coming up in Morey's planned talks with him, Megaw was pushing for Salamis, on the east coast, which he promoted as "the most impressive archaeological site in the island."

Of course, Megaw allowed, Salamis's magnitude of riches probably demanded a long and costly investment. Well, then, he went on, like a salesman flipping through his catalogue, "I must point out that there are many sites through Cyprus of smaller extent than Salamis which are worthy of the Committee's attention." In other words, *perhaps one of our cheaper models would do*. "Let me know the type of the site and the period in which the Committee is most interested. I shall be glad to give you particulars." Sandy Campbell visited Cyprus at the end of April, coming away hopeful. One appealing site presented "none of the difficult problems encountered at Antioch." Surface deposits above the ruins were relatively thin. The water table was way down below the surface. And any art treasures found were more apt to be Greek or Roman than recent Cypriot. It seemed to Campbell, he'd write Morey, "good insurance to have a rich alternative site in a peaceful country."

But Morey and his colleagues weren't ready to ditch Antioch. Yes, they'd have to get out if Hatay proved uncooperative. But why get out if they didn't have to? In June another spectacular mosaic, from the House of Menander, named for the fourth-century comic playwright, surfaced. "The damn thing just doesn't stop producing," Campbell wrote Morey of Antioch. Meanwhile, the State Department was telling them that Ankara would honor the original French terms after all. Maybe one strategy, as Morey outlined it to Francis Taylor, was to return to Antioch in the spring—but then, early in the season, ask for a division, and thereby gauge the Hatay government's cooperativeness. They'd get their answer in action, not words.

Campbell, back in the States, wrote Dick Stillwell, "I hope the terrible Turks will let us dig," inserting above the line—"and divide!"

—

On July 7, 1939, Hatay, the old Sanjak of Alexandretta, was ceded to Turkey, becoming its sixty-fourth province. Antioch was now Antakya.

Later, a detailed, multipage listing of all the mosaics found between

1932 and 1939 and their disposition among museums that for eight pages had cited Antioch, the Louvre, Baltimore, Worcester, and Princeton now began alternating simply between the U.S. and the "Turkish Government."

—

For the past two years, Antioch had seen French and Turkish troops, gunfights in the streets, and all manner of intrigue among Turkey, Syria, and France. Yet all the while, through 1938 and 1939, the American archaeological team managed to pull more ancient inscriptions, pottery, and mosaics from the ground. Malarial mosquitoes or not, they did get back to Antioch's old port, Seleucia, discovering a raft of particularly choice mosaics from the House of the Drinking Contest there. That villa sat at the east end of a large complex overlooking the old harbor. Later scholars would be intrigued not only by the mosaics themselves but by how cunningly the site had been arranged to leave guests with attractive sight lines—across the central mosaic itself, through the open courtyard in the next room, and out to a vista of mountain and sea just beyond.

Looking back at the Antioch dig from many years later, it is hard not to sense the urgency, the surrender to folly and haste, that marked the excavation's final year. Adib Ishak's own informal survey of that last "unblessed year" told of a shipment of mosaics bound for Beirut that faced no obstacle to leaving Antakya—*except* that, until Adib bribed the customs officer, the authorities barred "export" of the truck's gasoline. In June, a Hellenistic mosaic was unearthed while digging a Turkish machine-gun emplacement. Reports coming out of the Antioch dig were truncated and rushed. No comprehensive account of the last season was ever issued. The world was ready to dig trenches, not unearth antiquity.

—

It is Antioch, October 1938, a month after becoming part of the short-lived state of Hatay. The photo shows what at first might be mistaken for an ordinary traffic jam. Or even, impossibly, a species of gridlock. We see the peaks of distant mountains across the valley floor. A cityscape of mosques and minarets in the mid-distance. And in the foreground, a column of cars and trucks, maybe a dozen of them, rolling down the dusty road from Antioch. They are bound for Beirut, packed and piled high with the gear and supplies that had nourished the expedition for eight years. In their gray workaday functionality, they remind us of jeeps and other military vehicles, in retreat, ferrying home their war-weary troops from the front.

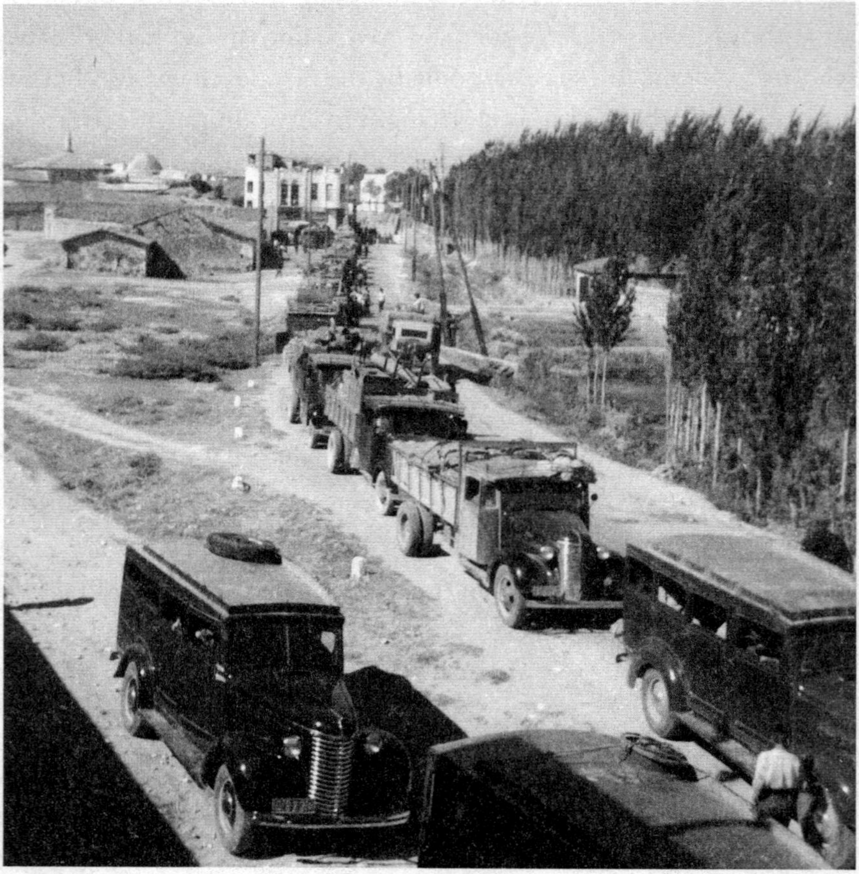

Clearing out from Antioch in 1938, cars and trucks bearing expedition supplies head for Beirut.

Part III

West

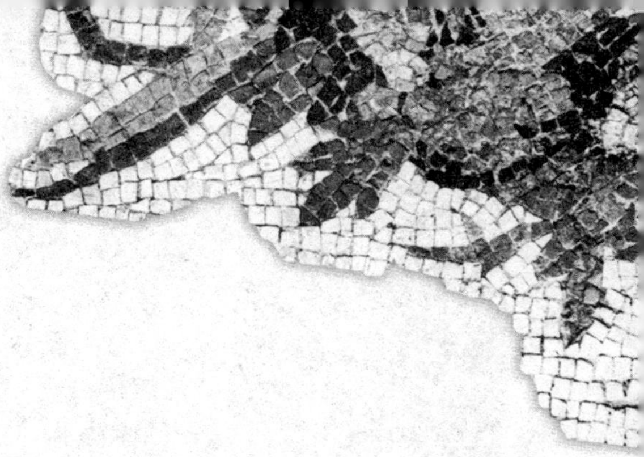

CHAPTER FOURTEEN

The Making of the Medieval

Set on a peninsula in south Baltimore, near Fort McHenry, Locust Point was once the city's own Ellis Island, point of immigrant entry for Poles, Irish, and Jews during the nineteenth century. Shot through with docks and rail yards, it was the embodiment of Baltimore grit and industry. Its ranks of narrow row houses went back to the 1840s. Now, in October 1937, at Locust Point's Pier 8, it was mosaics from Antioch that were being unloaded. It was still two years before Princeton would close up shop there. Many more mosaics and other baubles of archaeological treasure would reach Baltimore later. But just now, these products of the most recent division-of-finds, trucked down the coast to Beirut, packed and shipped like any other commodity, set into thick, steel-reinforced concrete cases, eighteen tons of them, were the first installment.

The middle and late 1930s were the first time ordinary Americans could see any of the mosaics themselves. In Baltimore, they went on display in the museum's new Antioch Court, which looked out through arched, floor-to-ceiling glass walls to a sculpture garden. About one hundred feet across on each of its four sides, its expanses of wall were adorned with mosaics. With the Dancing Maenad and the Dancing Satyr that had once flanked the Drinking Contest of Herakles and Dionysus in Atrium House;

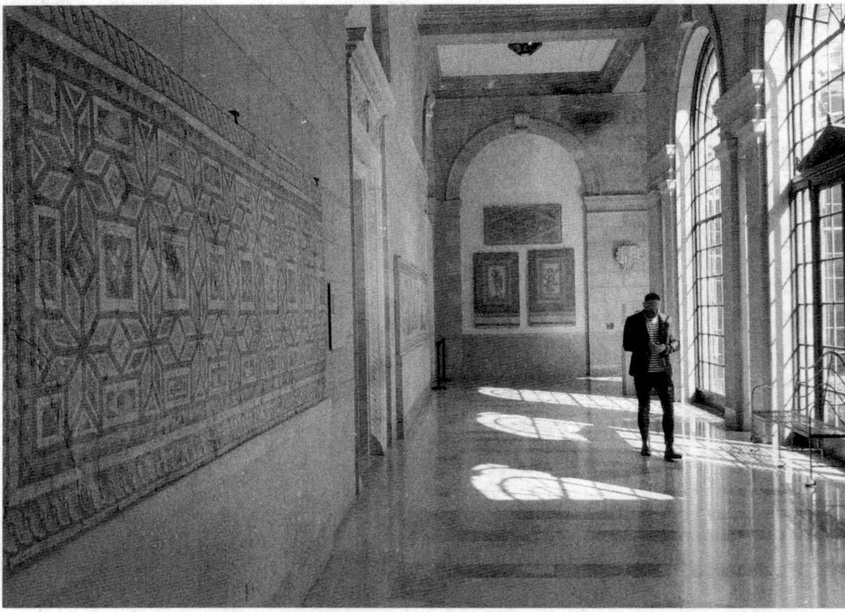

Antioch Court, Baltimore Museum of Art, as seen in a recent photo.

with a series of paired predator-and-prey animals, like Leopard and Goat; with figures from mythology, like Narcissus and milk-white Galatea; with untitled geometric panels not "about" anything, but whose abstract intricacies teased and tantalized the eye.

The mosaics were foreign country to many a middlebrow Baltimore museum visitor more at home with old masters or colonial Maryland period rooms. To introduce them to its new riches, the museum turned to Mr. Morey, by now the expedition's public face, in a way its publicist, equally adept at giving the mosaics nourishing context and saluting the host institution. In "The Antioch Mosaics at Baltimore," he described the third century CE as a dark age to the art historian, few examples of Roman art surviving since the destruction of Pompeii in 79 CE. "The excavation of Antioch has completely changed the situation with its wealth of fine third-century mosaics, and of these by far the choice examples have come to Baltimore."

Mostly, they arrived in good shape. But rust spots, from the steel rods and wire screening used to reinforce them from beneath, riddled many of them. Some were more seriously damaged, significant portions of the image missing, tesserae dislodged or lost altogether. Such sad, sorry losses, of course, undermined the viewing experience. What might be done about them? There was no cut-and-dried solution. Could new tesserae be gathered to fill in where the old had come out? That was one approach. But perhaps too permanent a one, worried museum director R. J. McKinney. Was "permanency" even a good thing? Maybe better to paint in virtual tiles—dry earth colors in an egg emulsion, say—that could be undone later if necessary.

A young local artist and technician, Roland Wehrheim, was engaged for the work, which he all but learned on the job. To mechanically fill in empty, ravaged areas with the opaque watercolor would not do. Better, he'd write, "to approach the mosaics in the same spirit in which they were originally approached, that of an artist creating a work of art. Each mosaic panel had to be considered as an incomplete composition." His job was to create a simulacrum of completeness. Getting the colors right was just part of it. "Of equal importance are the size and texture of the tesserae, and the rhythm in which they are set in the design," these to be hinted at or imitated.

Wehrheim would describe mosaics, as medium, as "simple, fascinating, and limited," a curious gathering of judgments, but true enough. Tesserae cut by hand from marble or limestone were inhibited by their "rather geometrical character." Yet together, he acknowledged, they yielded works of "great rhythmic and organic beauty. . . . These third-century artists and their immediate successors," he came to appreciate, "were neither naïve nor primitive but possessors of a great sense of style."

A tinge of damning-with-faint-praise flavored his account; it was still rare in the 1930s to pay tribute to this historically lesser art form.

—

Four hundred miles north into New England, Baltimore's sister subscriber, Francis Taylor's Worcester museum, welcomed its own sizable contingent of mosaic immigrants as well; they were put to work almost immediately, in February 1937, in a grand exhibition, *The Dark Ages*. The subject was pagan and Christian art in the Latin West and Byzantine East, from the breakup of Alexander's empire to the First Crusade in 1096. "Civilization—that is Hellenistic-Roman civilization—crumbled," visitors were advised, "but it died slowly."

On view were illuminated manuscripts, sculptures, textiles, and metalwork, but the show was largely framed by the Antioch mosaics. A pair of maps showed the extent of the Roman Empire in the second century and, beside it, much diminished, in the sixth century; the two spanned the very range of years represented so richly by the mosaics dug up from Antioch. The dozen or so at Worcester offered "for the first time in this country an opportunity . . . to observe the development of monumental painting from classical times to the Middle Ages."

On view was an eight-foot-square, second-century mosaic showing two actors from antiquity, Parthenope and Meteochos, drawn from an early Greek novel; a substantial fourth-century fragment representing Hermes with the infant Dionysus—"a prototype of the medieval representation of Saint Christopher and the infant Jesus"; mosaic fragments bearing Greek inscriptions for "Mother of the Muses" and "Winter Solstice." And then, of course, there was Worcester's showstopping early sixth-century hunt mosaic, pitched as the largest in any American or Western European museum, soon known simply as the Worcester Hunt. It was *set* as a pavement, on the floor, not on the wall like the others, in the museum's Renaissance Court.

Not until "the rise of modern New York and Chicago," the exhibition catalogue advised, "do we find a community so blatant, so wealthy, and so conscious of material comfort" as Antioch. "With us," it quoted Libanius, referring to fellow Antiochenes, "night is distinguished from day only by the difference of the lighting; diligent hands find no difference and forge on, and he who will sings and dances, so that Haephestos," the god of work, "and Aphrodite here share the nights between them." Antioch, the catalogue carried on,

> was the Broadway of the ancient world; no actor, gladiator, boxer, or courtesan could hope for recognition without the enthusiastic approval of the horsy young men about town. If one were to believe the ancient authors, life at Antioch was a combination of

> New Year's Eve and Saratoga [the lively upstate New York resort] with a touch of surrealism on the side.

The Dark Ages show pulled in big crowds. Perhaps its biggest draw was the Great Chalice of Antioch, displayed in a glass case under police guard, visitors allowed no closer than three feet from it. Dug up near Antioch in about 1910, then moved for safety to the U.S. during World War I, it had been heralded as the Holy Grail at the Chicago World's Fair in 1933. The claims were said to be backed by "a body of religious and scientific evidence designed to show the Chalice is actually that used by Christ" at the Last Supper. Did the museum, or its director, believe it? For the exhibition, it was styled "The So-called Great Chalice of Antioch" and, with what could seem calculated ambiguity, "cautiously assigned," as one review had it, to the "first centuries of the Christian era."

In a letter to Robert Woods Bliss of Dumbarton Oaks after the exhibition closed, Francis Taylor observed that a half dozen noted art historians had dated the silver chalice, or cup, or whatever it was, to sometime between the third and fifth centuries. "The chalice may have been an object of particular veneration at Antioch"; but he'd seen not a "shred of scientific or archaeological evidence associating the chalice with the Last Supper." Don't buy it for the cathedral, he warned Anson Phelps Stokes, canon of Washington Cathedral. The church could not afford to give "even tacit credence to the legends which have been so cleverly built up about it since its discovery in 1910."

Of course, Taylor, who would later ascend to the directorship of the Metropolitan Museum of Art in New York, where he enjoyed a reputation for hauling in the crowds, got to have it both ways: Offering "tacit credence" to the Holy Grail myth, after all, was the museum's police guard, its deferential glass case, and its three-foot keep-your-distance vigilance.

—

The year before *The Dark Ages* show, at a convention of the College Art Association held at the Met in New York, Rufus Morey spoke of the mosaics coming out of Antioch. The year's division had not yet taken place, but he'd seen enough to credit the mosaics with helping write "a missing chapter" in the history of late antique art. Pompeii and Herculaneum furnished examples of Mediterranean art up to the first century. But the next five hundred years, up to the early Byzantine period, at the threshold of the Middle Ages, were murky and obscure. A great gulf in style and sensibility separated the two epochs. The Antioch mosaics would help bridge it.

The split across those centuries, Professor Morey explained, could be seen "as a loosening of the old Greek grip on actuality and the growth instead of a symbolic view of the physical world. In art the change is plain—the third dimension, which still made things real in the first century A.D., had vanished by the sixth century." The rational composition through which "Greek art organized the details of a subject around a central axis or motif" gave way to an "unending sequence of equal accents whose only principle was rhythm." This he classed as "Oriental," referring not to China and the Far East, but the Near East of the Holy Land, the eastern Mediterranean, and Mesopotamia. The mosaics coming out of Antioch helped trace this transformation.

To the casual consumer of his talk for the College Art Association, or of kindred ideas he expressed for *The Dark Ages* exhibition, or in Baltimore, this could all seem like new, intellectually rich territory. And it was, this dark, uncertain space between artistic epochs. But in a broader sense, Morey was talking about transformation and change, a familiar and respected line of inquiry in all the arts and sciences, inspired by our natural curiosity about how one epoch, or fashion, or constellation of assumptions gives way to another. How does an embryo develop into a fetus? How does a worldview placing the earth at the center of the universe shape-shift into the Copernican Revolution?

Likewise in the arts. Art history and criticism are notoriously replete with movements, periods, and styles—Impressionism, Cubism, Art Deco, Abstract Expressionism, many more. The dividing lines among them are sometimes disputed. But they attest to the truth that in art, as in music and literature, as in every aspect of culture, fashions and understandings change: Influenced by other artists, by their own lives and experiences, by their patrons, by the Zeitgeist, artists treat new subjects, use new materials, see the world through new eyes. Their art looks different, and is viewed differently. Such was the influence of any new "school" or style.

And no less so in earlier times: Hellenistic art? Early Christian? Byzantine? However they might blur in any first canter through the landscape of art history, the differences among them were many and real. The classical art of the Greeks or the Hellenistic period that followed the death of Alexander differed much from early Christian art, and from the Byzantine art of the Middle Ages. Realistic scenes from mythology, lush with three-dimensional roundness and richness, gave way to a conspicuous two-dimensionality, figures parading in seemingly stilted formations across wall or canvas. The pagan yielded to the Christian, Dionysus and Aphrodite to arrays of Christian saints and church fathers. Across the five hundred years of what historians today call "late antiquity," art changed.

In broad outline, Greco-Roman art sought to express the fullness of a particular time, story, place, or person. The art of four or five centuries later placed less attention on precise rendering of faces and figures, tended to scatter objects, animals, and people across the painting's face. Look to the 79 CE wall paintings of domestic scenes recovered from Pompeii and you'd see something like the first. Look to the walls of a Byzantine church after the sixth century, with their almost identical religious figures arrayed across the wall, and you'd recognize the latter. For William M. Milliken, writing in 1947 as director of the Cleveland Museum of Art, Byzantine

> figures are not three-dimensional as in classical art. They do not have bulk. They cannot be contained in a cube. They are . . . flatter and usually rather impersonal in their treatment. They are placed against an abstract background, with a suggestion of limitless space.

Or listen to Jean Lassus, who went on to write a tome devoted to *The Early Christian & Byzantine World*. In it, he took his own fine turn at articulating the change: "The Hellenistic style is spacious, light, supple and graceful, full of flowing figures which move in a three-dimension world, achieved by *chiaroscuro* effects," bold contrasts of darkness and light to draw out shapes and figures. The "Eastern" style, on the other hand, "tends to present the world in two dimensions. Space is abolished and replaced by backgrounds of a single, strong color."

Others might place weight on features, effects, and practices they deemed more telling; practiced eyes might extract from a lifetime of study variant interpretations of what five hundred years had wrought. But that something considerable had happened across those centuries was indisputable. What wasn't so plain was just *how* it had happened. In what stages? Under what influences?

Most art historians of the era held that the great change took place across those missing centuries under the influence of Italy, Rome, and the Roman West, a broadly European progression. By one pithy summary of this argument, Christian art developed "from its presumed origins in the Roman catacombs, through the Roman basilicas of the fourth and fifth centuries, to the Byzantine churches of Ravenna—a downward curve showing the gradual debasement of imperial Roman art under Oriental and barbarian influence." In short, if you sought the origins of Byzantine art, you need hardly leave Italy.

But a controversial, fiercely opinionated Austrian art historian named Josef Strzygowski argued otherwise. Born in 1862, Strzygowski was the son of a cloth manufacturer, took up an apprenticeship in his father's mill, abandoned it, enrolled at the University of Vienna, then at the University of Munich to study art history. Over a dozen years or more he traveled widely through Italy, Greece, Russia, and Egypt, immersing himself in Byzantine and Islamic art. Then, in 1901, he came out with the polemical work for which he'd ever be known: *The Orient or Rome?: Contributions to the History of Late Antique and Early Christian Art.*

In a respectful if critical study of the book in 1910, Morey's predecessor as chair of Art and Archaeology, Allan Marquand, recapped Strzygowski's argument this way: "It is not to Rome, but to Alexandria and Egypt, Ephesus and Asia Minor, Antioch and Syria, Jerusalem and Palestine, that we must look for the solution of early Christian and mediaeval art." And Strzygowski had amassed the evidence to forcefully argue the point. To him, elaborately crafted sarcophagi suggested Eastern roots. So did catacomb painting, sculpture, carvings, decorated cornices, ornament. Carpets and textiles, too. Strzygowski attacked purveyors of what he depicted as the Roman orthodoxy. Wrote Marquand of him, only a little unfairly: "Whoever explains Christian art through the Orient is right, whoever raises the banner for Rome is wrong. This is the point of view for which Strzygowski becomes a violent partisan."

Over the next three decades the question gained adherents on both sides; here was "one of the better fights in twentieth century scholarship," cheerfully observes former Princeton archaeologist Christopher Moss, a close student of the Antioch mosaics. And Morey, a student in Rome around the time Strzygowski's book came out, was ideally placed to feel these scholarly winds from the East; he could hardly come away untouched. The first course he ever taught in medieval art aimed to trace the "final breaking up of the classical tradition and the subsequent rise of medieval schools under the transforming influence of Christianity."

This, then, was the transition zone that would intrigue Morey for much of his professional life. By 1934, he'd write, his department at Princeton already had a reputation for its interest in "the transformation of the ancient into the mediaeval," as manifested in Antioch, "center *par excellence* of such metamorphosis." There, Morey wrote in an article for the American Philosophical Society in 1936, "were joined the cultural currents of East and West, of Latin and Greek culture on the one hand, and the traditions of Semitic Arabia, Palestine, and Mesopotamia, together with those of Persian Iran, on the other." Antioch was a kind of mixing bowl, folding and refolding the East into the Greco-Roman world.

In the foreword to the Princeton dig's first published volume, he all but planted Antioch's importance in the soil of Strzygowski's ideas:

> Antioch has played a role in every theoretical reconstruction of the metamorphosis of antique into medieval art . . . a crucible in which these two traditions [Greek and Oriental] were fused into a new art, sufficiently original and strong to temper and shape the nascent forms of Byzantine art.

Earlier yet, in 1931, Morey had asserted that Antioch was so crucial to an understanding of medieval art that "the complete explanation of the latter can never be made" until it was excavated. Three years earlier, just beginning to marshal support within Princeton, he had tried to show how an Antioch dig fit the mission of the Art and Archaeology Department; it would illuminate medieval history, Hellenistic art and culture, and early Christian archaeology, all three of interest to the department. "It is probably not too much to say," he added, "that the current problems in Hellenistic art and history, and the much discussed question of the role of Syria and the Near East in the origin of mediaeval art, would be solved by such an excavation."

Dig in Antioch and stubborn scholarly problems would yield to scientific resolution and proof. Burning questions would be "solved," an explanation of early medieval art at last made "complete." This, nothing less, was what Morey hoped for from Antioch's mosaics. And as they started coming out of the ground, Morey put them to work.

To his eye, even the first group from the Island and its baths, forty or so of them, helped fill gaps in the art history of the Near East. By 1935, the trove was richer yet, all the better to track down changes in the Hellenistic style from the first through sixth centuries, "every stage of which is illustrated by one or another of the Antioch mosaics now displayed in the storerooms of the expedition's house, and already a focal point . . . [for] traveling scholars and tourists in Syria."

Consider, he said, the Judgment of Paris, dating to the early second century. To Morey, it was plain that "the preoccupation of the mosaic artist . . . was to imitate and achieve as nearly as possible the effects of easel painting." In the end, it *was* a kind of easel painting: "Green and blue glass cubes were added to the colors afforded by the stone tesserae to complete the easel's gamut, and the size of the pieces varied from minute specks to squares of a centimeter in dimension," working toward a gradation of tone to rival that of painting. The result? A more or less familiar Hellenistic landscape, a naturalistic scene resonant with life.

But now, he asked readers, look ahead two centuries. In one third-century mosaic, which showed a Greek soldier pulling an Amazon warrior from her horse, the deference to reality, the nod to nature, has weakened. "The landscape is reduced to a bare hill and a tree." The Amazon's horse is "foreshortened with angular stiffness," any natural overlap of figures, of depth, was gone, the image reduced to simple shapes turned toward the viewer in ways never seen in life, broadly artificial. In another mosaic—from Yakto, not the topographical border this time, but the hunting tableau within it—Morey noted the "broad simplification of light and shade," the heavy shading, the staring eyes, the frontal faces. These, to him, were plain evidence of the East, seen in "the drift away from realistic rendering toward pure design."

For Morey, the mosaics were like fossilized remains left behind from five centuries of titanic struggle among generations of mosaic artists. The Antioch mosaics spoke to the "transformation of this metropolis on the frontier of Greek civilization as it succumbed during the last days of the Roman Empire to habits of taste ingrained for ages past in the Oriental culture surrounding it."

Two years later, in October 1938, Morey signed off on a new, oversized book, *The Mosaics of Antioch*, which welcomed readers to the ancient city and to a choice sampling of its mosaics. Its publisher was not the usual university press, but an old British house, Longmans, Green, founded in 1724, that had issued, among other Sherlock Holmes classics, *The Hound of the Baskervilles.* Morey's book was a spacious, handsomely designed volume, studded with maps, charming pen-and-ink drawings, floor plans, black-and-white photos of the mosaics; and, as frontispiece, a hand-drawn color rendering, tile by individual tile, of a mosaic of Bacchus, god of fertility and wine, clad in panther skin, his head bearing a phallic symbol entwined in vine leaves and grapes. "The illustrations are livelier than those in previous publications," wrote one reviewer, "the descriptions full and sympathetic." Morey told of where and how individual mosaics had been found, commented on style and color, expressed delight in a visual joke here, a mosaicist's special expertise there. He wrote of "a dancing youthful satyr with a shepherd's pipe in hand"; of a bacchante clashing her cymbals; of a "symposium" of Fruit, Field, and Wine, each personified by a human figure.

But, invariably, he returned to the theme driving his book: Of one mosaic, where Mercury carries away the infant Bacchus, its composition,

Morey wrote, "points to the primitive manner of the East, the fractional representation which makes Egyptian figures, for instance, so beautifully clear in their parts, and so impossible as wholes." Typically, he seemed less interested in what a particular mosaic said of its own time than in what it meant for the evolution of Western art from its Greco-Roman first century to its Byzantine sixth.

Among Morey's references to specific mosaics, virtually none were untethered to this one overarching theme, Greco-Roman artistic sensibilities versus those of the East. He didn't let it go, Herr Strzygowski never far out of mind. An otherwise admiring reviewer, J. W. Crowfoot, writing in the *Journal of Hellenic Studies*, was downright skeptical: Morey argued that the mosaics "show a gradual Orientalisation of art during this period, Hellenistic Syria slipping into the embrace of the East." Well, his mosaics "may have been chosen with an eye [too closely wedded] to this theory." And that theory was one he, Crowfoot, didn't buy.

In almost all the Antioch mosaics Morey saw tension between *what had been* and what, in the churches, vaults, and canvases of the Middle Ages, *would be*; between the old Greco-Roman past and a Byzantine world forever shaped by the East, traces of both sometimes coexisting in the same mosaic. For him, a third-century mosaic from Daphne, of Diana and a rearing lion at which she aims her arrow, reminded him of a Hellenistic landscape; a column rising up from the foliage recalled the Judgment of Paris. Here was "evidence enough of the tenacity of Greek tradition, in spite of the Oriental tendencies in Antiochene art which we have just noticed." Another mosaic showed a "nostalgia for the disappearing naturalism of Hellenistic art," yet hinted at the art to come.

Morey's tone was not didactic, moralistic, or badgering, not quite. But he *was* relentless, much as he'd been ten years before in corralling resources for Antioch. "In the Orientalizing of the Western Mediterranean that was accomplished in the fifth and sixth centuries of our era," he concluded the book,

> historians of art have long suspected that Syria and Antioch played a major role. The evidence was lacking, so long as no authentic

> monuments of Antiochene art were available for comparison; the hundreds of paintings which the mosaic pavements have provided have filled this lacuna, and produced the material for a new chapter in the history of Mediterranean art.

No one or few of the mosaics from Antioch composed Morey's "new chapter." It was all of them, together, those from the villas and the baths, those from the Island, from the slopes of Mt. Silpius, from Daphne, from Seleucia, all the three hundred.

CHAPTER FIFTEEN

The Three Hundred

In 2022, some months before the earthquake early the following year that reduced much of the city to ruins and took thousands of lives, scholars from universities and museums in Turkey, France, and elsewhere in Europe, the U.S., and the Near East descended on Antakya for a weeklong conference devoted to the Antioch mosaics. They compared those from Antioch with those raised from sites in Portugal and Constantinople, today's Istanbul; noted the many species of birds appearing in the *Megalopsychia* mosaic from Yakto; reported on restorations of Antioch mosaics at the Louvre; teased apart lines of influence between Antioch and the rest of the ancient Near East. Conference-goers were bused to the site of the ancient hippodrome, whose contours and dimensions Sandy Campbell had traced almost a century before, the stubs of a few crumbled piers still poking from the ground; to Seleucia, Antioch's ancient port, twenty kilometers down the Orontes; to Hatay province's new archaeology museum, where mosaics enthusiasts feasted on vast, unending rooms of them, down on the floor, up on the wall, everywhere you looked.

Critics of the Princeton excavations would decry what could seem the madcap hurry of "this big thing" Mr. Morey had championed, its seeming overreadiness to veer from the dig's original objectives for the sake of the mosaics. Lassus glimpsed such failings, Robert Schirmer did, and so did Henri Seyrig. Still, those three hundred mosaics borne of Antioch made for a great haul of evidence, seeds of provocation, *data*. They were lifted from the earth between 1932 and 1940, and ever since, whatever their physical and legal status, they belonged to the world—to study, understand, inspire, and inform.

Six decades after they were unearthed, pencil point–sized bits of glass tesserae from several Atrium House mosaics were cut out with a diamond-edged scribe and steel scalpel, embedded in epoxy, ground down with silicon carbide paper to expose their interiors, polished with cerium oxide, vacuum-coated with a carbon deposit, and analyzed in a laboratory of the Metropolitan Museum of Art with an instrument known as a dispersive X-ray spectrometer. Yellow tesserae, it turned out, stood apart from green by their differing proportions of antimony oxide and lead oxide. All told, Antioch's tesserae differed little from those earlier recovered from Pompeii, but derived from a wider variety of sources, differences found even within individual mosaics. There, in the lab, was one way to take the measure of the mosaics. Over the decades since the 1930s, there would be as many as the intellect could conceive.

In 1935, in the pages of the *Bulletin d'études orientales*, Jean Lassus indulged in a charming little exercise. In 1932, he'd been among the first to look closely at the Yakto mosaic. Now he stopped for a new look at the street scenes and human figures of its topographical border, comparing them with photos of street scenes in Antioch from his own time. "Dans les Rues d'Antioche," he titled his experiment, In the Streets of Antioch.

At one site on the border, two men sit facing each other across a small table upon which we see checkers, *jetons*, or other game pieces. One of them shakes what are probably dice, the other makes a hand gesture, holding up a finger, pointing, perhaps celebrating a moment of good luck. The image is rudely executed, but it's good enough that Lassus can see it as almost identical to what he's seen in the cafés of Antioch himself. He offers a photo as proof. "My photograph," he writes, "was taken in the most frequented of these establishments. . . . The well-off customers are dressed in European garb, like the old players were *à la romaine*." The likeness is uncanny—the two players, bent over the game, engrossed, 1,500 years apart, yet as one. Looking back and forth between the ancient mosaic image and the photo, figures 4 and 5 on the same page of Lassus's article, each bolsters the other, the ancient scene clarified and affirmed by the modern, the new inheriting the authenticity of the old. Lassus sees similar doubling in mosaic scenes of street merchants and butchers in the local souk, among shops lining the street, even in articles of clothing. Perhaps, he concludes, "the gap between Antiochs old and new may be less absolute than we might have thought."

—

A proper art historian or critic could look at the dice players from the Yakto border or any other mosaic from Antioch, tell its story, compare it to others, note anomalies, draw insights; scholars have been doing that since 1932. And yet, perhaps the most lasting mark of the Antioch expedition lies not in any one of them but rather in all of them at once, in their very number. We've seen how Mr. Morey relied on the scope and span of years the mosaics represented to illuminate the passage of Hellenistic into medieval art. Since the 1930s, Princeton University has poured prodigious resources into editing, organizing, sorting, publishing, and later digitizing expedition records, its efforts seemingly mated and matched to the dig's own considerable scale.

A few years ago, an article about an accomplished American mosaicist noted that her biggest, most ambitious work of mosaic art, for a hotel restaurant in New York, required sixty-five thousand tesserae; my own largest mosaic, about the size of a biggish desktop monitor, needed two thousand. By my back-of-the-envelope calculation, the recovered Antioch mosaics were together the work of 50 *million* tesserae.

In Antioch, once local landowners came to see the value that the excavators attached to the mosaics, the occasional random find became a flood. And with it, a taste for number, quantity, began to seep into expedition records. As we've seen, a 1937 year-end report listed the "number of mosaics found, lifted, and cemented," the number "found and left in position," the number "ready for division." The dig could be reckoned as so many trial trenches dug, so many million tesserae laid, so many photographs taken, so many feet of sediment stripped away, so many laborers digging out so many buried villas. And all this counting left its stamp on the expedition, its numerical profligacy becoming part of any elevator pitch on its behalf: *No, they didn't find any palaces, but they did come back with all those mosaics, you can't believe how many. . . .* Some of the wonder of the dig, what we are apt to *mean* these days by "the Antioch Mosaics," and the very conceit of this chapter, rests on these numbers.

Scientists often scoff at mere "anecdotal evidence"—a single observation or experiment, one delicious gossipy tidbit—that might at first seem to speak volumes, yet may be written off as proving nothing. After all, maybe it's an outlier, just simple coincidence. Researchers ask, "What's your sample size? What's your *n*?" Too small and even a tempting line of evidence might be dismissed as merely "suggestive." A larger pool of data promises, statistically speaking, to reveal truths that small *n* muddies or hides.

Antioch's *n* was about three hundred—three hundred mosaics created, buried, and recovered.

Across eight years in Antioch, the excavators found scarcely any mosaics reflecting Christian themes—almost no crosses or other Christian symbols buried in the mosaic rubble. There was plenty of Dionysus and Narcissus, Hercules, Hermes, and Apollo, all the stuff of Greek myth. But despite Christianity's roots in Antioch, recorded in the New Testament and historical accounts alike, and though the emperor Theodosius I had made it the state religion in 380 CE, the mosaics better showed off Antioch's resilient paganism. No single mosaic told this story, or could tell it; but hundreds together did.

Early in my own evolving fellowship with the mosaics, as I encountered them on museum walls, online, or in the pages of books, I developed genuine intimacy with only a few of them. But with time, seen repeatedly and in varied contexts, they together worked their way into me, with their gods and goddesses, warriors, heroes, Greek inscriptions, animals wild and domestic, food, drink, revelry, jewels, scenes sweet and grotesque, wild hair, piercing eyes. And it was not just individually that they reached into my imagination, but in concert. I was reminded of one of those little novelty flip books you sometimes see, with its thick wad of miniature cardboard pages, stapled at one end, bearing a parade of images: Flip the pages just right and you get a brief animated cartoon, three or four seconds' worth, a living holistic impression of Mickey Mouse or a belly dancer, the product of no one image but of all of them.

The three hundred, together, bestowed this different kind of understanding. In his book *Gods of the Upper Air*, Charles King told how, in the early 1920s, a number of bright young social scientists came together under the influence of a Columbia University professor, Franz Boas, a father of modern anthropology. Boas and his followers decried too-easy judgments of "primitive" cultures. Refusing to dismiss them as alien and lesser, they insisted instead on seeing them up close, living among them, for months and seasons at a time. Margaret Mead went to Samoa. Zora Neale Hurston ranged through America's Black South, her studies fueling her later novel *Their Eyes Were Watching God*. In time, after a thousand mornings or a hundred shared meals among native peoples, faulty first impressions yielded to the sheer *muchness* of this layered experience, conferring new truths. So it was, or something like it, among the three hundred: In time, patterns, themes, repeated subjects and styles emerge and, as for Boas's young disciples, the mosaics turn you into something like an old Antioch hand yourself—novice anthropologist, adventurer, time traveler.

—

Consider the Erotes, the winged, Eros-inspired, nude youthful figures we met in the prologue at the House of the Boat of Psyches. To a twenty-first-century eye, they can seem downright wacky; if you encountered them in a single mosaic you might write them off as some bizarre fourth-century aberration. But they were no aberration. In the mosaics, you see them everywhere. By the count of Mississippi State University art historian Lori P. Neuenfeldt, Eros and Erotes appear in twenty mosaics from the House of the Drunken Dionysus, the House of the Green Carpet, the House of Menander, and others from the second to the fourth centuries. Their very ubiquity said something of the world out of which they came. For Neuenfeldt, they attested to the patron's ties to his classical heritage.

Or take "personifications," mosaics giving life, color, and weight to abstractions or ideas. About a dozen of the breed emerged from Antioch in the 1930s. They were not one-offs or rarities. They were almost commonplace. Often they showed a well-coiffed and bejeweled woman of imposing aspect at the center, a word in Greek inscribed above or beside her: Like *Tryphe*, luxury. *Apolausis*, enjoyment. *Soteria*, meaning safety, or deliverance from harm. Among such mosaics, it was almost always just the one word—inscribed in Greek, never Latin. *Ktisis*, from a large fifth-century mosaic recovered from the House of Ge and the Seasons in Daphne, means creation, foundation, or generative force. In this one, now on a wall at the Worcester Art Museum, the female bust is almost lost within an intricate geometric array of diamonds, squares, and wedges, each rendered in its own pattern of variously colored tesserae.

Fifteen hundred years ago, you might have passed by any of these without an errant thought—a mosaic underfoot, mere decoration. But sometimes, too, we can be sure, it would insinuate itself into your imagination, get you thinking. For Americans of our time, analogous inscriptions might refer to *Freedom*, *Justice*, *Choice*—ideas too abstract and open-ended to mean just one oversimple thing. "At least a part of the value and importance of these mosaics in antiquity," Glanville Downey would write of personifications, was that they had "for different people, or even for the same people in different moods and circumstances, different meanings." In their very ambiguity, they inspired reflection.

Appearing again and again among the mosaics is the god Dionysus, ubiquitous in the life of late antiquity. Bacchus to the Romans, he stood for both the pleasures of drink and its price in morose inebriation. According to Brazilian scholar Gilvan Ventura da Silva, Dionysus figures in no fewer than eight mosaic panels from Antioch. A Turkish scholar, Inanç Yamaç, counts nine. We meet a drunken Dionysus, falling all over himself, propped up by a satyr half his size; a slovenly and chubby one; a Dionysus reclined on a couch, hoisting his cup, vying with Herakles in a drinking contest. He is everywhere, becoming more real the more we encounter him. Ultimately, I was drawn into the thickets of French historian Paul Veyne's book *Did the Greeks Believe in Their Myths?* His answer was elusive, more shaded, certainly, than yea or nay. But now, pausing at the gates of Antioch, where

Dionysus loomed so large, with its Theater of Dionysus, its many mosaics representing him, the question could seem all the more natural to ask, if no easier to resolve.

For Ventura, the pervasiveness of Dionysus in Antioch's mosaics, marked "a people who . . . did not hesitate to celebrate as much as possible the delight of being in the world." More than half a millennium after the death of Alexander, and long after Julian the Apostate's failure to frustrate the new Christian faith, the pagan gods and the legendary Homeric heroes were a living presence in Antioch; the mosaics said so. It wasn't just Briseis and Achilles, from the *Iliad*, showing up on a mosaic here and there, or Eros and Psyche in the House of the Drinking Contest; if the mosaics were any guide, the Greek gods were vividly present in every aspect of their lives.

Another persistent presence in Antioch was its hunting mosaics, and a fine haul of them there were. Like the personifications, they were their own *thing*, a genre prominent in Antioch and the Empire. Pop culture today reminds us of the gladiators in the Roman Colosseum locked in bloody combat with wild animals. In the hunt mosaics we see more such mayhem, if often stylized and not too gory. If you're interested in the long, checkered relationship between humans and the rest of the animal kingdom, these mosaics are a good place to stop, look, and think.

The *Megalopsychia* mosaic from Yakto, within its more famous topographical border, was one of them, with its gazelles, boars, and lions and their human, spear-bearing predators. Likewise the Honolulu Hunt, coveted by the Honolulu Academy of Arts in the 1930s. And the Worcester Hunt, grandest of the lot: At its center stands a lone human figure at exaggerated ease, hand on hip, triumphant, leaning comfortably on his staff or spear, unmoved by the slaughter around him, or else relishing it. Fruit trees jut toward the center from the mosaic's corners, marking it off in quadrants. We see a leopard simultaneously speared by a horse-mounted hunter and one on the ground. Another hunter, a big cat about to pounce, is saved by a spearman.

Again, a single expression of the genre might rank as a one-of-a-kind curiosity. But the six that have been counted at Antioch say more about the city and its wealthiest residents. To art historian Irving Lavin, who dedicated a long 1963 paper to them, the hunting mosaic spoke to "salient elements in the existence of the rich, provincial proprietors: the land upon which their wealth was based and the leisure activity which their wealth permitted." It was the fashion of proud, important men, eager to flaunt their wealth and social position, each perhaps seeing himself as that heroic central figure from the Worcester Hunt.

—

The hunting mosaics from Antioch were *about* hunting. Most of the other mosaics were about something, too. They had subjects one could address, just as friends discussing a film they've both seen or a book they've both read have something they can talk about, a real subject, character, or human theme: *Now, why does Dionysus here look so shabby and miserable?*

But many of the three hundred—or parts of them that formed the outer reaches and borders of otherwise figured mosaics—weren't "about" anything at all. They were geometric, ornamental, abstract, exercises in design. They transformed otherwise empty space. They teemed with ribbons, entwined cables, weirdly thick interlocking I-shapes, diamonds, ornamented squares. They contrasted with more figural works in a way not so different from how Abstract Expressionism, say, turned its back on likenesses of people and nature for an abstract grandeur of its own. Indeed, like other examples of modern art, the geometric mosaics have often been treated with disdain.

In 1983, Jean Lassus, fifty years past his earliest days in Antioch and by then an elderly gentleman, was thinking back to the excavation, recalling one of the very few churches uncovered and the surprising lack of interest in it. It was paved in *opus sectile*, a Latin term referring to a wall or floor made up not from tiny tesserae, as in real mosaic, but from much larger, hand-cut pieces of limestone or marble fitted into a broadly scaled design. The design was purely geometric; to Lassus it was sober, elegant, and original. But in the end, he reported, the excavators chose to recover only a small piece of it, bearing an inscription, and rebury the rest.

So it was, lamented Lassus, that geometric mosaics once found and briefly viewed often disappeared all over again. Back in France, he went to see one of his professorial masters, who he hoped might make him feel better about the loss. He didn't. "I have never, in the course of my career," declared the senior man, "attached the least value to the conservation of geometric mosaics."

Mosaics, then, were marked by a kind of class divide. The abstract, geometric, and purely ornamental were routinely discounted or dismissed. The figural mosaics, with their human portraits, animals, nature, and scenes from mythology, were what everyone wanted and could talk about. Though built up from pieces of the same stone, marble, and glass, they were something like real paintings. It required artfulness and finesse to represent the idealized likeness of a woman from an elite family. To faithfully depict eyes, mouths, folds of drapery, the subtlest curves and flow. Here was art worthy of art, innately superior to the geometric mosaics for which Lassus's master had no use.

In my own mosaic work I've tried a few purely figural depictions, including faces. But I've done many more mosaics of a purely abstract or geometric nature. Some of them seem to me original or interesting and give me pleasure. Not so my few figural attempts, all of them unsatisfactory. I can't seem to make lips look like lips. Or render soft shadows in hard stone. If innate difficulty be the measure, then, Lassus's senior colleague probably got it right.

Practically speaking, of course, as backgrounds, borders, and in whole panels flanking figural ones, large geometric fields of tesserae were necessary and important: They covered broad expanses of floor with space-filling designs that, pattern established, could be readily repeated and extended out to the far reaches of the frame. There it might give way to an ornamental border, one or more bands of embellishment, sometimes rigidly geometric, sometimes a sinuous intertwined growth of grapes, leaves, or flowers, lending to the whole a dignity and finish.

The work of background and border could be done by less accomplished artisans not enjoined to work out intricate detail anew: As work progressed and the mosaic grew, it wasn't an ever-fresh visual problem to solve, but an old and familiar one, one's task but to repeat the overall pattern or lightly improvise. No new fold of a garment to puzzle out, no glint

1

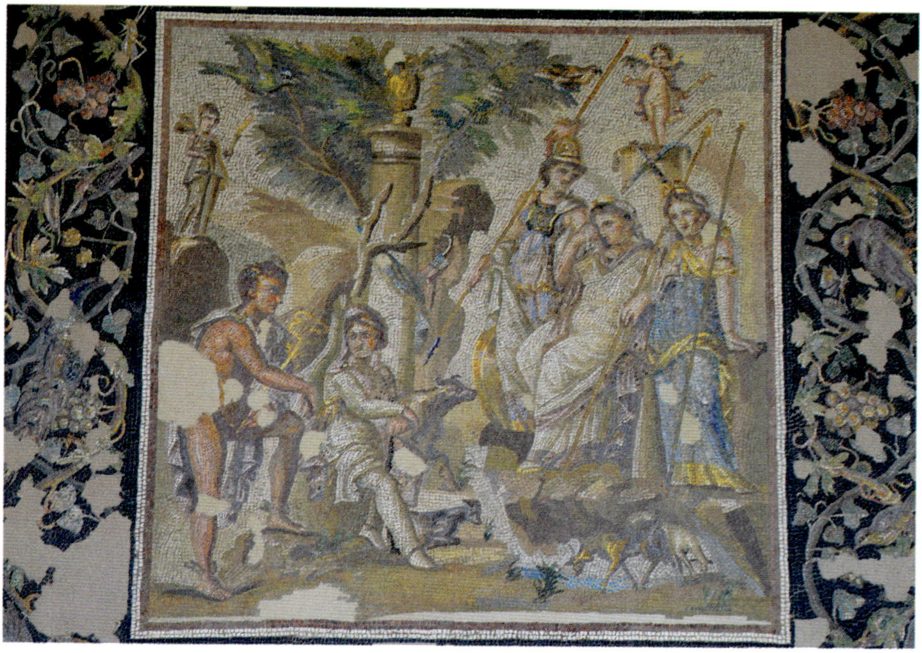

The Judgment of Paris mosaic. The 1932 discovery of this mosaic, and others of similarly high quality that together make up the triclinium, or dining room, of a Roman villa, secured a crucial early success for the Antioch expedition.

2

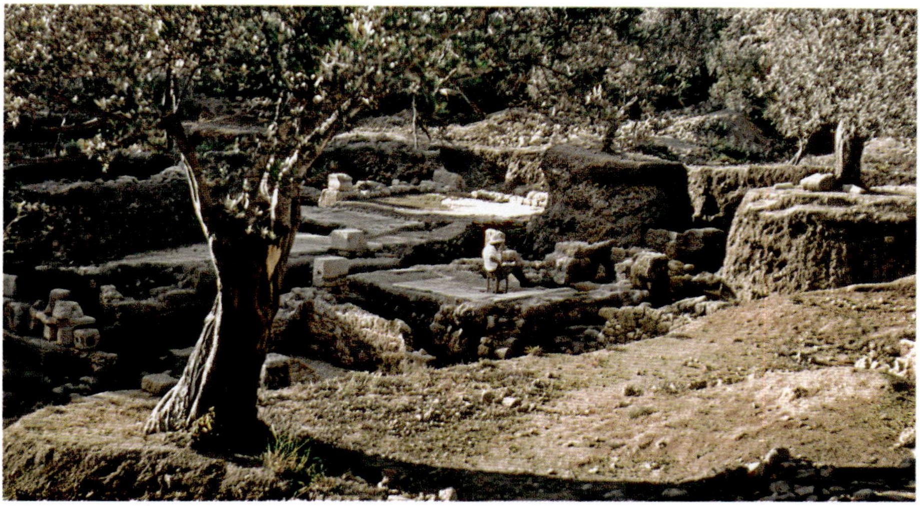

G. E. Kidder Smith was still early in his career as an architectural photographer when he undertook to take color photographs of mosaics and other finds coming out of Antioch. Most served simply as records and historical documents, several of them appearing in these pages. But Kidder Smith also took a few handsomely composed vistas of the excavation in repose, such as this one, which shows field director Sandy Campbell at the site of the House of the Menander in Daphne.

3

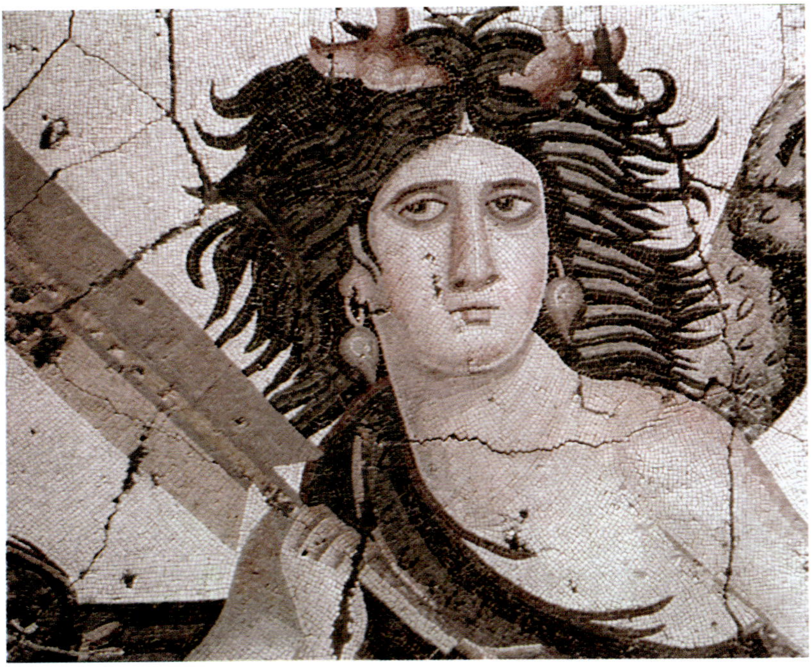

4

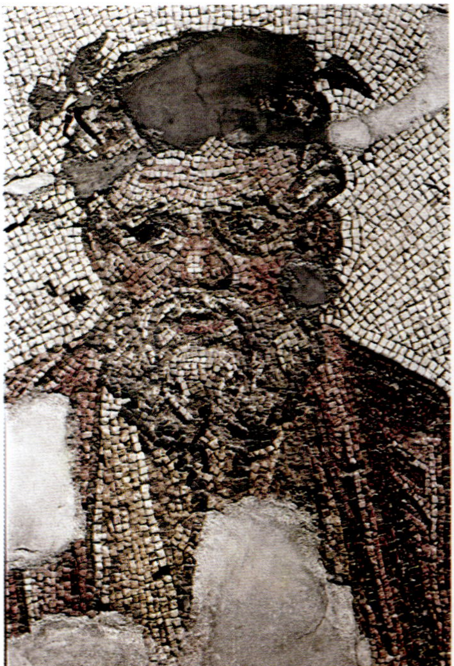

5

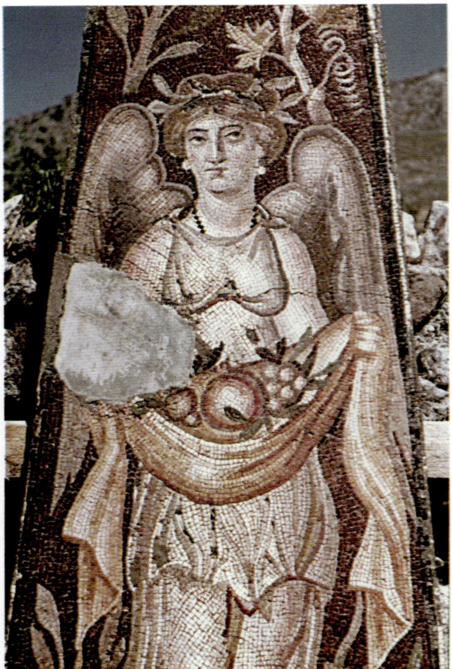

A portrait gallery: In these images culled from Princeton's Kidder Smith collection, faces rendered in tesserae, modelled from life, memory, or imagination, arrest our gaze from across the centuries.

6

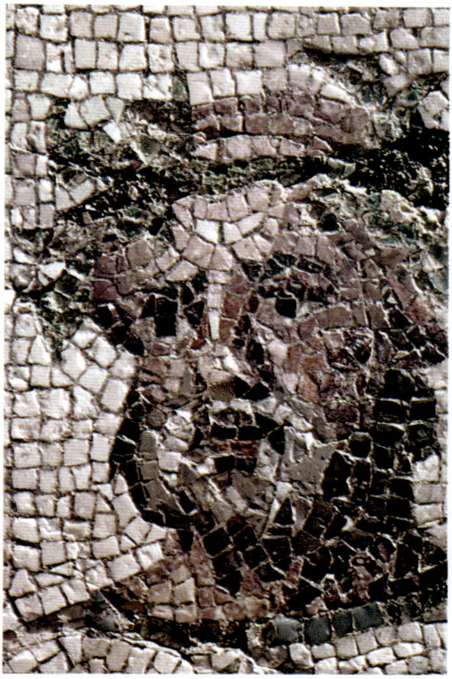

7

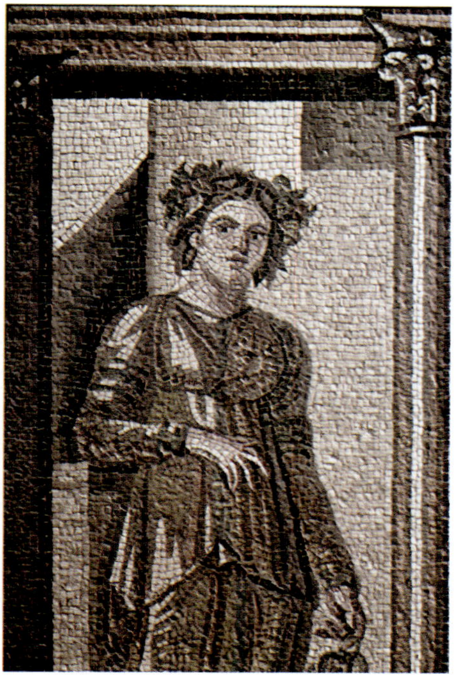

8

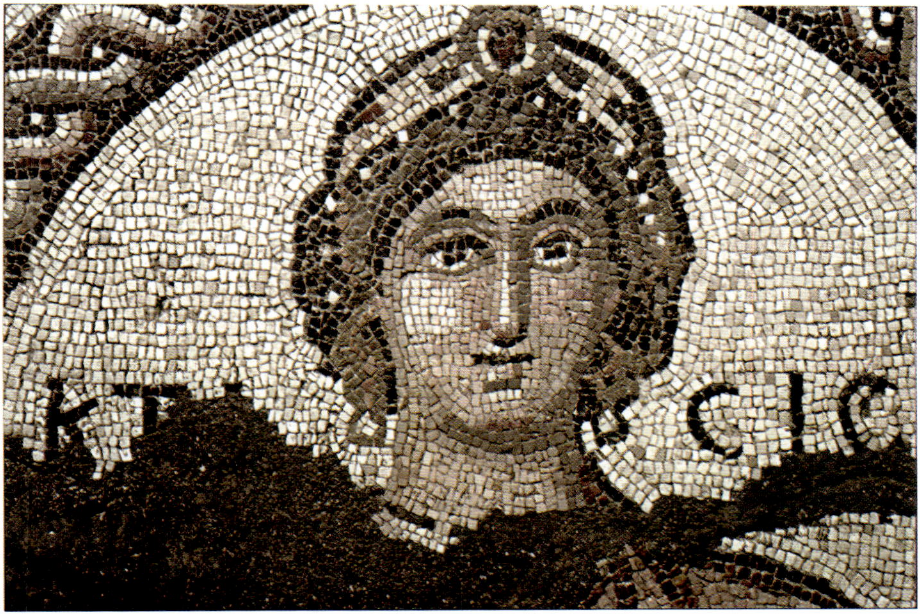

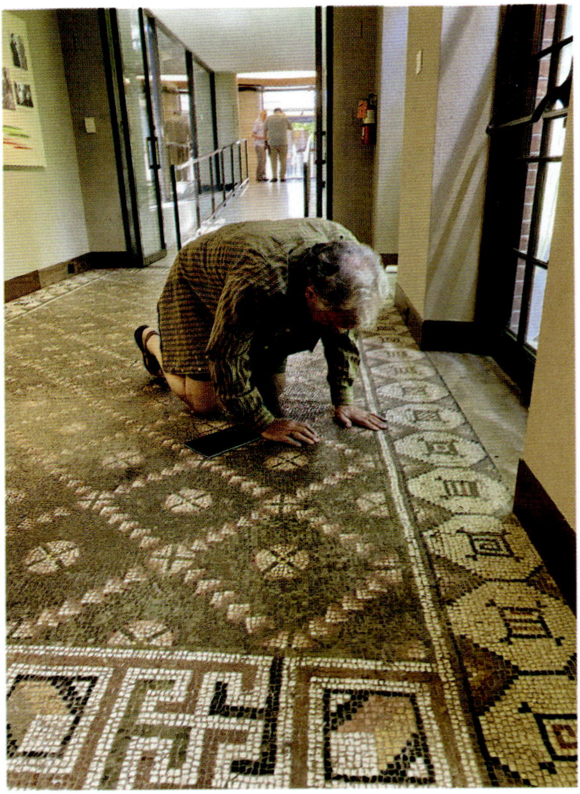

9

Most "pavements," or floor mosaics, from Antioch have wound up on museum walls. But the Dumbarton Oaks Museum in Washington, D.C., which joined in support of the Antioch excavations a few years after they got underway, exhibits several of its mosaics back where they started—on the floor. Visitors shuffle and stroll across them every day. One of them, celebrating *Apolausis*, pleasure or enjoyment, greets visitors as they enter the museum from 32nd Street NW. Another, this geometric one called the Green Carpet mosaic, which is almost seventeen feet long, seized the interest of the author.

10

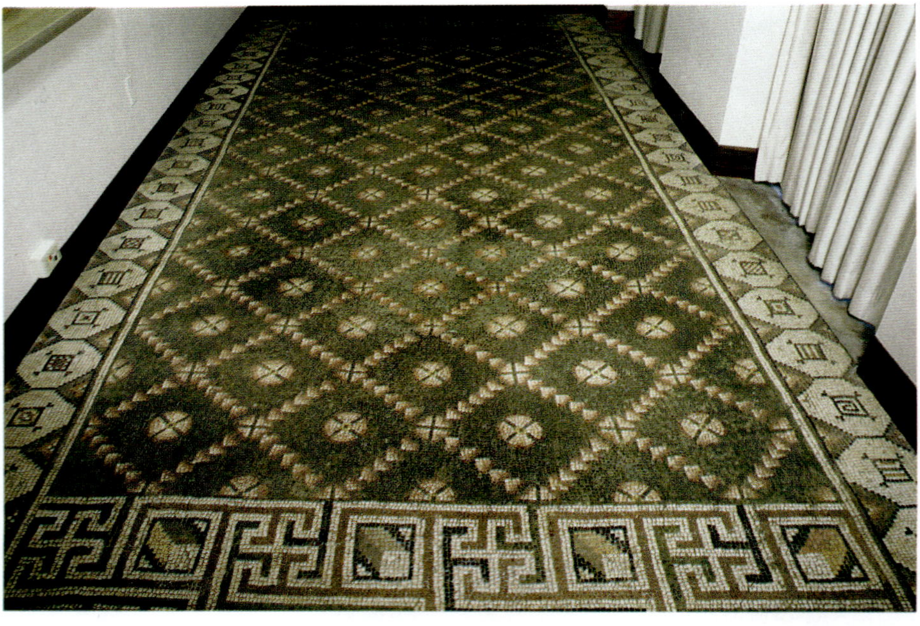

11

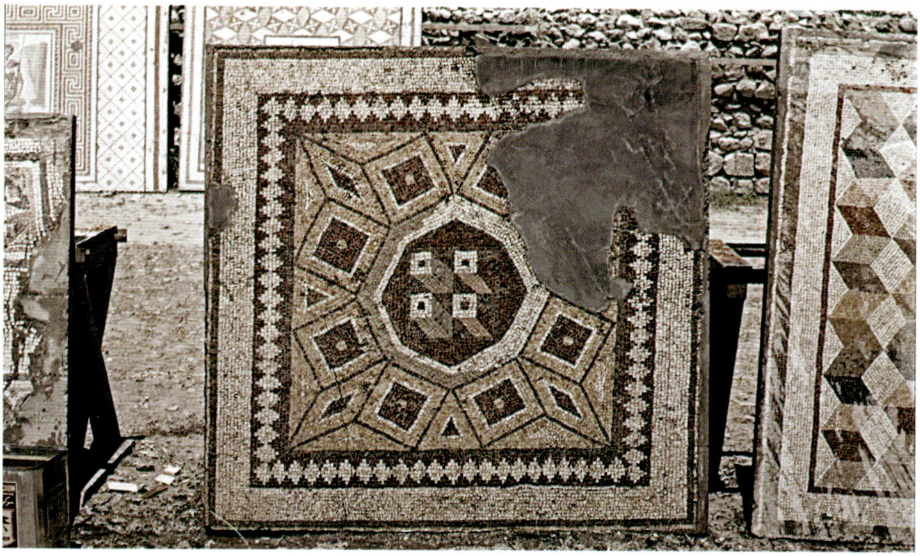

Field of mosaics: Midway through their passage from underground to museum, the mosaics stood propped up against walls and supports on the grounds of the expedition headquarters. In 1937, so many visitors came to see them and sign the guest book—and sometimes disrupt the work of the dig—that visiting hours had to be limited to two hours a day.

12

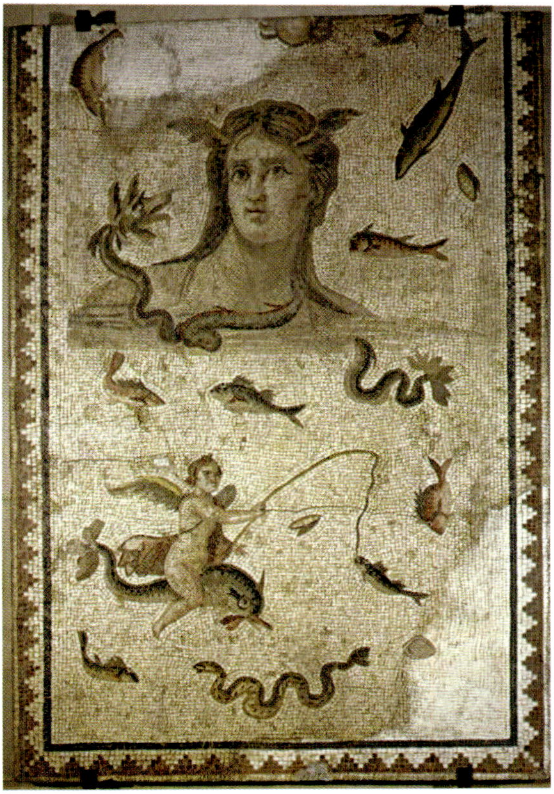

Tethys (also known as Thetis), wife of Oceanus (also known as Okeanos), was one of the Titans, who, long before Homer, preceded the rest of the Greek pantheon. Here we see her, wings erupting from her brow, surrounded by sea creatures and Eros-like infant figures called Erotes. One of them, straddling a large sea creature, can be seen out fishing himself.

13

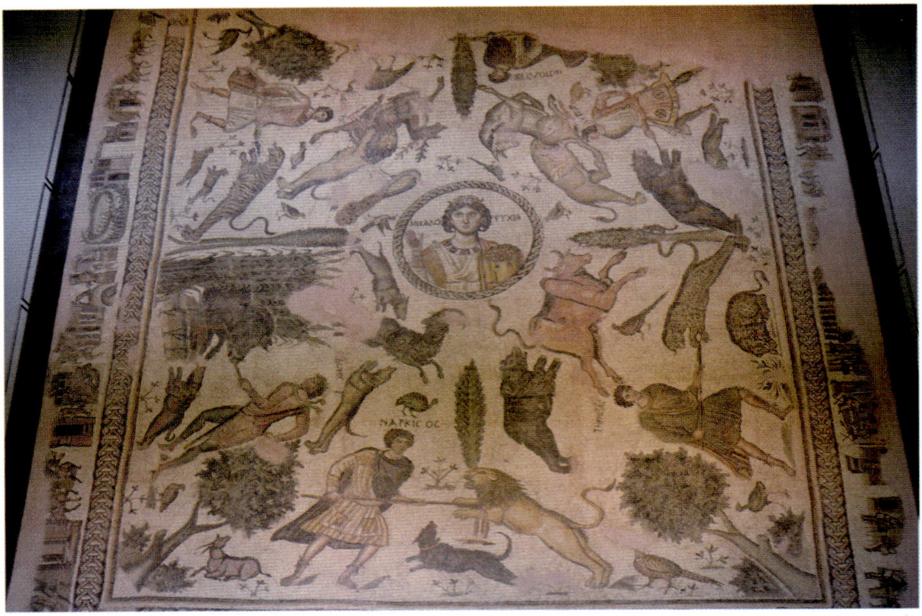

The Yakto mosaic, shown above, resembles at least three other Antioch mosaics in that it is devoted to scenes of the hunt. But this one, outside its decorative border, includes elements quite divorced from animals and hunting—namely, a cartoonlike series of images that scholars have interpreted as a kind of guide or map to ancient Antioch and its suburb, Daphne. A brief length of this "topographical border," below, shows what an inscription records as an Olympic stadium.

14

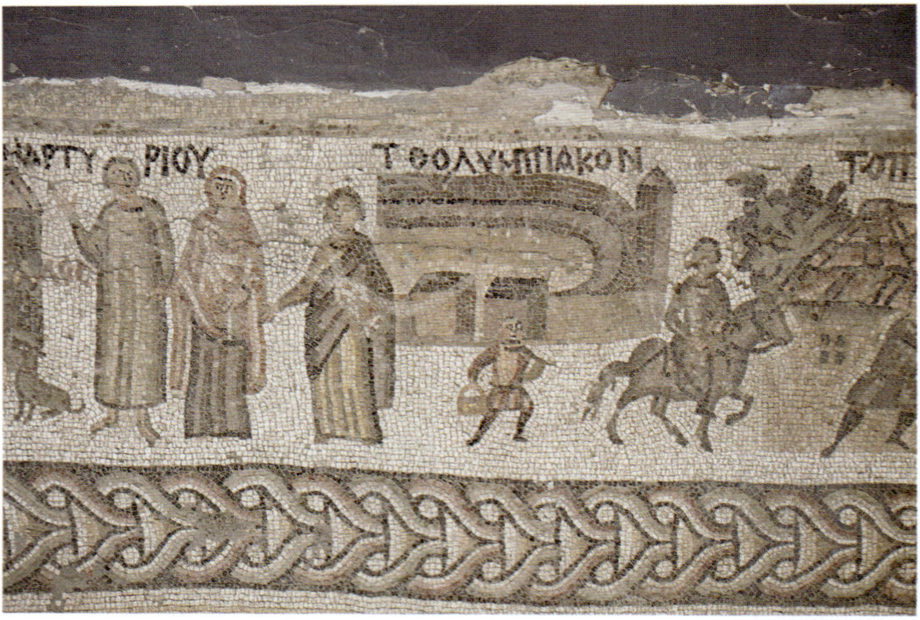

15

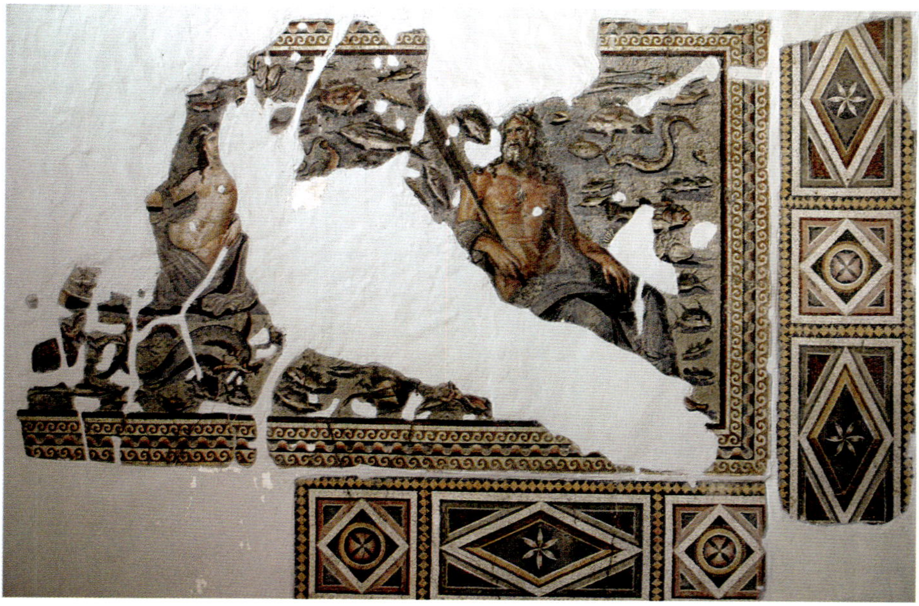

This image represents a fragment of a mosaic depicting Thetis and Oceanus today displayed on a wall in the Hatay Archaeology Museum. But in fact, Thetis is scarcely to be seen, half her face, some of her body, and much of the original composition failing to survive the centuries. Damaged mosaics like this, many of which were recovered from Antioch, present museum professionals with difficult questions of how best to conserve, restore, and display a work of art parts of which no longer exist.

16

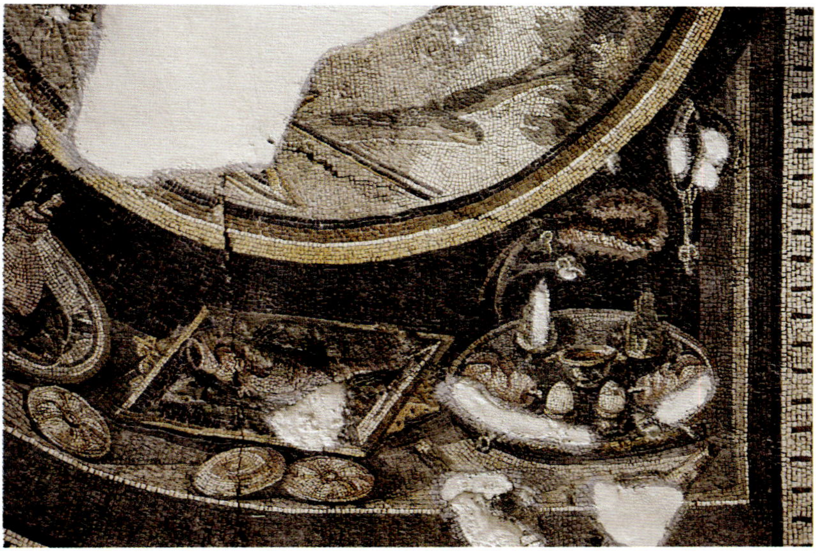

When Jean Lassus, who represented the Louvre and France, first set eyes on this mosaic, he was moved to write out, like a restaurant menu, what he took to be a typical meal in third century CE Antioch.

17

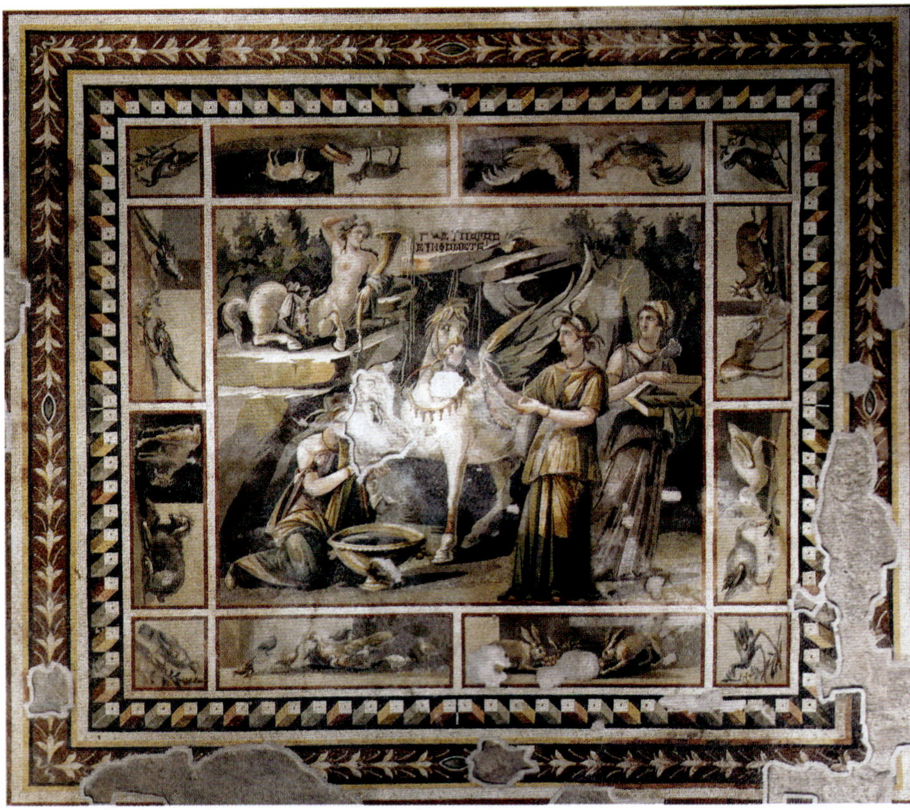

This mosaic, picturing Pegasus, the winged horse of Greek mythology, was found in Antioch three quarters of a century after the excavation closed down on the eve of World War II. An excavation led by Turkish archaeologist Hatice Pamir discovered the mosaic on a site intended for a large hotel. Construction halted. The excavation continued. The hotel was built on top of it. The Pegasus mosaic and other broad stretches of mosaic were left in place, where today they can be viewed by hotel guests and visitors.

of a necklace, no play of a horse's leg. You could manage with less detail, with larger, hence fewer, tesserae, less cutting, less careful setting into place. Numbers told the story, or part of it: The head of Dionysus in one of the Atrium House panels required 523 tesserae per area unit, the geometrical border only 197.

Still, many of the geometric mosaics recovered from Antioch were strikingly inventive, boasting shapes within shapes, bizarrely convoluted, some of them reassuringly symmetric, others just enough "off" to dizzy you. The sinuous curves and waves, intersecting circles, parabolic look-alikes, and other mathematical shapes could be dazzlingly beautiful and beguiling: You look, and you keep looking, three dimensions seeming to arise wonderfully from two, the retina overwhelmed. It doesn't take a math geek to appreciate them—or, for that matter, to note their sometimes daring contrast with more conventional figural regions in the same mosaic.

Take, for example, a third-century Dionysus and Ariadne mosaic recovered from Daphne in 1935, making up the entry to a triclinium. In the myth, Dionysus sees the sleeping Ariadne, abandoned by Theseus after she'd helped him escape the Minotaur, and falls in love with her. She's shown in a white tunic, adorned by a green glass necklace and golden pendant. Competent enough, if barely: One scholar judged their heads "stiff and meaningless." In any case, the mosaic would be the poorer without the two large geometric panels that flank it. To one side is a kind of checkerboard array, five by five, each small square divided into triangles of differing shades, in white, black, and earth tones. The other is also built up from squares, again in five by five, but this time with eight-pointed stars superimposed, happily relieving the otherwise static array. The whole, Ariadne and her checkerboards, is much better than its parts.

Sometimes, geometric borders, boundaries, and backgrounds stole the show altogether. Consider an early fifth-century mosaic found in 1938 on the slopes of Mt. Silpius above Antioch, originally covering the floor of a vestibule in the Bath of Apolausis. It went first to Worcester, but was later sold to the Getty museum in California. Mosaic Floor with Animals is fourteen feet long, stands almost six feet high, and does indeed include animals—a hare nibbling on grapes, a long-billed woodcock, two partridges.

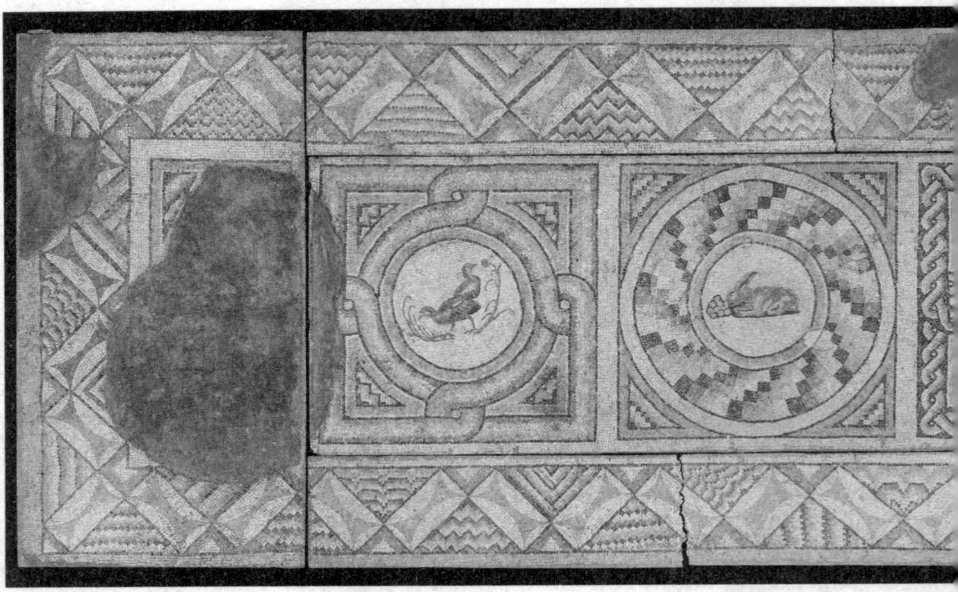

This ca. 400 CE mosaic, found in the Bath of Apolausis on the slopes of Mt. Silpius just east of Antioch, went first to the Worcester Art Museum, before being sold to the J. Paul Getty Museum in 1970. Compared to the extravagant geometric patterns around, above, and below them, do the creatures seem like afterthoughts?

Yet these poor creatures seem an afterthought, little diverting you from the geometric playfulness all around them. The mosaic's "dominant characteristic," writes Alexis Belis in a book devoted to the Getty mosaics, is "its mesmerizing assortment of geometric patterns" executed in shades of gray, pink, ocher, black, and white—entwined cables, traditional guilloches, a circular pattern of rays of color inducing a kaleidoscopic effect.

In the archives of the Antioch excavation in Princeton today lies a visual inventory of geometric motifs, dozens of them, in color, appearing in mosaics from Antioch and elsewhere. Each design comes with cross-references to where else it could be seen in the ancient world. Each gets a name. Like "Bead and Reel," or "Oblique Squares with Rainbow Shading," or "Egg and Tongue," or "Amazon Shield." The names don't tell you much, but the act of naming them does somehow ennoble them.

When, during the 1980s, Canadian scholar Sheila Campbell studied the Antioch mosaics, she put together her own inventory, a fifteen-page

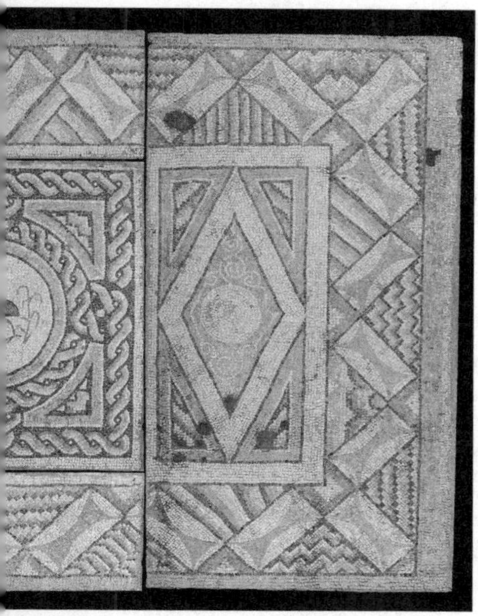

feast for the eyes that included close to a hundred motifs, each with descriptive names, like "Twisted Ribbons," "Looped Guilloche," "Grid with Diamonds," and "Laurel Garland." Almost poetry. Some, like "Checkerboard of Scales" and one of several versions of "Overlapping Circles," she found in only a single Antioch mosaic; others, like "Grid of Fleurettes," in half a dozen or more. "Wave Crest," which looks about like you'd think, a wave of tesserae rolling over onto itself, appeared in seventeen.

Does this recurrence and repetition sap the stature of geometric mosaics, conjure up an antique assembly line? Is it evidence of the one-of-a-kind originality we expect of art extinguished by the need to fill up floor? Or, more benignly, of the healthy sharing of visual ideas among fine craftsmen?

Beyond their odd or charming names, what was there to say about these intricate designs, shapes, forms, and geometries? To Michael Padgett, retired curator of ancient art at Princeton, who for thirty years helped preside over the Princeton legacy of the Antioch mosaics, it seems so obvious as to need no explanation: Say you're a professor, in class, or you're a museum docent or curator, lecturing on this mosaic or that. You're pointing out features in a mosaic like Drinking Contest, with all its varied and complex design, its mythological figures, the play of light across the cup, its links to similar scenes depicted by ancient artists, and pretty soon you've got a good story to tell students or visitors. But then, turning to the geometric motifs that frame the rest of it, what then? What's to say about a circle, or loop, or rhombus, or wave?

CHAPTER SIXTEEN

Doro in America

Three hundred mosaics came out of Antioch, and Theodoro "Doro" Levi would become intimate friends with most of them.

Levi was an Italian archaeologist, born in Trieste in 1898, educated in Florence and at the Italian Archaeological School of Athens, a veteran of digs in Crete and Mesopotamia. He was director of the island of Sardinia's art and antiquities, professor of archaeology at the University of Cagliari, widely published, of the highest reputation. Back in the 1920s, he'd shuttled across Greece and Italy with his student friend Gilbert Bagnani, exploring, getting into scrapes, romantic and otherwise. In 1928, he married a woman of Greek descent, Anna Kosadinou, who'd nursed him back to health after a car accident. Sixty years later, film footage of Levi captures him as an old man, a few years before his death, reliant on a cane to navigate cobbled European streets, but trim and smartly dressed, a picture of Old World dignity.

But Doro Levi was a Jew, and so, in the shameful year of 1938, we must disrupt our account to tell a darker story. Hitler had locked the Jews of Germany, and then Austria, in tightening chains of cruelty and constraint. Now his Fascist lackey, Mussolini, issued an Italian edition of Hitler's racial laws, which booted Levi from the position in elite Italian scholarship and culture he had worked hard to attain. While visiting his friend Bernard Berenson, the influential art historian, at his rented summer villa outside Florence, Doro received a telegram brusquely expelling him from his place in an upcoming archaeological expedition to Greece.

Around this time, Robert Woods Bliss and his wife, Mildred Barnes Bliss, wealthy collectors of Byzantine art who, since 1936, had helped support the Antioch venture, learned Levi would soon be out of a job. They knew of him already through their friend Royall Tyler, diplomat, historian, art connoisseur, and an organizer of the first international exhibition of Byzantine art in 1931. Tyler advised them on all things artistic and cultural, long affectionate letters among the three of them often given over to new curatorial finds. Earlier in 1938, Tyler had written Mr. Bliss about lectures Levi had recently given at Dumbarton Oaks, the Bliss estate in Washington, D.C., soon to become Harvard's center for Byzantine studies. Levi, he wrote, was "a fine type of unworldly, disinterested scholar," one ever eager to help others "without bothering his head about what is due to himself." Now, eight months later, Fascist Italy's racial laws pulled tight around him and his wife. The Blisses, in Switzerland, got the news by telegram:

> ITALIAN DECREE EFFECTIVE OCTOBER 16 DEPRIVES LEVI OF PROFESSORSHIP
>
> SITUATION DESPERATE SINCE STIPEND THEIR ONLY INCOME COULD [LEVI'S] SERVICE AS FIELD ARCHAEOLOGIST POSSIBLY BE UTILIZED BY ANTIOCH COMMITTEE

A few weeks later, Tyler laid out Levi's predicament for Mr. Bliss: He would be out of a job, lose his salary, probably his pension as well; he had no private means. "This after having risked his neck by going to Italy (from his native Trieste) during the war and enlist[ing] as a volunteer in the Italian army. . . . The urgency is great. It is expected that one of the next steps will be to deprive Jews of their Italian citizenship and to take away their passports."

Levi astonished him: "Not a trace of bitterness. Just serenity and calm." But now he needed help. Could Bliss find him a job at an American university? This was essential if Levi was to get out of Italy; a U.S. visa required a formal invitation. "There is one favourable point," Tyler added with blunt sagacity: "Doro is the only Italian archaeologist who is a Jew, so there'll be no competition from that quarter."

The following month, Bliss heard more from Tyler of Doro's troubles: "I am so deeply distressed about it that I can't refrain. He is such a good creature, and of the very highest quality as an archaeologist." By then, Bliss had already written Harvard, his alma mater, as well as the Institute for Advanced Study, the recently founded think tank. Harvard offered to name Levi professor of classical archaeology—but would need a large contribution from the Blisses toward Levi's salary to do so. Advanced Study could, with Bernard Berenson's help, find a slot for him immediately, for the second half of the 1938–39 academic year. This proved the more workable alternative.

In the end, Mr. and Mrs. Bliss put up $3,500, the equivalent today of at least $75,000, to settle Levi in America. "I was touched deeply by what Robert has done for Doro," Tyler wrote Robert's wife, Mildred, in a letter on November 18. "What may come to the Jews in Italy may be guessed by what is going on in Germany," a reference to the eruption of destruction and death, Kristallnacht, visited on Berlin's Jewish community a few days earlier.

On November 22, Tyler wrote Robert Bliss with the text of the cable he'd just sent him:

> DORO & WIFE PROFOUNDLY GRATEFUL ACCEPT PROVIDENTIALLY OPPORTUNE CABLE & TELEPHONE INVITATIONS ARRANGING FORMALITIES DEPARTURE EARLIEST POSSIBLE & WILL MAKE ANY ADVANCES NECESSARY.

On January 5, 1939, Levi arrived in the United States, bound for Princeton, where he would spend most of the next six years, mostly given over to the mosaics from Antioch. Eight months after his arrival in the U.S., the Germans invaded Poland, and the world was at war.

—

Just before the war broke out, Jean Lassus, fresh from Antioch, found himself, now a French army captain, serving on the Maginot Line, the elaborate network of forts, artillery, and underground railways that ran along the border with Germany; after the carnage and humiliation of the Great War, it was supposed to keep France safe. "A curious thing," Lassus would look back to that moment just before the declaration of war: "The Maginot Line is the shield of France. But a professor of archaeology"—he, himself!—"presided over it," or a stretch of it. Early one morning, the telephone rang: War had been declared at last. He recalled the corresponding moment from 1914, when he was eleven, knew what was happening, but had no responsibilities. "At 37, I did have some—for 1,200 meters of French frontier," and the machine-gun emplacements to defend it.

First ensued a strange indeterminate period, "the Phony War," months and months with little combat. When he wrote Dick Stillwell on February 25, 1940, Lassus was still in uniform, the border quiet. Four months later, when he wrote Mr. Morey, the Maginot Line had been rendered moot by the German invasion of the Low Countries, well to the north, and then France itself. That was in May. Within weeks, the Germans occupied more than half of France. Eight *départements* east of the Rhône were held by the Italians. Hitler visited Paris to bask in the glow of his victory. Lassus was plunged into a period of confusion, fear, and mortal danger that would last all through the war. "My wife, my sister, my children, near [the town of] Dreux, under terrible bombardment, had to leave, on foot, along the road, without their bags. After a hundred kilometers on foot, the children on peasant carts, then by truck, they were able to find the means of reaching London." As for himself, he wrote Morey, after the severe bout of dysentery that had landed him in a hospital in Clermont, he was safe and on his way back to health, at least for the moment.

World War II halted the excavations at Antioch, but not all at once. Four months after the declaration of war but before the fall of France, Jacques Jaujard, director of the French national museums, could still write Morey of prospects for the coming year, as if no war intervened. In Antioch itself, the Committee was represented as late as 1940. "Now I can send you a few facts to go on until more is known," Sandy Campbell wrote Adib

Ishak in Antioch on March 26. "During these times we must live from day to day." He hoped that "with good luck we may be meeting in a couple of months and working together again. Inshallah," if God wills it.

Before the Japanese attack on Pearl Harbor, Campbell made the rounds of North American cities and museums—New York, Ann Arbor, Cincinnati, Toronto—lecturing on the mosaics, talking them up. Morey encouraged him. A round of new expenses attending the abrupt departure from Antioch, with its "emergency division" of finds, had left them with a sizable deficit. Fortunately, Morey wrote Fred Waagé in late 1938, Smith College "was taking one of the river god panels" for $2,500. The Committee was "negotiating a similar transaction" with the Met in New York for $5,000. A market was materializing for mosaics from Antioch.

In 1941, the director of the Baltimore Museum of Art, Leslie Cheek Jr., wrote Campbell with a tricky question. Rob Garrett had suggested the museum "dispose of a few of its handsome Antioch mosaics by writing to other institutions" and offering them the chance to buy them. For example, Vassar College and the Cleveland Museum of Art. But Cheek knew Princeton hoped to sell off some of its own Antioch holdings, too. "We do not want to interfere with your own negotiations," he wrote Campbell, or ask prices out of line with those quoted by Princeton. He had four mosaics in mind to sell, for anywhere from $2,500 to $5,500. Would Baltimore's plans conflict with Princeton's?

Campbell wrote back that two potential buyers on Cheek's list were indeed weighing purchases from Princeton. For those two, could Cheek withhold his offer? As for Cheek's prices, they seemed "justifiable." But the Committee, he needed him to know, was offering up to one-third off, "to dispose of them quickly."

Early in 1941, Fred Waagé, back at Cornell, was giving lectures on "The Excavations at Antioch, Syria: The Old Age of the Ancient World." By late 1941, after Pearl Harbor, the war and its insatiable demands overtook everything else. Glanville Downey, then at Yale, wrote Morey that he'd "been made second in command of the fire-fighting" squad . . . . "After the holiday we shall have to train volunteers and [practice] . . . with more or less live incendiary bombs." The following fall, Morey wrote

Waagé about some boxes of sherds from Antioch: Don't send them to Princeton; "There seems to be no cubic inch of spare space in McCormick Hall." The university wanted them to clear things out "in order to make room for the Navy."

During these years, too, reaching back to the Nazi rise to power in 1933 and all the way to the end of the war, a New York–based Emergency Committee in Aid of Displaced Foreign Scholars helped bring vulnerable scholars and artists to America. Among them were Martin Buber, Emmy Noether, and Thomas Mann. Beginning as early as 1935, plaintive letters, recommendations, and testaments from Central Europe began to pile up on Rufus Morey's desk in Princeton. Most of them handwritten, they came from noted art historians, old friends, former colleagues. They were sad and desperate. "Dear Morey," they began, or "Dear Rufus." One came from mosaics scholar Henri Stern. A biographical sketch he included with his appeal noted his mobilization by the French Army on October 1, 1939; his demobilization on July 18, 1940, with the fall of France; and the loss of his academic position to the new Vichy French racial laws that September.

—

Doro Levi was one of the lucky ones, avoiding the worst disappointments and horrors faced by his fellow refugees.

During the first two years of his stay in America, the Antioch excavation's prospects were uncertain. For a time, as we've seen, the Committee had judged Cyprus a worthy alternative to Antioch; in that scenario Levi's name had figured all along: If the Committee did turn to Cyprus, Robert Bliss wrote Royall Tyler on March 31, 1939, he thought it likely, "judging from what Morey told me in a brief talk a few days ago, that we will make use of Doro's unusual qualifications." Even most of a year later, with war declared, a Cyprus dig was alive enough that the École du Louvre's Jean Charbonneaux could advance Levi's name as its director. As Levi remembered it later, he'd been named to the post when, "at the last moment," the calamitous fall of France erased all thought of it.

At first, Levi was at loose ends in America. His wife was stuck in Italy, his livelihood was uncertain. "The Institute," director Abraham Flexner wrote Bliss early in Levi's tenure, "took unlimited pains to bring him to this country on the assurance which you and Mrs. Bliss have made good, namely, that $3,500 would be placed at his disposal for the present year." But what then? Interest in him by the Blisses and Tyler, Flexner wrote, had planted in Levi the "natural supposition" that a secure position, an academic home, was something to which he could look forward. Thus far, however, nothing.

During parts of 1940 and 1941, Levi lectured at Princeton, Harvard, and Michigan; on Etruscan art, Minoan art, excavations in Sardinia; to students and to the general public. But he was still a man without a country. "It may be a bit discouraging for him that nothing worthwhile has turned up," Mr. Bliss wrote Tyler a year after Levi's arrival in the States; universities, it struck him, took an interest in archaeological expeditions, but not in archaeology itself, as a discipline, limiting Levi's options. Levi "will have his chance, nevertheless, but he will have to bide his time." For a while, it seemed Levi might be reduced to teaching Italian to undergraduates, "just as a means of keeping alive until some better opportunity offers," noted Advanced Study's next director, Frank Aydelotte. Baldwin Smith pictured poor Levi stuck doing "odd jobs," like working on "the Antioch material."

—

"I should be very grateful to you," Levi wrote Sandy Campbell, if, while writing up his own Antioch work, he could "send me in a few words" something of his findings; "they will offer me the greatest help for developing my own study on the art of mosaic." Information he sought for each mosaic-yielding villa or bath included "datable objects" found at the site, coins, evidence of earthquake damage. But dipping into the project now, he couldn't be sure he'd be able to continue or complete it.

Then the stars aligned. Levi won a prestigious Guggenheim Fellowship, which, beginning in May 1941, let him give himself entirely to the mosaics and later request further support from the Institute for Advanced Study. The job now falling to him was a deeply informed art-historical study of the Antioch mosaics—"entrusted" to him, he would write with evident gratitude, by Mr. Morey. A round of scholarly volumes devoted to the dig, while still underway, had already come out from Princeton; but these hardly supplied the last word on the mosaics.

At least for a time during the next few years, Levi lived in a house on Wiggins Street a few blocks above Nassau Street, a ten-minute walk to McCormick Hall, where most of the Antioch materials were housed. Those bearing on the mosaics—the reams of field reports, photos, descriptions, statistical summaries, sketches, maps, and colored drawings—were the raw materials of his intellectual life in America; he'd rarely get to see the mosaics themselves, many of them still in Antioch, Beirut, or German-occupied Paris. Levi was mostly cut off from European scholars, from the Princeton excavators, from Antioch itself. It was just him and his book.

An author doesn't always know just what shape his book will take. But by March 1943, certainly, Levi did: "It will not only illustrate one of the most imposing groups of monuments . . . discovered by American archaeological research in recent years," as he described it to Aydelotte. It would "sketch for the first time the history of Roman mosaics." And it would help "fill the gap of our knowledge of the dark period between the art and civilization of antiquity and [that] of the Middle Ages." That, of course, echoed Rufus Morey's scholarly fixation, and Josef Strzygowski's, about the origins of medieval art.

"Under the ruins of a large building, of which only scanty and confused traces are left, the remains of a house of the early Roman Age were found." This was Atrium House, from the first season. "A room of this house has given us one of the most important mosaic pavements among those discovered at Antioch. . . ." And so it began, with Levi turning his attention to the Judgment of Paris, the Drinking Contest of Herakles and Dionysus, and Aphrodite and Adonis. He considered whether they and two smaller mosaics from the same room made for a single work of art; or else were best thought of as individual *emblemata*—works of figural art made in outside workshops brought separately to the site and slipped into a larger, room-sized tableau. Either way, they were held together, almost literally, by meanders, vines, and steplike patterns of tesserae known as crowstep—the classic designs and geometries often making up the borders of Roman mosaics.

At one point, he turned to a mosaic depicting Briseis's Farewell. This is the classic moment in the *Iliad* when Briseis, Achilles's lover—or concubine, or slave—is surrendered to Agamemnon, at the king's insistence, igniting in Achilles the rage that burns through the story. Levi notes "the handsome youthful head" of Patroclus, Achilles's dearest friend, "bent sadly over one shoulder," gently urging Briseis toward her unwelcome fate. She "advances reluctantly, still turning her head backward toward her beloved Achilles," whom we cannot see, lost in a part of the mosaic defaced by the centuries. Here was just the first brief pulse of attention Levi gave any subject. Soon he was alluding to black-figured vases, a Pompeian fresco, and the Ambrosian Iliad, a fifth-century illuminated manuscript, all of which represented the same poignant scene.

In the mass of detail Levi marshaled, the sheer range and depth of his learning, his willingness to venture forth into other times, places, and arts—his four-hundred-page "Description and Interpretation" of Antioch's mosaics reads like the last word on its subject. It isn't, even for Levi himself. Two-thirds of the way through volume one, he breaks away from individual mosaics themselves to broader themes—ornamental style, the representation of human figures and animals, principles of composition used in the mosaics—another two hundred pages' worth.

Levi didn't overesteem the mosaics he surveyed. Those unearthed from Antioch, he wrote, were not all spectacularly good. Indeed, scholars often deprecated the medium out of "contempt for an art whose products—we will gladly admit it—are mostly of modest artistic value and are the work of artists of a rather low category." *Ouch*. Mosaics were aesthetically limited. Their tesserae could never make for a true painting. Why, you couldn't even enjoy "an integral view of the wide horizontal surface of a pavement" while standing atop it, as you typically were. Then, too, there was its "hardness of lines and changes of colors and the disturbance caused by the breaking up of lines into the web of tesserae." All undercut mosaics as an art form.

Still, he allowed, "we must be grateful to the Tyche of the art historians," grateful to fortune, "that the solid technique of mosaic preserved for us at least a partial testimony of so many treasures of ancient art fatally condemned by the fragility" of painting: Paint flaked. Canvas and paper tore or burned. Tesserae endured.

When finally published in 1947 by Princeton University Press, *Antioch Mosaic Pavements* was a great oversized volume of 650 pages with the ungainly heft of a library atlas, printed on thick, glossy paper and weighing in at five pounds. That was volume one. Volume two bore hundreds of black-and-white photos. Levi's text fell in thick paragraphs down both sides of each double-columned page, often crashing into a block of microscopically printed footnotes at its base. For each mosaic, he might draw connections between it and art found at Pompeii; comment on the "flatness" or "roundedness" of a figure represented within it; note the dates of coins retrieved nearby. He theorized about how the one Psyche of ancient myth—we met her in the prologue—could multiply "into a band of Psyches as work and play companions to the Erotes." He wrote about the depictions of Negroes and dwarfs among the mosaics, about fishers and hunters; of mosaic portraits and their similarities to mummy portraits found in Naples or Berlin museums; of trellises, quatrefoils, meanders, and other elements of geometric decoration. To the vines, tendrils, flowers, and fruit that often bordered figural mosaics he devoted twenty-eight pages.

Only in his book's foreword did Levi slip free from the jungle of detail he'd inhabited for the past six years to hint at what moved and motivated him.

> A teacher and friend of mine recently expressed bitter disappointment because his excavations on an island of the Aegean—which we first roved over together in our explorations, and where still my nostalgic thoughts often return—did not entirely fulfill his expectation: "Alas, Fortune did not smile on Science, as is only to be expected, because she is an enemy of method!" Far from sharing this pessimism on the ways and accidents of archaeological discoveries, I believe, on the contrary, that Fortune is friendly to method, and in the long run smiles, and yields to it, if method includes—as it must—insight, discipline, perseverance, and also alertness, that is, readiness to grasp capricious Opportunity by the hair, as she passes near in her fugitive flight.

—

Levi's knowledge was extraordinary, but so were his industry and patience. He was in a foreign country, away from most of his friends and from his wife, who was stuck in Europe for the duration; a 1941 letter reported her ill. When the Germans marched into Athens, his patron, Mrs. Bliss, wrote him, "The thought of the Swastika flying over the Parthenon puts steel into one's heart." But outwardly, Levi retained his composure, writing back: "I try only to concentrate on my work," the mosaics. He did relish the comfort and freedom from distraction of his American years. He was aware of his good fortune, and not shy to say so. He had a driver's license, a car, a new place to live in town, on Moore Street, a few blocks from campus. Later, at Advanced Study, he appreciated its resources and conveniences; he wrote the Blisses of its "hospitable quarters, comfortable quiet studios near the library, excellent food."

A former student and friend of Levi, Clelia Laviosa, an Italian archaeologist a generation younger than he, would write that Levi would remember this time "as one of the most stimulating in his life." "The spirit of cooperation with which he was received" touched him. So did the chance to "exchange ideas with specialists in the most diverse fields." He was sometimes a dinner guest of Albert Einstein at his house on Mercer Street. On the eve of his return to Europe a few weeks after the German surrender, he wrote of how sorry he'd be "when the moment comes of leaving Princeton." After the war, Laviosa reported, "his mind would often nostalgically go back to the days spent in Princeton's 'Antioch Room.'"

At the behest of friends in early August 1941 he traveled to Dublin, New Hampshire, for a vacation at a "quiet house among the woods and the lakes, at the foot of Mount Monadnock." It was called Five Chimneys, his hosts were musicians, and it was just what he needed. "After many weeks of hard work in a very trying damp weather," he wrote the Blisses, "I thought I felt a little tired. . . . After this short rest I hope soon to be able to take up my work again with renewed energy."

—

"The amazing series of mosaics" from Antioch, wrote Clark Hopkins in the *Journal of Near Eastern Studies* in 1947, had now received their due in the "two monumental volumes of Doro Levi. This is the outstanding work on mosaics of the Roman Empire." Hopkins, who had directed an important dig at Dura-Europos, on the Euphrates, in Mesopotamia, regretted Levi's extravagance of detail. "The Princeton volumes," he wrote, "do not err on the side of economy." This fact no one could fail to see, though most put a warmer gloss on it: "In the sheer density of its language, [Levi's book was] . . . at first difficult to penetrate," wrote Belgian mosaics scholar Janine Balty, "but, pushing ahead, it seduces by its clarifying intelligence, perceptiveness, and intuition."

Hopkins, however, saw a deeper flaw in Levi's work, in "the whole problem of Eastern influence at Antioch. Levi keeps his eyes fixed on the West; he fits the mosaics into the long arc of Roman art." His view of its decline across the centuries was insufficiently open to what Hopkins saw as "a new artistic feeling and a new stylistic manner," born of influences from the East. These Levi resisted. "An escape into the Orient" to explain the uncertain roots of mosaics was, he wrote, unwarranted. Likewise, "If an external influence on Hellenic art" for certain ornamental patterns "must be sought, we need not turn to the East for it." As Karen C. Britt, a scholar of medieval and Byzantine art, put it, Levi "steadfastly refused to admit the possibility of eastern influence for any of the motifs that occur in the mosaics." Thus, almost half a century after Strzygowski, the fires of the old debate had not been extinguished, and the Antioch mosaics still figured in it.

In the end, Levi helped immortalize the Antioch mosaics—if not by the grace of his pen, or even the acuity of his insights, then by the depth of his devotion to his subject. Almost from its publication in 1947 and in all the years since, *Antioch Mosaic Pavements* would serve as the real scholarly culmination of the Franco-American excavation, a towering bastion of information, interest, and insight about the mosaics, and point of departure for all subsequent study.

Sometime after his return from America in the late 1940s on the first ship to bear civilians back to Italy, Doro and his wife, reunited, stood for a photographic portrait that captured the two of them looking happy, proud, and at peace. They stand together, hands clasped, in a tiled court in Athens, warmed by the summer sun. They are beautiful people, their posture impeccable, he in a vested suit and tie, she in a trim print dress and heels. Seeing Levi like this, extricated at last from the wreckage of fascism, the war, and his own herculean labors, it is disquieting to think of him back in Princeton, removed from the light of day, a little too lost in his mosaics for his own good: His life, from before 1938, has been restored to him.

Doro's book turned out to be about the last thing he would have to say about mosaics. Save for one article in an Italian encyclopedia, Janine Balty would note in a 2001 essay titled "Doro Levi—Fifty Years Later," he never returned to mosaics, instead bringing his archaeological intellect to bear on Minoan Crete. And yet, "passing like a meteor across the field of ancient mosaics, then little explored," his years in America proved him "a true pioneer . . . raising questions still at the center of our thinking."

CHAPTER SEVENTEEN

Anonymous Hands

The art historian and mosaics scholar Christine Kondoleon has sometimes referred to what she calls "the Antioch Workshop." By this she means no specific and identifiable group of working mosaicists, but rather an abstract entity, a construct, representing Antioch's place in the mosaic art and practice of its day.

But would we not love to step inside the real thing, a mosaic workshop of the third or fourth century in all its bustle of human activity?

For all Doro Levi's scholarship, neither he nor anyone else had ever identified such a workshop. But in an article in a French-language journal in 1997, a Purdue University professor, David Parrish, proposed to fill the gap. He admitted his conclusions were provisional. He was modest about his claims. He called it his "*atelier proposé*," his proposed workshop. Still, his paper bore a whiff of bravado. For it could seem there was some definite workshop he had in mind, perhaps located on a particular street, staffed by a named boss or lead mosaicist.

It didn't come to that, but what Parrish did turn up was intriguing enough. Among the Antioch mosaics, he identified several with striking likenesses suggestive of a common origin, the same intellect, style, or sensibility behind them. Its most telling marker, its very signature, was its

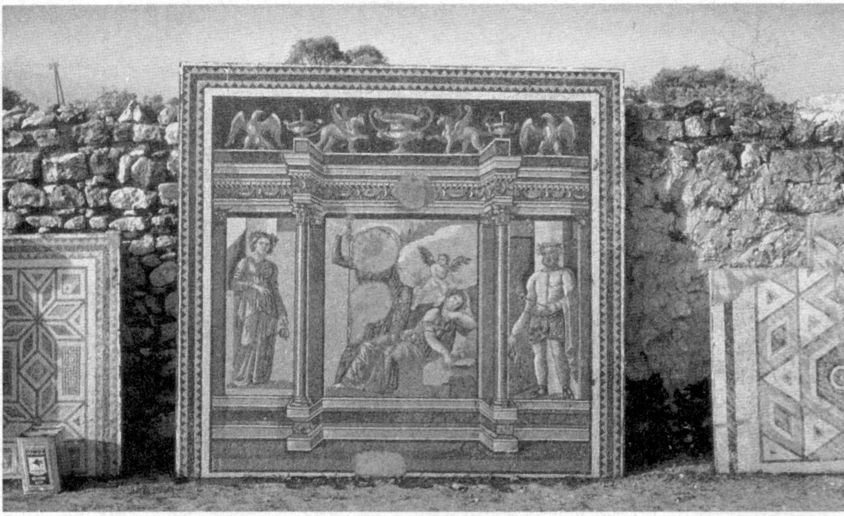

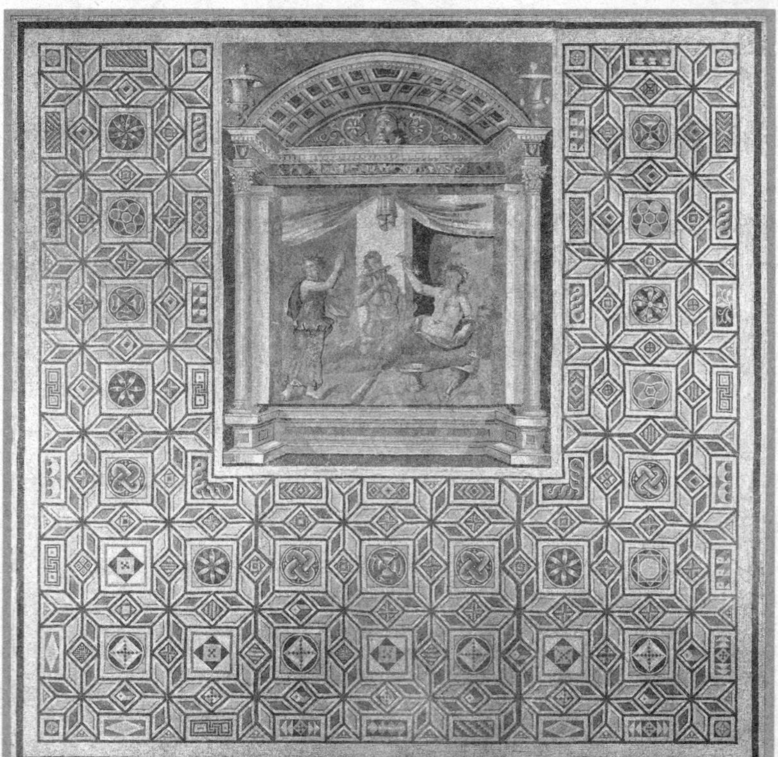

Were these two early third-century CE mosaics designed and made in the same Antioch workshop, perhaps by the same men? Close comparison of the two, especially their elaborate architectural frames, led a Purdue University professor, David Parrish, to suggest as much in a 1997 paper.

penchant for setting its mosaic subjects in architecturally lavish settings. Like a picture within a frame, except that the frame was part of the picture.

One mosaic, from the House of the Drinking Contest in Seleucia, represents the god Dionysus with the mortal Herakles. But this scene of orgiastic drinking, cups raised high, takes up only half the panel's total area. The rest depicts the ornate structure framing it—"real" columns and stone pediments jutting out toward the viewer. It is lit so realistically, writes Parrish, "that you see the play of light and shadow at the base of the columns." Drinking contests were a staple of Roman mosaics, several other examples, as we've seen, being found in Antioch. But never set on anything like such a stage.

Yet one does appear in another Antioch mosaic, this one today installed at the Hatay Archaeology Museum. It shows Dionysus as he discovers the sleeping Ariadne, daughter of King Minos of Crete. Again we step into the mosaic from a specific place—more columns, these resting atop footings that set off three paneled niches. A decorative cornice of mythical creatures parades across the top. "The taste for very carefully rendered architectural illusion" in the two mosaics, writes Parrish, suggested to him they were "products of a common workshop." Similarities in their geometric borders—especially the squares and diamonds of their complex ornamentation—bolstered the impression. So did their overall proportions, color palettes, tile density, and materials. So did Doro Levi's dating of them both to the first half of the third century. For Parrish, the evidence testified to a single mind, eye, or guiding hand.

In Doro Levi's book, only a single footnote in discouragingly small type mentions mosaicists by name. None hailed from Antioch, though one mosaic from Crete, for example, bears the name of a mosaicist from Daphne. A mosaicist whose name does come down to us, through Pliny the Elder, is Sosus of Pergamon, creator of The Unswept Floor. This cheerfully transgressive mosaic marvel portrays chicken bones, nuts, lobster claws, and other culinary debris littering a tile floor after a big meal. Today, we'd want to know more about him; we fuss over artists, wish to hear of their creative struggles, see the telltale signs of their light and genius. With the Antioch mosaics, though, we do so in vain. "Beautiful work by anonymous hands." That's how Gilvan Ventura da Silva has described the mosaic riches of Antioch. Wall labels in the Baltimore museum's Antioch Court credit each mosaic, with no further elaboration, one after another, to "Unidentified Artists."

As an amateur mosaicist, I know, more or less, how I make what I make. I look in books and on museum walls at what others have done. I get ideas, of subject, composition, color, materials, and design. I reject most, settle on one or a few. I establish the mosaic's dimensions. I select or cut to size a substrate, a solid base on which to lay down tesserae, or perhaps an existing surface, a shelf or sill I want to embellish. I make sketches. I play with colors, select a palette, order tesserae if I don't already have enough. Finally, I start laying down tiles, following some rough internal compass. Sometimes I heed misguided hunches that take me off course. The result often disappoints. But at least I can account for the mosaic's evolution, trace something of how I got there.

But who, we might ask, made *Opora, Agros, and Oinos*, or Fruit, Field, and Wine, a mosaic recovered from the ruins of a villa in Daphne? In an article for visitors to its new home at the Baltimore Museum of Art, Rufus Morey was moved to a spirited description of this ambitious work, which he called possibly "the most important piece of third-century painting in existence." Eight feet high, ten across, it represented an after-dinner symposium bringing together personifications of the three agrarian elements, together with geometric and ornamental designs surrounding the main figural image:

> It is a work that looks backward and forward—still Greek in the ease with which it turns the annual beneficence of the earth into a cheerful humanistic allegory—the cultivated fields impersonated by a reclining banqueter who holds a wine-cup and embraces his companion, Fruit, a half-draped female with lap filled by real fruits, and head and neck encircled, like Field's, by leafy garlands. Wine is personified in a satyr of the type that one finds among the followers of Dionysus in Bacchic scenes—a squat and aged figure with body wrinkled and misshapen by age and good living, holding

the Bacchic thrysos [the god's traditional symbol, an ornamented fennel stalk] in one hand and proffering a wine-cup in the other.

Morey decided that the "formulas of simplification" that marked its design, edging away from the more naturalistic rendering of earlier epochs, made it "something of a landmark in the history of antique painting, the first of our mosaics to indicate the contribution of Antioch to that shift toward two-dimensional design" into which the art of the West was moving.

Maybe so, but Morey doesn't raise the question that might seem to come first: *Someone made this mosaic. Who?* Was it the work of a gifted artist of rare intelligence and feeling? If so, who was this Michelangelo, this Picasso, this master mosaicist? Or maybe the mosaic is better credited to a team of artisanal drudges who, with no broader vision or inspiration, toiled long, hard, and ably; maybe one artist focused on our poor, slouching bearded Dionysus, much the worse for wear, others assigned the more virtuous *Opora* or *Agros*? Or maybe we should look to the owner of the villa, who put up the money, perhaps suggesting, or decreeing, particular design features. And what are we to make of the trio of theatrical masks lying beneath the central scene, striking portraits of open-mouthed anguish that draw your eye once it's finally turned away from the central grouping? Or of the wandering ribbons of guilloches and waves that take up as much space as the three agrarian figures? By what accretion of individual or collective labor did this spectacle come to be? *Who made this mosaic?*

Did the mosaics coming out of Antioch qualify as "art" in the first place, or as something lesser? Many of them, figural and geometric alike, are simply stunning. They can be found in some of the top-ranked art museums of the world. Museum directors and curators pay good money for them, exhibit them in lofty, well-lit galleries. Yet even so, mosaics carry a taint. Because, as anyone can attest, some aren't any good. And because the artists who made them maybe weren't, after all, *true* artists, as we conceive them today. Provoked by the question, Katherine Dunbabin, one of the premier mosaic scholars in the world, says, "I think perhaps we need to recognise that most mosaics might be better classified as the work of 'artisans' or 'craftsmen,' rather than 'artists.' Or perhaps rather, that the modern concept of art is something that was entirely foreign to antiquity."

Certainly there was plenty of room for artisanal excellence among the Antioch mosaicists, for exactitude and close workmanship. When the Princeton excavators measured the presumably rectangular shapes of the Atrium House pavements, they found opposite edges almost perfectly parallel, off by only two millimeters in seven thousand. On the other hand, some mosaicists doubtless just laid down tile patterns as sketch or boss decreed. At the same worksite, then, one might find ham-fisted menials from one end of the spectrum, gifted artists from the other—a split that discourages any impulse to force the mosaicists of old Antioch into one oversimple category.

—

If there was a place in a late Roman mosaic where high art met less exalted craft, it was where the *emblema* left off and the rest of the mosaic began. The *emblema*—from the Greek, meaning one element introduced into another—was the featured figural portion of the mosaic. Here were the fine scenes from mythology that so entranced Doro Levi and other scholars, the nobly attired women, the Greek inscriptions nodding to Pleasure, *Megalopsychia*, or other Hellenic ideas, the superbly wrought images that, from a distance, might be taken for actual paintings. Much evidence suggests that *emblemata* were often made separately, then brought to the site on trays and set into the larger work, any awkward edges between them artfully erased. Beyond the *emblema*, the mosaic typically gave way to broad swaths of background, ornament, and geometric pattern generally easier to execute. By this crude breakdown, at least, the *emblema* was the work of the real artist, all the rest that of ordinary artisans.

> There is every evidence that the *emblemata* were set into the pavement as ready-made units and that they are the works of superior craftsmen. It seems reasonable to assume that these panels, for which we reserve the designation *emblemata*, were purchased

> separately in special ateliers. The less important figure and geometric panels were probably made on the spot by craftsmen of varying ability.

So wrote Sandy Campbell in his field diary sometime after the discovery in 1934 of Fruit, Field, and Wine, which he saw as "perhaps the finest and most important *emblema* that we have uncovered so far." It might be interesting, he went on,

> to study the development of the ateliers of Antioch to determine at what period their craft declines to the level of the ordinary mosaicist who worked on the spot in the production of stiff, flat, stereotyped scenes and geometric patterns. Obviously it will come at the time when the taste for representational art gives way to the Oriental preference for decorative art.

In this last, of course—that "obviously"—Campbell echoed Morey's, and Strzygowski's, ideas about the Eastern stamp on medieval art.

Two years later, in 1936, Lassus was reviewing the first few seasons of the dig for a French journal. The mosaics count stood at 239. The excavators had mostly stopped raising geometric panels. They focused now on the better figural ones, especially the *emblemata*—whose artistry, it seemed to Lassus, duly "conforms to the traditions of Hellenistic painting: picturesque décor, skillful composition, adroit perspective." But things were changing. In third-century mosaics from a single Daphne villa, he noted, three exhibited that familiar Hellenistic realism, but a fourth did not. And another third-century mosaic, Dionysus its subject, "makes one already think of Byzantine mosaics." The once-clear line between *emblema* and periphery was fading. By the fourth century, *emblemata* were being executed on-site, like the rest of the mosaic. Thus, Lassus asserted, "*l'artiste et l'artisan se confondent*," artist and artisan became indistinguishable.

Ancient mosaicists have sometimes been thought reliant on pattern books of familiar motifs, perhaps handed down from generation to generation in drawings and sketches, even scraps of papyrus. But here again, any neat split between artistic inspiration and mere mechanical execution falters. As English archaeologist and art historian Jocelyn Toynbee wrote in a 1950 essay:

> The method of treatment and the combinations of even the most commonly recurring individual figures and *genre motifs* impress us by the extent to which they vary from one mosaic to another. It would seem that the function of cartoons and pattern-books was to provide mosaicists with ideas, compositional schemes, and examples of stock, or typical, figures, while still leaving something to the individual craftsman's (and his patron's) taste and initiative. They did not set rigid models to be slavishly followed.

Among mosaicists today, the old Latin terms for how tesserae are worked into mosaics are still heard. For example, *opus vermiculatum*, closest to painting and most apt to inspire oohs and ahhs from a viewer, refers to fine "wormlike" patterns, using the smallest tiles, to express detail and nuance. In *opus tesselatum*, we recognize wide expanses of background, larger tiles, less intricacy and, probably, skill. When the emperor Diocletian in 301 CE decreed maximum prices for commodities and categories of work, he distinguished between just such levels of skill and practice, as well as between mosaic work on floors and walls. In his 1938 book on the Antioch mosaics Mr. Morey blithely pronounced one panel of a mosaic "done by the artist in charge and . . . distinctly superior" to the others, those being "executed by an assistant."

In the end, attachment to any too-simple notion of individual mosaic workmanship seems misplaced. Inscriptions on some Roman mosaics (though not specifically from Antioch) furnished Katherine Dunbabin strong evidence for "the communal production of the overall work, rather than the skill of the individual craftsman." For Brazilian historian Gilvan Ventura, one conclusion seemed certain: "The practice of the profession was not lonely, [but rather depended] on a teamwork under the leadership of a more skilled or experienced craftsman." The largest room-sized mosaics from Antioch are hard even to *imagine* as the work of a single artist; they're just too big. Overall, for much of what we admire in mosaics, most scholars today credit broader social entities, collective, not individual—teams, crews, workshops.

But not, typically, workshops established at fixed locations, as in shop fronts or the memorable Old World "ateliers" of our modern imaginings. Even a trough of cleanly cut tesserae found in early Islamic Jerash, in today's Jordan, dating to about the eighth century CE, failed to persuade its discoverers it was anything but a temporary cache, serving that one particular job, a house renovation. For Jocelyn Toynbee, evidence of traveling mosaicists, of local materials in figural compositions, of decorative surrounds that formed a pleasing unity with the *emblemata*—these to her all suggested "artists working in situ, in the actual buildings for which the pavements were designed," not in workshops of their own.

So now we see men converging on the site, men of varied levels of artistry, skill, and experience, some of them perhaps slaves. Many acclaimed mosaic artists today are women; but no evidence comes down to us that women made mosaics in Antioch, or that they enjoyed the autonomy to do so. The men cut tesserae, lay out designs, mix mortar. Some are local. Some have traveled from elsewhere. All are coupled to a need, as in any business venture, to get on with the job, get it done, and fast, clean up the dust and mess, and clear out, perhaps by a looming deadline, so the patron and his friends can enjoy their handiwork. All this suggests a fever of some urgency, a scurrying-about.

As in most workplaces in the centuries since, like the bustling shops and factories of the Industrial Revolution, there was probably much grist for conflict among mosaicists and their bosses. The genesis of ideas, the dispensing of jobs, the assignment of tasks, the distribution of wages or profits, the organization of production, the delegation of responsibility, the setting of how well and how fast jobs were to be done, must often have seen interests clash, lines of authority challenged. Antioch's mosaic workshops were not the free artists' studios of our collective imagination, but places of work beset by the economic and social stresses of their time. For all we cannot say about mosaic workshops in Antioch and the rest of the Empire, we can say that much.

—

Later, long after Antioch's fall from its heights during the Empire, mosaics showed up in glorious array on the walls and high vaulted ceilings of Byzantine churches—distant, godly, glittering. Yet the craft's very roots were back down in the ground, in the stone and dirt, right there with foundations, sewers, and graves.

Roman architect Vitruvius's influential first-century BCE tome *On Architecture* served as a primer for temples, theaters, villas, and baths. In it he described in detail how, long before the laying of tesserae, a floor's bed was to be prepared. First comes a bedding,

> composed of stones not smaller than can fill the hand. After the bedding is laid, mix the broken stone in the proportions, if it is new, of three parts to one of lime; if it is old material used again, five parts may answer to two in the mixture. Next, lay the mixture of broken stone, bring on your gangs, and beat it again and again with wooden beetles into a solid mass. . . . On this lay the nucleus, consisting of pounded tile mixed with lime in the proportion of three parts to one. . . .

This was hardy, practical work, well shy of anything aspiring to art.

And once the bed was laid down, was making mosaics not a little like playing with children's blocks? Hadn't every tessera—the sine qua non of mosaic art—once been cleaved from the earth's own beds of stone? Didn't every floor mosaic, as Irving Lavin wrote, "serve the ignominious function of being walked on"? A fine, museum-quality mosaic might be likened to a poor boy from the old neighborhood who's made good, yet still bears some lingering stain of his lowly past.

"While admitting that a large number of mosaics are products of secondary quality," Doro Levi wrote in the introduction to his magnum opus, "we will not commit the exaggeration of denying to all of them any aesthetic value whatsoever." Good of him to concede as much, but his concession only points up the ambiguous place of mosaicists in the art and aesthetics order, of their claims as artists and craftsmen, of whether what they did could ever count as fine and good.

Writing of mosaics from Macedonia, art historian Ruth Kolarik would observe that many suffered from rough workmanship, tesserae crudely shaped and laid, floors laid by men who could follow patterns, "but lacked basic mosaic-making skills."

Of Roman mosaics from the ancient Cretan city of Paphos, Christine Kondoleon, then curator at the Worcester Art Museum, pronounced many not very good. Their makers sometimes reproduced a model with scant comprehension "of its significance or symbolism." They produced "muddled or diluted compositions." One she studied extensively was "filled with curious errors and . . . presented in a dry and uninspired manner."

In her book-length tour of *Mosaics of the Greek and Roman World*, with stops in Italy, North Africa, Britain, Syria, and Turkey, including Antioch, Katherine Dunbabin at one point visits southern England. An intricate mosaic, fifteen feet on a side, found by a blacksmith in 1963, shows a figure, perhaps Jesus, in a central medallion lying within four concentric rings of guilloches. Its outermost ring brushes up against, and merges with, similar semicircular rings surrounding it on four sides. In three of the four, this fusion works: With notable grace the rings unite with their neighboring semicircles. But then, at the fourth, they fail to touch at all; the guilloches never meet up, like bridge spans built simultaneously from both riverbanks that fail to meet in the middle.

Swinging over to North Africa, Dunbabin explores another, more obvious mosaic error, in a large third-century panel today at Tunis's Musée National du Bardo. Two sections of geometric border, both executed in the same intricate pattern, meet—but disjointedly, one range of the pattern running smack into the wrong part of the other, like an earthquake rift in the earth's surface. It's a blunder so plain you might spot it from across the room; Dunbabin guesses it stemmed from two workmen starting at opposite sides of the room, or some kindred failure to work out the geometry beforehand. In any case, it's a wonder the floor wasn't torn up and redone on the spot. Maybe the patron thought to preserve the gaffe as a charming nod to human imperfection.

I don't recall failings so egregious among Antioch mosaics I've seen. But, among the three hundred of them, surely every other kind of error and imperfection, sloppiness and shortcoming, turns up. The topographical border of the Yakto mosaic, iconic as it is, does not, in its depiction of dice throwers, stadiums, and street scenes, seem notably refined. The lettered inscriptions on many mosaics seem sloppy, like hand-lettered signs in a neighborhood coffee shop, the deltas, psis, and kappas of the Greek set down almost haphazardly. In a geometric mosaic, a double row of north-going gray tiles abruptly swerves east for no apparent reason, as if a road made to bypass an invisible house.

How much do such errors and transgressions bother us? Sometimes less than you'd think. Up to a point, anyway, mosaics tend to forgive errors and irregularities. What might seem clumsy from a foot away—a skewed square, a wavering straight line, a right angle that isn't—may disappear, and often does, when seen from across the room.

In a closely reasoned 1978 essay, French scholar Henri Lavagne made much of the split vision that so enriches mosaics. In mosaics, each tile is placed beside another, distinct and apart, by itself nothing much to appreciate; yet, at the same time, it is "subsumed" in the larger composition of which it is part. Or viewed otherwise, a mosaic rests on a "discontinuity of material that disappears to the viewer who sees the ensemble and not its detail." Lavagne imagined a deficient class of viewer "whose spirit is too narrow" to see a work of art in its totality, who sees in it "only accidents, absurdities, disturbances, and annoyances." A broader view reintegrates and restores its coherence. In this delicious doubleness resides something of the art and charm of mosaics.

In 1937, a mosaic panel was lifted from the upper level of the House of the Phoenix in Daphne. Approximately square, about six feet on a side, it today hangs in the light-filled modern cafeteria of the Institute for Advanced Study in Princeton, on the north wall just past the alcove where you turn in your lunch tray. It shows intricately interwoven cables, mostly in tiles of black, white, and beige, looped around white circles. It is no aesthetic marvel. Its colors are muted. It includes no recognizable human or otherwise natural figure. It can come across like a warped chessboard. Yet somehow, when I saw it in 2023, it moved me.

Its presumably "geometric" pattern is, by any norm of mechanical precision, irregular—circles imperfectly circular, visual objects that sometimes jump out smartly from their backgrounds and sometimes slip back into them; abstract "flowers" that don't look like flowers. It is a mosaic ruled by variation, exception, and peculiarity as much as by pattern. Kathleen Mary Coleman, a professor of classics at Harvard, wrote how its "looping cables give the impression that the circles are tilting to the right"—she's right, they do—contributing to the queasy confusion of the whole.

It is abstract, this mosaic, and does not at once reveal its secrets. But as with cloud patterns in which you see, or find, recognizable images, stick around long enough and you see things afresh. For me, it was swirling crowds moving through and against a backdrop of city grids, streets, and

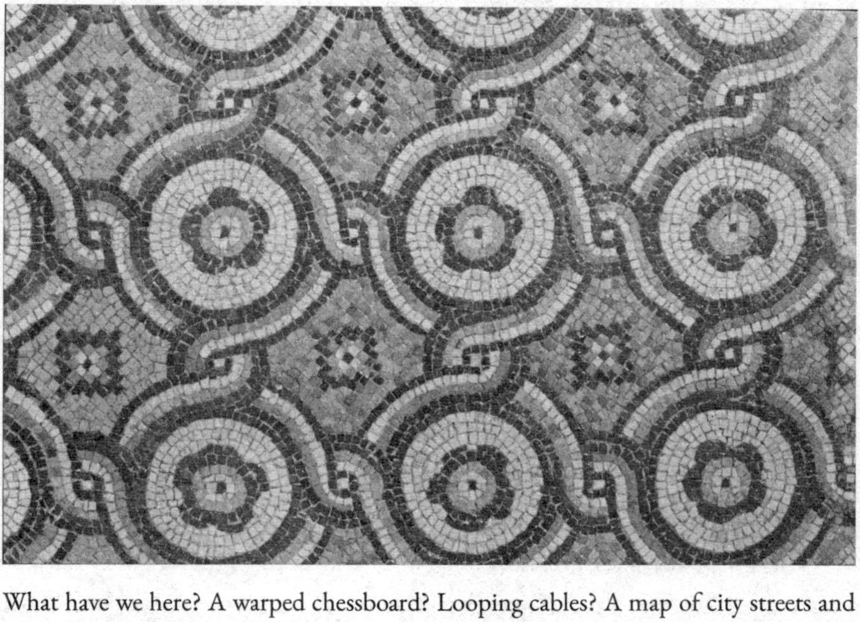

What have we here? A warped chessboard? Looping cables? A map of city streets and squares? The abstract geometries so pervasive among the Antioch mosaics can stir the imagination. Today this fragment, extracted from the floor of the House of the Phoenix in Daphne, occupies the wall of a cafeteria at the Institute for Advanced Study in Princeton.

squares, geometric order and squirming chaos in tension, like life itself—real life, sloppy life, overriding ordered rules.

In painting or drawing, appreciative viewers sometimes comment on the perfection of a work's execution, that it looks just like the wooded glen or maidenly princess it's supposed to represent, even the lightest brushstroke contributing to its fulfillment. Mosaics aren't like that. The finest *opus vermiculatum*, the technique most suited for fine-grained likeness, using the smallest, most intricately fitted tiles, can't come that close. And maybe we wouldn't want it to. Second-century BCE Roman satirist Lucilius, Professor Dunbabin tells us, once invoked this mosaic extravagance to mock an orator's "over-elaborate or artificial diction."

Elizabeth James, a British scholar of ancient history and archaeology at the University of Sussex, in 2022 visited the Art and Archaeology Department at Princeton to give its Kurt Weitzmann Memorial Lecture. She was a champion of mosaics, she made it plain, terming them "the most magical form of art." Her interest was more in wall mosaics than floor pavements like those at Antioch, and more in Byzantine art than late Roman. But she had much to say about the "quality" of mosaics generally, and what made them "good" or not. At one point, she cited an Austrian art critic's assessment of two Byzantine mosaicists, one an acknowledged master, the other a lesser-known young Venetian artist "only recently schooled in the technique of mosaics." To compare them might require language like "the pattern of the medium-brown hair is a little coarse," or "the shadows in the face are heavier." But was there an echo here, James asked, of the tired old assumption that good art is realistic art? In any case, she stressed, such judgments were apt to arise from looking at mosaics close-up. And that, she argued, wasn't the best way to weigh their merits: "We need to look at mosaics from where they are seen, rather than from where they were made."

Close-up, mosaics are never perfect; and some are way less perfect than others. To me, a mosaic reassuringly neat and even, all the grout lines equally fine, indistinguishable from a painting, would hardly be a mosaic at all, the impress of human hands too distant and indistinct.

As a mosaics maker I am never in such firm command of the craft that my final work matches my original idea. Mostly, I adapt my design as I go along, letting it slip into its evolved form. "When you make something, whatever the design or concept," James said in her Weitzmann talk, "the thing itself changes. That is the alchemy of making. You don't start with the finished idea in your mind: It is the thinking-about and working-through that brings the germ of an idea to a fruition that is often not where you started from." I was pleased to hear that; it accorded well with my limited experience as a mosaicist, and with my larger experience as a writer.

On the other hand, I am not so indulgent of my failures that I always just let them go. Even when I think I'm finished and the mosaic is all cemented, grouted, and done, some choice I've made—a run of blue tesserae reaching too aggressively into a yellow field, or tiles too crudely delineating a figure—bothers me. Bothers me enough to haul out hammer and chisel and whack away at the offending tiles, knocking out four or five of them, and redo the section, filling in with tiles that better belong. At that point, the new tesserae are part of the final work, while the original ones no one ever sees again—which is nice, like a writer's failed words mercifully expunged and replaced with something better.

—

Once cut to fit, edged into place, and set in mortar, it's hard not to be impressed by a tile's stony solidity. With painting or drawing you can imagine each stroke of brush or pencil point as tentative, ineffably shaded, artistry marking every speck of surface, the final work the result of a million small acts of addition, gradation, and erasure. But with mosaics, there's no edge to feather, no line to lighten, nothing to erase, blend, or paint over. Just one tile after another, laid down into its bed of receptive mortar or cement. Each fragment of stone or glass, cool to the touch yet somehow warming, becomes for the viewer, as it was for the artist, the product of a deliberate, individual act.

These days, a beginner's early purchase, soon after being won over to mosaics, is apt to be a "hammer-and-hardie," two tools used together, inseparable, like Tom and Jerry. The hammer's blade is a single, broadly arched swath of heavy steel, each end culminating in a solid cutting wedge. The hardie, a staple of blacksmith shops of yore, is another beefy chisel blade, traditionally set into a tree stump, stubby blade pointed straight up. Much of the fine trimming of tesserae can be done with any of several specialized hand tools. But the initial sizing is apt to be done with this one—stone or glass held in place between two fingers against the upthrust chisel blade, smartly smacked by the hammer. The stone cleanly severs when you do it right, or else, if you don't, splits uselessly. Contributing to the appeal of these tools is their irresistible echo of former times. A fourth-century CE stele uncovered from Ostia, the ancient port of Rome, shows men leaning into their work with hammers much like those used today, cutting tesserae, a pile of them meanwhile being hauled off to the worksite.

Today, you can go online to order manufactured ceramic or glass tesserae, all more or less regular, for your mosaic project; usually they're a centimeter or so square, sometimes labeled for American buyers as three-eighths of an inch, which is close enough. A species of especially prized rough-cut glass tiles from Italy or Mexico, known as smalti, usually comes in pieces a little larger, an irregular centimeter and a half or so on a side, but once cut for use they often wind up about the same centimeter square. When a trove of hand-cut tesserae was discovered in Ostia, the excavators found some variation in size among them, but not much. Among the thousands they measured, the most typical was about a centimeter square; this was two thousand years before the metric system established the centimeter and the meter as basic units of length.

One's fingernail measures roughly a centimeter across, too; whether a child's thumb or a grown man's pinkie, here is human scale at its most familiar and recognizable. No matter how large a mosaic, once you get down to tesserae, all the action is down at this fingertip scale, every detail rendered in tiles you can pick up with your fingers or gather together, a few at a time, in your palm, each tile bearing the ghostly presence of the hand that set it in place. Liz James, the University of Sussex archaeologist, tells of an expert mosaicist who told her "he didn't have to look at the tessera he picked up; he just knew from the feel what it was like and where it would fit."

There were times in the writing of this book when, slipping into creative doldrums, I walked over to the Baltimore Museum of Art to get back in touch with some of the Antioch mosaics. Like Europa and the Bull. Or the Dancing Maenad, her garments all awhirl, that once graced Atrium House. Or the peculiar Peddler of Erotes, which depicts a poor man who keeps nude Cupid-like beings in a wooden cage and sells them. I'd always come back from my visit to the museum refreshed, readier to write. And it was not the mosaic images alone that did it for me. It was the raw tesserae themselves.

Early on, I'd collected many books stuffed with color or black-and-white photos of the mosaics. Yet those pictures would dim in my recollection, while the actual mosaic tiles lingered with me—a mosaic's thousands of tesserae, side by side, sunk into their mortar bed, never so tidy and regular as they appeared from afar. Somehow, they seemed to *demand* that you draw up close; then step back to see what you'd just seen through new eyes. It was as if, however you looked at it, from farther away or closer up, you were missing something.

Sometimes I'd place myself unnaturally close, inches away, from those bits of stone and colored glass. It was an intimacy that seemed a little goofy, even to me, yet it left me feeling closer to the creators, the "anonymous hands" who selected those tesserae, cut them to size, and set them right *there* in the design, not somewhere else.

Mosaics are just another two-dimensional art? Not entirely; tesserae rarely form a perfectly flat, smooth, unvariegated surface. They poke up from their bedding. They gleam and sparkle spectacularly with even slight alterations in ambient light. Sometimes they seem almost sculptural, quasi-three-dimensional. In their stony hardness, they seem peculiarly permanent, even if, like all things of this world, they are not.

And in this, their physical truth, they challenge the tyranny of disembodied image, whether on paper or—ubiquitously, interminably, monotonously—on the computer screen. However excellent the means of reproduction, however fine the pixels that represent them on the screen, images today so often seem counterfeit. Living tesserae offer silent, transgressive testimony to their insufficiency.

CHAPTER EIGHTEEN

Antique Stones

The sounds of cranks and winches echo through the empty gallery. For years, a large mosaic has hung on this wall of the Wellesley College museum. Now it's to be moved, mechanical know-how and keen calibration mustered on its behalf.

The mosaic was given to Wellesley in 1936, a gift from the Committee to the Boston-area women's college, to honor one of its faculty, Sandy Campbell. It's a geometric mosaic, a handsome example of the genre, discovered in room 21 of the Yakto complex in Daphne. Eight squares, one edge of each forming a hexagon, the interiors of each adorned in different patterns, are set around a central medallion. The medallion consists of thirty-two radiating wedges of color, in shades of brick red, brown, and black. Four diamond-shaped "lozenges" penetrate the composition, one from each corner, each inserted into the otherwise open spaces left by a pair of squares.

After twenty-two years hanging on a wall in the museum, the mosaic is to be moved, though if you didn't know better, you'd say it couldn't be done: It's just too awkward, too big—almost perfectly square, thirteen feet on a side, and much too heavy to yield to brute human strength. But planning for the move, overseen by a team of structural engineers, has been underway for two years.

Now, flanked by two motorized scissor lifts, which raise and lower aerial work platforms, the mosaic is gripped at four points along its edges and wrangled down from the wall on the fifth floor, through a cutout, to the third. There, it's settled onto a wheeled carriage that takes it from one end of an otherwise vacant gallery to the other; pivoted into a right turn through a short corridor into another room; slipped into and through the next room, all the while perched at an unlikely angle atop its carriage. Finally, it's lowered gently onto a spot previously prepared for it on the second floor, its new home.

—

HARBORSIDE
Warehouse Company, Inc.
Exchange Place, Jersey City, N.J.
January 11, 1940

This receipt certified delivery, from the SS *Exeter* to the company warehouse, of a shipment bound for the "Dept. of Arts," Princeton University. It listed storage fees of four cents per hundred pounds per month, handling at six cents per hundredweight.

The shipment consisted of eighty-two cases of "Mosaic Art" and weighed 132,512 pounds.

—

When they aren't being shown off to admiring museum visitors, the Antioch mosaics can be a real bother. Mostly, they are big, formidably physical objects. That owes in part to the tens of thousands of tesserae that make them up. But also, to the bulky substructure, typically reinforced concrete, needed to support them on wall, floor, or in transit, and so sustain them as works of art and not heaps of loose, tinkling tiles. One hears of thieves stealing into museums, brazenly slicing priceless paintings from their frames and spiriting them away. Not so much with the great floor mosaics of Antioch. Even a relatively small one weighs a thousand pounds. And all through their lives, their sheer bulk figures in decisions bearing on them, sometimes almost laughably so; they can seem too big and clumsy for their own good, yet need to be lifted, cleaned, mended, packed, shipped, guarded, and otherwise fretted over like a baby.

In February 1949, Jean Labatut, a French-born architect on the Princeton University faculty, learned that neighborhood children had broken into his barn on Snowden Lane and upset crates of mosaics stored there for the past few years. The next morning the mother of one of the young hooligans came round to apologize, as did the boys themselves a few days later. They had gotten in by breaking a window and had knocked over the mosaic crates. "I hope," Labatut wrote Baldwin Smith, Art and Archaeology's postwar chairman, that

> the impact caused by the fall of the heavy boxes has not provoked the loosening of any of the elements [tesserae] in the mosaics. As you know, the boxes containing the mosaics are protected by tar paper nailed at the top of each box against the chance of water leaking through the roof of the barn. . . . It is advisable that they be put back into a vertical position.

Princeton buildings and grounds people were soon dispatched to set them aright.

A few months later, perhaps motivated by the Labatut barn incursion, Smith wrote the Louvre asking what he, and Princeton, were supposed to do with several mosaics assigned to the Louvre in the last division. These included two geometric panels and the head of a Medusa that, in the hurried eve-of-war departure from Antioch, had been shipped to Princeton. Part of that last batch, Smith explained, "is now stored in a barn," likely Labatut's, outside town. The department faced "a very serious problem of storage." They'd hoped to sell off some mosaics, but the market had turned flat. For now, it seems, they were stuck with them.

—

In their friendly letters back and forth, Princeton's Richard Stillwell was "Dick," and Eugenio Batista González de Mendoza was "Gene."

Batista was a Cuban architect who'd moved to New York in 1927, studied at Columbia and Princeton universities, and later became professor of architecture at Princeton. He returned to Cuba to form an architectural practice with his cousin and then, before the Castro revolution that deposed dictator Fulgencio Batista (no relation), became dean of the school of architecture at Havana's St. Thomas of Villanova Catholic University. Now, in 1955, Villanova was buying, for a pittance, a few of the Antioch mosaics.

One was a richly ornamented octagon linked to squares at each edge, each featuring its own intricate and distinctive pattern. "Dear Gene," wrote Stillwell, successor to Baldwin Smith, on August 8, "I am glad that you like the mosaic, and delighted that Fr. Spiralli [of Villanova] did, too. His check arrived safely." The sale was routinely settled.

But getting the mosaic to Havana was another story. Stillwell wondered if Batista had "any suggestions as to the best way of sending the pieces. You understand, of course, that the packing and freight will not be inexpensive." One option was to haul them down by truck to Key West, Florida, then load them onto a ferry to Havana. Maybe less chance of breakage that way. In the end, the North Atlantic and Gulf Steamship Company got the job, though its officials didn't quite know what they were shipping. Their paperwork described the mosaics as "antique stones, probably engraved or otherwise" or "plaques."

The Quaker Export Packaging Company of Philadelphia was engaged "to pick up these slabs at Princeton," move them to their own shops, box them for shipment, and deliver them to the pier. At $4 per hundred pounds, the 6,500 pounds of mosaics would cost $260 to ship. Of course, there was also a wharfage fee of so much per hundred pounds. All told, North Atlantic's district traffic manager figured the bill, less insurance, at $535. This, he allowed, was "purely a guess"—and already five times the amount of Father Spiralli's check.

"As you rightly suspected, the estimate for transport has alarmed the whole angelical field," Gene wrote Dick the following month. "Please hold the mosaic for us a little longer and await further instructions."

Two weeks later, he wrote Stillwell again, assuring him that the Cuban university had signed on, that the way was clear, that Princeton could ship. By December 1, the mosaics were on board the SS *Hadrian*, bound for Havana.

Twelve days later, Gene wrote Dick: "The mosaic is finally here, and we are running around in circles, looking for a bank easy to rob, in order to pay the shipping company. They want almost twice as much as their estimate."

—

In any mosaic's journey from where it was first laid down, across the seas, across the centuries, and ultimately to a museum wall, floor, or storage room, every sort of abuse could be visited upon it. A mosaic was not unduly delicate, but it was not unbreakable, either.

Even before disappearing underground, it could be warped or broken by earthquakes, destroyed by rampaging armies. While still in the ground, it could be sorely bruised by subsequent construction, by walls and structures of crushing weight built atop it or toppling down onto it. Drowned by floods, it could be buried under tons of sediment. And sometimes, whatever it suffered in fifteen or twenty centuries underground was less than what it endured later, at the hands of desperate looters. Or, while being lifted from the ground by earnest archaeologists and the workmen in their service. In his 1938 book, Morey would recount the methods used to pull mosaics from the ground and embed them on new, reinforced concrete bases. "The result is an indestructible monolith." This was an optimistic appraisal at best.

The Committee's March 13, 1940, minutes told of several mosaic panels cracked, pieces broken off, all suffered during excavation, the result of "haste because of delay [of the] division and declaration of war." In one case, the cement backing had not had time to dry. There'd been too few big trucks to get them out of Antioch, the military having confiscated many of them; the small ones left were overloaded, causing serious damage to three mosaics.

In 2003, California's J. Paul Getty Museum, a leader in conservation studies, issued a telling taxonomy of mosaic injury. Its "deteriorated tesserae" category, for example, included tiles disaggregated, eroded, exfoliated,

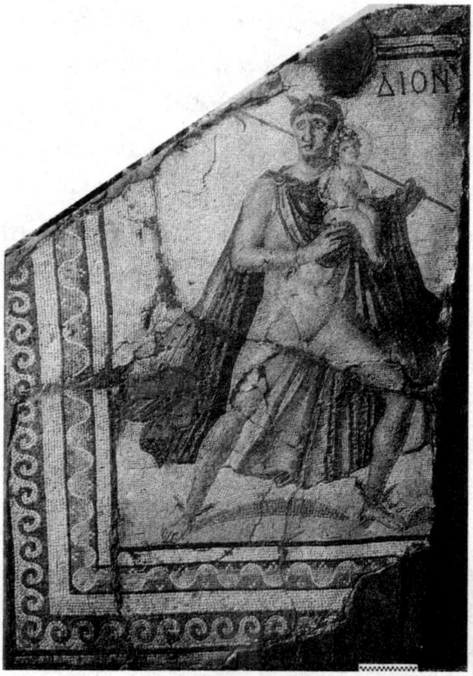

Hermes, with winged hat and herald's staff, carries baby Dionysus. This late fourth-century mosaic, which today adorns the Worcester Art Museum's Renaissance Court, shows the infant god surrounded by the sort of nimbus or halo that would often embellish the infant Jesus and other holy figures in Byzantine art. Shown here are both the mosaic soon after its excavation in 1933 from Bath D in Antioch, and as conserved and on display today.

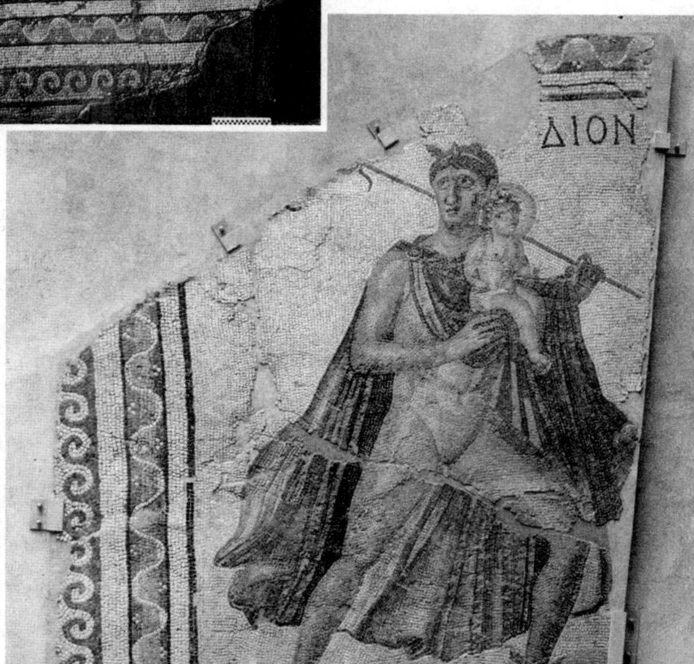

fractured, and pitted. But often, the tiles themselves were not broken, chipped, or discolored; they were simply gone, the bedding layer that once held them in place cracked and crumbled, intact tiles shed, the design itself rendered unrecognizable. An otherwise intact tableau corrupted by swaths of featureless void.

Even once they'd reached their destinations, mosaics were subject to varied regimes of care, display, and use. One, the Worcester museum's great hunting mosaic, was for a time covered over and used as a dance floor. A late fourth-century mosaic, of male and female heads set within a meander pattern, became in 1949 the threshold of a campus building. People trudged across it every day, as they might have two millennia before. But its new home was northern New Jersey, which meant extremes of icy cold all but unknown in Antioch. It suffered severe damage before being removed to the Brooklyn studio of Leslie Gat. "We got it out just in time," she told a *Princeton Alumni Weekly* writer in 2012. It was "about to break into nine pieces," tracing the rusting rebar underneath used to reinforce it in the 1930s.

Leslie Gat was a conservator. Today, painting conservators preserve Picassos and Rembrandts. Paper conservators stabilize and repair ancient manuscripts, old books, and drawings. Those, like Gat, who care for mosaics, along with jewelry, sculpture, and the like, are known as objects conservators.

In a letter to Rufus Morey on May 23, 1932, George Elderkin wrote from Antioch of the imminent "raising" of an Atrium House mosaic panel. "It will be set in cement, panel by panel, except the damaged parts which will be set on a layer of plaster of Paris with a supporting base of cement." This, he added, "will permit of 'ironing out' the very uneven surface by some specialist later on."

Seven decades later, near the end of the century, mosaic panels from Atrium House did indeed get close attention from "some specialist." Her name was Paula Artal-Isbrand, and she was working on a large, ambitious exhibition, featuring the Antioch mosaics, set to open at the Worcester Art Museum. The panels from Atrium House, which had been split up and dispersed to no fewer than six different museums, were now to be reunited, and Artal-Isbrand was to ready them for installation and viewing.

Over the years, areas of loss had been treated differently by the recipient museums. Some, Artal-Isbrand would recount, "had left them untreated, others had painted them over, replicating the missing designs, and still others had removed some of the concrete and filled the losses with neutral colored mortar." Concrete backings from their original treatment in Antioch had sometimes cracked. "Dirt and grime covered all surfaces to some degree." For the big show, she needed permission from each museum, each with its own conditions. One asked that its mosaic simply be cleaned, no more. Another wanted its painted "fills" to remain just as they were.

Artal-Isbrand, her colleagues, and her interns faced every sort of problem. Sometimes cracks appeared in the tesserae themselves, not just between them. Some panels had been coated with varnishes that had noticeably yellowed. Two panels even had vestiges of small roots, from their long lives underground, still attached to the surface. In some instances, tesserae had been covered or obscured by the concrete overspill from adjacent fills.

> Areas of poorly adhered tesserae were reattached or consolidated as necessary. Lost mortar around detached tesserae was replaced with bulked adhesive colored to resemble the bedding mortar. Cracks on the front were strengthened with consolidant, and a newer, very dilute acrylic coating was applied.

So recounted Artal-Isbrand. As in a hospital physician's hectic day on the wards, each ailment, aesthetic or structural, slight or deeply troubling, demanded diagnosis and treatment. All in a day's work, yes, but conservation of Worcester's mosaics, from both long before and long after the exhibition, ranged over nine years.

As we've seen, sometimes it wasn't just that some tiles had flaked, discolored, or faded; rather, they were simply gone, leaving blank, unsightly swaths of missing design. How best treat such ragged empty regions? Fill them in to the best of your ability, maybe fudging it with tesserae freshly cut or perhaps collected elsewhere on the site? Or paint them in to resemble tesserae? Or leave the great emptiness smoothed over in a formless gray wash?

One solution, especially with geometric panels, was to paint in the voids to mimic intact neighboring sections. Figurative panels posed more of a problem; there was nothing to mimic. Was the conservator's fidelity to the original, leaving her reluctant to alter, sully, or usurp it in any way? Or to the museumgoer confronted with ugly gaps that degraded the viewing experience? Or to some minutely calibrated balance between the two?

At a 1999 lecture bearing on conservation issues, Polish archaeologist Wiktor Daszewski broke in to remind his colleagues that redoing mosaics was nothing new, that ruptures and breaks had been tackled down through the ages. Sometimes "with utmost care," but in some instances, too, going so far as to add "new motifs . . . introduced regardless of the original composition." Then, as now, even the "right" answer was sometimes unsatisfying.

An earlier chapter told of a Baltimore conservator filling large gaps in a mosaic by painting in tesserae look-alikes, different enough from surviving tiles not to be confused with them, but close enough to preserve the viewer's overall response to the mosaic. "Opinions may differ regarding methods of restoring these ancient mosaics," wrote Baltimore Museum of Art director McKinney at the time, "but it is our opinion that we have followed the safest course until greater knowledge of the subject is available."

Among conservators, opinions *do* differ. Sometimes the approach taken nods more to art, sometimes to science. Knowledge grows and with it new technologies, new materials. Fashions change, reflecting the assumptions and expectations of the age. These days, whatever the conservator does is supposed to be tentative and reversible.

And doing nothing is always an option. A second-century mosaic from the House of the Calendar, a bathhouse part of a mountainside villa outside Antioch, today hangs on a wall of the Hatay Archaeology Museum, depicting Oceanus and Thetis, two Titans from Hesiod's *Theogony*. Ruddy-faced Oceanus appears in all his considerable male glory, barechested, with wild sprigs of hair and beard, vast eyes. Of his sister and wife, Thetis, enough was left for Doro Levi to write of her, "Her face is oval in shape, the lips full and slightly compressed, the eyes large and staring; and her hair clings to her cheeks as if wet. The long tresses fall to her shoulders in thick curls." In fact, across the large, ruined void from Oceanus, Thetis is not all there. Her face and nude body are both half-missing.

And yet, one can view a devastated image like this and appreciate it. Major portions of its geometric border, in appealing array and comforting in their familiarity, are well-preserved. That helps. So does the panel's intact fields of teeming sea life. So does the provocative gap between the anonymous artist's surviving virtuosic work and the gray disrupted void beside it; the tension is tantalizing.

In the years since this mosaic was lifted from the ground, conservators might well have treated it otherwise, perhaps filling in its empty regions with color and design. They did not do so. To leave this damaged mosaic largely as it was represented a choice, and not an unworthy one.

CHAPTER NINETEEN

For Sale or Trade

It was 1949, the war was over, and Henry S. Robinson was trying to establish a museum in almost the dead center of a rural, mostly empty American state. He and his wife, Rebecca, a Bryn Mawr graduate in archaeology, found themselves in Norman, Oklahoma, a town settled in the great Land Rush of 1889; there the state university was founded two years later. In the 1930s the university decided it needed a teaching collection of classical antiquities to enrich the minds of its students. Harvard's Fogg Museum as well as the Museum of Fine Arts in Boston were persuaded to loan or donate some artifacts.

But now, Robinson, a Princeton man, was going one step further. After a visit to Princeton in October 1949, he wrote Richard Stillwell, the new head of Art and Archaeology, about a mosaic he coveted for Oklahoma that he suspected was bound for the Louvre, along with certain other mosaics, which he listed by number. "We shall be much obliged if you can give us the prices on the above five items." They could hardly afford all five, but maybe two? If, that is, the prices could come down. "The Classical Division of the Museum has rather limited funds."

Sure enough, the Louvre did want that first mosaic, allocated to it in the most recent division and thought bound for a choice spot at the French embassy in Washington. In a letter to Robinson a week later Stillwell quoted the prices of the other five: Among them were two small geometric panels, at $75 each (perhaps $1,000 today); a big mosaic of Thetis at $250; and another big one, of Cilicia, thought to be a female personification of the Roman province of that name, dating to the second century, at $700. The Royal Ontario Museum, Stillwell put in, seemed interested in that one.

Well, he'd have to think about it, Robinson wrote back. In the meantime, he wished to raise a point, "though I am not certain about the propriety of my mentioning it." While earlier reviewing a list of Princeton's mosaic offerings, he'd noted prices penciled in beside them. For example, the geometric panel

> M 194 j (from House of the Evil Eye) was marked $40.00; but I note that you have [now] priced it and the accompanying panel M 194 k at $75.00 each. Is there any possibility that these panels could be sold at the lower price or that the prices of any of the other pieces we listed could be brought any lower? I am afraid that I have not lived long enough in the Near East to have become sufficiently brazen as a bargainer and to be able to ask this question without some qualms.

But ask it he did.

No, Stillwell replied, those notations were early provisional figures; the prices quoted now were correct, the current price. "At that, it is practically giving them away when you consider prices which have been paid for other mosaics." But now Stillwell backed off, keeping the deal in play: "I am sure that we would be glad to consider meeting you part way, and if you wish to suggest what you could hold as a fair price, we would be glad to give it due consideration."

Maybe Robinson and Stillwell weren't brazen old Near East hands, but bargainers they were. Robinson offered $650 for Cilicia and a small geometric, provided Oklahoma could pay in installments, across three years.

Princeton agreed.

The deal went through, and soon the mosaics arrived in what passed for the Oklahoma museum, the university's old ROTC building with its adjacent stable.

—

Early in the Depression, as he struggled to line up financial pledges for Antioch, Mr. Morey found wealthy patrons and institutions loath to contribute. Yet in the end, the Depression made the Antioch venture possible, thanks to the worldwide drop in workmen's day wages, typically a dig's largest expense. Later, as the excavations ground on, periodic divisions-of-finds among the Americans, French, and Syrians left mosaics haggled over and traded like Pokémon cards among teens. Objets d'art they were, our mosaics. But they were always economic objects, too—valued, bought, sold, traded. Invariably, they bore a price tag. From the time they were first conceived or commissioned to when they wound up on the floor or wall of a twenty-first-century museum, the Antioch mosaics were never long detached from the acquisitive impulses of our species but, indeed, often aroused them.

All through late antiquity, they were coveted luxury objects—a public luxury bestowed by an emperor or provincial administrator, or a personal luxury enjoyed by denizens of elite enclaves like Daphne, but a luxury in any case. Not just in Antioch and Daphne but all across the Empire, in Gaul, in Britain, in northern Africa, if you were someone of means and consequence, you likely had a handsome villa, with commanding sight lines from one room to another, bubbling fountains, views of the surrounding landscape receding into the distance. And often a fine mosaic—or two, or three—to beautify it. Your visitors were apt to be left in wonder, you yourself left feeling pretty good about your wealth, taste, and position.

Though materially just stone and glass, mosaics asserted wealth. Around the year 391, in a synagogue in Apamea, a hundred miles south of Antioch, an inscription on a surviving floor mosaic honored the wealthy women who made it possible. One of them, named Ambrosia, "gave 50 feet of floor." We don't know how much surface area that represented. We do know the mosaic was costly enough that signing on for even a piece of it got your name recorded for posterity.

French art historian Jean-Pierre Caillet has tried to reckon the cost of fourth- to sixth-century Italian mosaics as so many gold solidi for so many square meters of mosaic. But his more telling conclusion was that a mosaic representing a human face, ornate drapery, or other technically challenging subject might cost twice one that was all squares and octagons. Much, or most, of a mosaic's worth, then, lay in the skill and artistry its design and execution required.

A mosaic was difficult to do well, took substantial time and trouble to do at all. As a sometime mosaicist I've made two dozen or so small works, the largest being about nineteen inches on a side. It took me months to stumble my way through it. True, I was in no great rush. And my modest skills limited not only the worth of what I did but the ease and quickness with which I did it. Even so, just nineteen inches square, and the work of months! Some mosaic pavements dug up from Antioch were a hundred times bigger, the work of whole teams of artisans, and, of course, incomparably better.

Could such magnificent creations as emerged from Antioch ever be anything but costly and rare?

Doro Levi seemed to think so. In *Antioch Mosaic Pavements* he asserts that among the towns and cities of the Roman Empire "there was practically no house, with even a minimum pretense to comfort, that entirely lacked mosaics." In his later *A History of Antioch in Syria*, Glanville Downey didn't challenge Levi's claim. Conservator Lawrence Becker, who has worked closely with many of the Antioch mosaics, likewise expresses sympathy for the idea; mosaics, he says, "were not that uncommon."

Were mosaics, then, really so widespread in the homes of the Empire's broad, comfort-seeking classes? Could there be such a thing as "middle class" mosaics? Michael Padgett, former curator of ancient art at Princeton, thinks not: A mosaic in your house *meant* you weren't middle class. You might reckon mosaics as commonplace, but only in the sense that a Mercedes-Benz or Maserati is commonplace among the well-off today. Either way, Levi's broad reading of the sway and prevalence of mosaics in Antioch may be misleading.

So, even, may be our supposition that the mosaics shed fresh light on the world out of which they come. They do, of course, but like so much art from their time and ours, most of that light falls on the favored few. John Chrysostom, the fourth-century Christian polemicist, bishop of Antioch between 386 and 397 CE, and author of Bible-thumping homilies and sermons, portrayed Antioch as one-tenth rich, one-tenth poor, the rest in between. For the Antioch of infamous excess and opulence he had only contempt. In this he was unlike his contemporary and teacher, Libanius, who was more complacent, apt to view Antioch from a comfortable perch on high. Chrysostom directed his gaze to the city's less lucky precincts. He saw not the great porticoes of the city's bustling main street that intrigued Jean Lassus, but down into the narrow alleys abutting it. There, as University of Notre Dame theologian Blake Leyerle has drawn the scene, one could hear the wife berating her slave, the chattering teeth of the street beggar. "Chrysostom," she wrote, had "spot-lit the normally darkened spaces of the city"—that Doro Levi had overlooked as well.

Archaeology is often unkind to, or unappreciative of, ordinary men and women—if for no other reason than that they leave less for archaeologists to find. In this, the Princeton expedition of the 1930s was no exception. In a 2000 essay devoted to the houses of Antioch, John J. Dobbins noted that "not one single whole block of houses has been uncovered" there; no ordinary housing, it seems, nothing like apartment houses, or modest row houses, or little cottages. "This means that we cannot address such questions as: Where did the poor live? Were elite houses located in mixed-use neighborhoods as they were at Pompeii?"

J. R. Perkins, author of *Antioch Actress*, imagined just such an unremarkable Antioch house, the one where Cynthia, his novel's protagonist, was born. It was

> an uneven walled structure of stone with an oriel window projecting over the street. Below the window was a heavy door, massive and scarred as if heavy blows once rained upon it. The sill was worn; the lintel sagged slightly. The upper story of the house had two small windows; the roof held a penthouse, reached, as Cynthia explained, by an inner stairway. . . . "I slept up there when it was hot."

Perkins's novel may not adhere to every standard of historical accuracy, but the very fact of his attention reminds us of ordinary lives little represented by the mosaics dug up in the 1930s, and of the skewed impressions of daily life thus left behind.

We can't know whether ordinary householders had tidy little mosaics in their homes the way almost anyone today might have a pretty rug. It is charming to think they did, but evidence of it from the 1930s or since is scant. The mosaics from Antioch's great villas and public spaces give a satisfying glimpse of the ancient city, but one inevitably distorted by wealth and privilege.

—

In the early 1970s, finding itself overstocked with mosaics, the Worcester Art Museum resolved to sell off some of them, and did. Buyers included three colleges—Amherst, Oberlin, and the Rhode Island School of Design. It decided also to sell another, more ambitious specimen—a fourth-century mosaic standing almost six feet high and fourteen feet across, recovered from a bath at the foot of Mt. Silpius in 1938, one we encountered in an earlier chapter: The diminutive woodcock, rabbit, and partridge it depicted could seem the least of its appeal; its wonderful geometric ornamentation much more of it. Worcester turned to a New York dealer, who found a buyer for it at the J. Paul Getty Museum in California, for $40,000. "When removed from dead storage," wrote Louisa Dresser, the curator who'd visited the dig for the Worcester museum in the 1930s, the mosaic "proved to be in a fine state and more handsome and impressive than the photographs" promised. As Worcester needed no more mosaics, she judged the sale prudent. With the proceeds, they'd be able to buy a sculpture for their Education Wing.

When excavators first descended on Antioch in 1932, only five institutions could look ahead to a share of the riches expected from the dig—Princeton, the Baltimore and Worcester museums, the Louvre, and a planned Antioch museum. Today, the mosaics are spread among more than two dozen institutions. This broad dispersal became its own story, almost the first thing you'd find to say about the Antioch mosaics. As early as 1940 and the Committee's publication of its third volume, its editors already felt the need to set down in one place where they all were. A few years later, in 1947, Doro Levi's book updated their whereabouts. And when, in 1996, Princeton curator Michael Padgett reviewed the place of ancient art at Princeton, he observed that the university's Antioch holdings had "proved curiously peripatetic, having been repeatedly moved, exhibited, lent out, relegated to storage, and sold to other institutions."

—

It was 1965, Michigan State University had an art gallery, and its new director, Paul Love, had been asked to upgrade it. The university's art department had begun placing art on view in 1930. But "not having a permanent home," as a capsule history of the museum tells us, its collection "bounced around the campus," at one point split among several temporary Quonset huts. In 1959, the Kresge Foundation gave it money for a new art center and gallery, which soon had a new full-time director. Love brought a relish to his job. When, on March 18, he wrote Dick Stillwell, still head of Art and Archaeology at Princeton, he reported that he was "busy building a collection out of scraps." To serve humanities and art history courses, he'd forever been forced to borrow from the Detroit Institute of Arts. But now, "on an uncertain budget, I am proposing to remedy such matters." Remedying it, that is, by buying art. And he had his eye on the Antioch mosaics, for which he asked to be kept in mind.

> I must also ask a question. I mentioned the uncertain budget. In view of the latter, could you give me even a glimmer of a glimmer as to what the asking price for such fragments of mosaic might be?

And so they were off, Dick Stillwell once again absorbed in a deal. The range was considerable, he replied to Love, but $200 to $500 was typical, transport and packing extra, borne by the purchaser.

That, Love wrote back, was "within the range of possibility."

Two months later, he advised Stillwell that he hoped to visit Princeton in June. "If, by any chance, the material is to be offered to other institutions, I should like to have the opportunity of seeing it early."

Love visited Princeton on June 16 and three days later wrote Stillwell, rather grandly: "You may inscribe the name of M.S.U. on the Thetis mosaic," recovered from the Portico of Achilles in Seleucia during the expedition's 1939 season. It wasn't a primo example, at least a third of the image having failed to survive the centuries. But the face of the water goddess, Thetis, was unmarred, her name inscribed in tesserae. The price was $750, ten or fifteen thousand today. Love thanked Stillwell for doing such a good deed "for a collector who is trying, almost overnight, to build a collection of some stature."

—

The good news—and to Michael Padgett, among others, it was very good indeed—was this: The mosaics, an "unexpected bonanza" of the expedition, had for centuries lain underground, where no one saw them. Now they hung on walls or were bedded down on floors, preserved and protected, where tens of thousands of people from every walk of life could, and did, see them. As University of Texas art historian John R. Clarke similarly makes the case, "that they ended up in museums worldwide added greatly to public awareness of the amazing accomplishments" of the artists and their patrons. That we can today see so many of them in the halls of the Hatay Archaeology Museum covering every spare wall and floor, or at the Louvre, or in American museums from New York City to Honolulu, each the happy beneficiary of this mosaic diaspora, counts as a great social gain. Yes, the mosaics were luxury objects, but now they could be seen and appreciated by all, even in Lansing, Michigan, or Norman, Oklahoma. In short, all the buying, selling, and trading had done little harm and much good.

But all along, an opposing voice could be heard, one that framed the flow of treasure from East to West as yet another painful legacy of colonialism. Back in the late 1930s, we learned earlier, Mr. Morey heard from Turkey how the locals had come to question the good intentions of the West, their priceless relics lost to the wiles of "subtle foreigners." Through this reground lens, archaeology could be read as the riches of ancient cultures—Egypt, Italy, Greece, the Holy Land—ceded to Paris and New York. And the mosaic diaspora from Antioch? More of the same old story.

Writing of the Antioch mosaics, historian Peter Brown lamented how they'd been "hauled out of the earth with little attention to the walls and doorways that had framed them," the sites that birthed them likely obliterated. The whole business, archaeology, could seem downright brutish and coarse. Grabbing artifacts and spiriting them away, writes Oklahoma State University historian Sarah Griswold in a review of archaeological practice during the Mandate period, "had been the core objective and raison d'être of archaeology, at least as Europeans had practiced it, for most of the nineteenth century." But during the interwar years, some began to wonder "if the foreign removal of artifacts, even if they made it *legal*, was best": The surviving mosaic now sat pristinely on a museum wall, while its original site beside the sea or on a hillside plateau was left desolate—a sad twist on that horrific vision from America's Vietnam War, of the village destroyed in order to save it.

In 2012, more than six decades after publication of Doro Levi's monumental treatise, another Italian art scholar, Claudia Barsanti of the University of Rome, recounted the familiar facts of the mosaic diaspora from Antioch, but seethed with vitriol in the telling. Barsanti, who died in 2017, told of archaeological "loot" divided among the Committee sponsors. She lamented the "cavalier" breakup of Atrium House. She stood aghast at how the Worcester museum sold off some of its mosaic panels to other museums and "without . . . apparent reason dismembered the panels from the Corridor of the Aion House," found in the final year of the dig; told how similarly "hard-boiled" policies marked the actions of the Baltimore museum and of Princeton University; observed how not even a choice mosaic once gracing a courtyard in the Constantinian Villa with allegories of the four seasons "managed to escape this archaeological treasure-hunt." Against the seemingly neutral backdrop of where this or that mosaic had wound up, or how the many mosaics of a particular villa had been divided, Barsanti sounded a sharp note of protest, using a vocabulary of butchery and carnage. As Barsanti herself wrote, her article made for a "review of atrocities." She seemed less troubled by legalities than with archaeological judgment, fairness, good sense, and good taste: In the removal and dispersal of the Antioch mosaics, she was saying, too much had been lost, too much harm done.

Oh, all that was just "a lot of moral posturing," another art historian, Christine Kondoleon, said when asked to comment on Barsanti's jeremiad. The Princeton excavators had done as well as they could, dealt honestly. The divisions-of-finds reflected the existing partage system. Everyone played by the rules, nothing untoward about it. *Come on*, she continued, referring to England's, and Lord Elgin's, notorious plunder of precious fifth-century BCE marble sculptures once adorning the Parthenon, "this was *not* the Elgin Marbles."

Yet Kondoleon, as we'll see in the next chapter, was sympathetic to some of the same currents of complaint that marked Barsanti's sweeping denunciation.

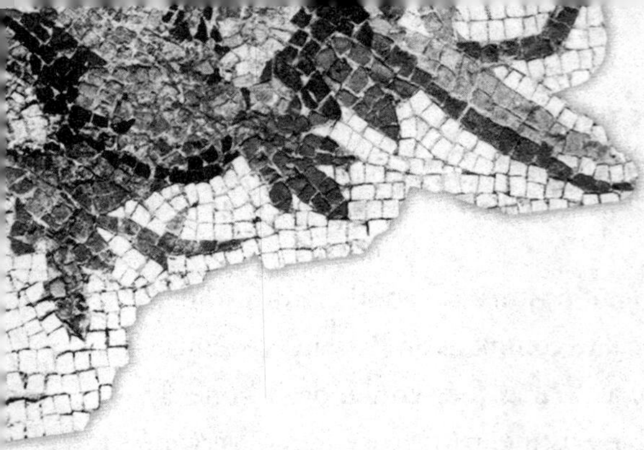

CHAPTER TWENTY

Off the Wall

In the year 2000, mosaics recovered in the 1930s but later widely dispersed were reunited in a major exhibition determined to deliver Antioch from the shadows of the centuries. *Antioch: The Lost Ancient City* was largely the creation of Christine Kondoleon. She herself would allow that it "made my name," leading her to a position overseeing the Greco-Roman galleries at the Museum of Fine Arts in Boston. Scores of men and women from museums, foundations, and private studios around the world had a hand in the exhibition. But the force and imagination behind it owed most to Kondoleon.

She was not a retiring figure. She had large enthusiasms, threw out ideas to everyone. She could be prickly and dismissive. But many who worked within her orbit saw in her a gift for reaching people with her intellectual passions. "She had an incredible ability to get people to express themselves creatively," recalls graphic designer and painter Victoria I, among those who worked with her on *Lost Antioch* (as we'll refer to the exhibition here).

Her chief collaborator on the show was Lawrence Becker, an objects conservator. He had started out as a paintings conservator but, after his first year in graduate school at NYU, had gone on an excavation in Egypt, coming home hooked on the mysteries of ancient materials, things he could actually get his hands on. "It was one of the few fields that left room for both mind and hand." In 1992, when he met Kondoleon, he was senior conservator at the Virginia Museum of Fine Arts.

Then in her thirties and in her first museum job following a stint as chair of the art department at Williams College, Kondoleon was down in Virginia with a colleague to study a third-century Antioch mosaic—a group of four six-foot-high panels representing the four seasons. Working closely with her, Becker was "immediately struck by the real dialogue" Kondoleon sparked. So often, it seemed to him, it wasn't like that; curators could be petty dictators. Inevitably, the two connected.

By 1995, Kondoleon had finished the four seasons project and, in part to be closer to her ill brother, had taken a position closer to Boston, as curator of ancient art at the Worcester Art Museum. Not long after, Brooklyn-born Becker, who'd by now had his fill of the South, joined her. There they formed a working troika with James Welu, who had come to the museum twenty years earlier as a specialist in Dutch and Flemish painting and in 1986 became its director.

Worcester had slipped a peg from its nineteenth-century heights as a humming, prosperous city. And despite two new wings, built in 1970 and 1983, so had its historic museum, though it was still New England's second largest. With its hundredth anniversary approaching in 1998, Welu resolved to leave his mark. He planned to reinstall the galleries devoted to ancient art, the better to show off the museum's substantial stock of Egyptian, Greek, and Roman art. But needed, too, he and his two new colleagues resolved, was some big, new, eye-catching show. Its subject, it seemed self-evident—the Worcester Hunt mosaic was all but underfoot every day as they passed through the museum's Renaissance Court—ought to be Antioch.

Of course, that could mean anything, and to settle on Antioch as the subject didn't guarantee something fresh and memorable. But to Kondoleon, as she'd write later, the sheer "quality of the holdings at Worcester encouraged me to suggest an ambitious show." Not, though, one limited to the museum's own holdings. On the contrary, they would gather up pieces of Antioch, mosaic and otherwise, from museums scattered near and far, bringing together in one place some of what for six decades had lain in pieces and apart.

In our day we've become accustomed to experiencing art and culture in disconnected snippets. A few bars from a popular song. A book excerpt. A trailer from an upcoming film. These can afford interest or stir resonant memories, but may leave us feeling only thinly connected, disconcertingly so, to the original art. Kondoleon and her colleagues resolved to portray Antioch "thickly," restoring something of its living context.

Lost Antioch was shaped in the service of this one broad, noble idea.

—

As it evolved, the exhibition ranged over Antioch's religious diversity, architecture, homes, baths, domestic life, and entertainment, much of it revealed through objects. There was a bronze and gold Antioch "psyche," or amulet of good fortune, from the second century; a larger-than-life (if headless) second-century marble statue of Hygeia, daughter of Asklepios, god of medicine, found in another of the Island's baths; a hammered silver plate and a shallow concave bowl from the House of Menander in Daphne. There were pitchers and jars, gold amulets, enamel buckles, coins bearing the likenesses of emperors and Alexander the Great, board games, candlesticks, mosaics.

Most every Antioch mosaic installed in a museum had a name, a serial number, and a page number in Doro Levi's book. So it was natural to see each as a work of art like any other, like a painting on its stretched canvas, worthy of close study of subject, colors, composition, with links to other art of the same or other eras. Art history at its most traditional.

But the mosaics were both more and less than art. They had never hung on ancient walls. Each had once served something larger than itself—a bath, public building, or private villa. They would never be so whole and connected, rooted in place and time, *attached*, as they had been 1,500 years before. In writing of his "pavements," Levi typically broke them down by the houses in which they had been found and to which he gave names—House of the Buffet Supper, House of the Ram's Head, and the like. In their first lives, the mosaics had lent them identity. They had contributed to a coherent aesthetic or architectural experience. But then later, exhumed, cut up into pieces and panels, lifted and removed, dispersed to museum galleries and storage rooms, they'd been left sundered from their birthplaces. Children all gone from home.

Claudia Barsanti was not the first to lament the "dismemberment" of the Antioch mosaics and the obliteration of their original context. Jean Lassus, for example, had been troubled, too. Returning to print almost fifty years later to express his lingering reservations, he wondered whether it was right to carve up a mosaic pavement made of seemingly independent panels. The question, he nimbly noted, had been posed the moment William Gad's team of specialists took over the lifting of each pavement. For just then it became "necessary to define the number of pieces to separate one from the others." The art itself would never be the same thereafter.

More than in Lassus's day, museum practice and art history had begun to lament such losses of context. So now, in the late 1990s, as Kondoleon and her colleagues thought through their exhibition, context became central. In dealing with the mosaics, she told me, "I refused to treat them as works of art," as they'd always been seen in the 1930s. Art history was still art history and Doro Levi was still, as she says of him, "a genius. . . . I had to memorize that book to do my [doctoral] thesis." But now, for *Lost Antioch*, she makes it sound, she was beyond them. Even by 1994, with the publication of her earlier book, *Domestic and Divine: Roman Mosaics in the House of Dionysos*, based on excavations in Paphos in southwestern Cyprus, Kondoleon had plainly taken up the new, broader thinking, which she called "contextual interpretation." "Within today's world of scholarship," one critic observed of her book, "the laurels generally go to works emphasizing obtuse critical theory and readings of the object removed from the limitations of its original context. . . . In contrast, *Domestic and Divine* is a breath of fresh air." It drew from traditional art history, but also "from more recently developed interdisciplinary explorations of experience, viewership, and kinaesthetics firmly grounded in the time of creation."

Now, five years later, Kondoleon and her colleagues brought a similar sensibility to their Antioch story: The mosaics weren't only works of art. They were works of Antioch life. You couldn't just line them up along the walls of the museum, say a few more or less interesting words about each; or simply compare them, however fruitfully, to similar works from different epochs or cultures. For these mosaics had helped form the settings and backdrops of everyday life, if for a narrowly wealthy stratum of it. Remove them from their context, show them alone and apart, and they were just pretty pictures. And that's just what Kondoleon didn't want to do. Better to situate each artifact in a version of its original setting so that a museum visitor might imagine herself a guest at one of the great houses of Antioch, perhaps taking in the mosaic from a particular vantage point, looking over and beyond it, across the room, to a distant vista.

—

The show opened at Worcester in October 2000, moved to Cleveland for three months in March 2001, then Baltimore that September. Altogether, it drew two hundred thousand visitors, and found further expression in two big, beautiful books. In Worcester the exhibition was heralded as "the most ambitious and significant undertaking in the . . . Museum's 102-year history." In the months leading up to it, visitors had been able to watch conservators, in public view, work on some of the mosaics, in some cases redoing repairs or treatments done in the thirties. The Baltimore edition opened a few days after the World Trade Center attack of September 11. A symposium, "Antioch at 70: An Excavation and Its Impact," brought speakers together to discuss specific mosaics, tell of the Butler and Morey tradition at Princeton, and offer a verbal portrait of favorite son Robert Garrett.

To bring it all off took five years.

As director of the Worcester museum, Jim Welu had to remind Kondoleon that they didn't have money in hand to fuel her every ambition; she'd have to go out and raise a lot of it herself. Says Kondoleon: "He just let me loose." Over the next three years, they were awarded grants from the Kress Foundation, the Rockefeller, and the National Endowments, both for the humanities and the arts. They got a million dollars from the Mellon. As for all the support they garnered, recalls Paula Artal-Isbrand, the conservator who worked most closely with Becker and Kondoleon and has maintained links with the museum since, "Jim couldn't believe it." They pushed, they didn't stop. They visited the Princeton archives, Paris, Antakya. Kondoleon recalls no special difficulty, as a woman, navigating the world of museums and foundations. "Welu had faith in me," she says. "He was no problem." Then, too, at many of the foundations, women by now often held key positions. "Christine was ambitious," recalls Artal-Isbrand. "She wanted to show what she could do. She wanted to do something stunning."

Early on, much of their new funding went toward a new conservation department for the museum. Many of the mosaics and other pieces bound for the show had lain untouched since their recovery; they were hardly ready to go on view as is. For Artal-Isbrand, *Lost Antioch* was the first project in which she had played so central a role. Just getting her hands on the mosaics was a high. So was watching Kondoleon work her magic.

For the exhibition to fulfill her vision, Kondoleon needed the Judgment of Paris, one of the crown jewels of the dig's first year. Since the 1930s it had hung on a wall at the Louvre, where curator Catherine Metzger presided over it. At least at first, Metzger was unreceptive to loaning it out. "We're never taking it off the wall," Kondoleon remembers her saying.

Museums, of course, frequently loan their treasures to other museums for special exhibitions. When the time comes, a "courier" from the lending museum descends on the recipient museum to oversee the artwork's unloading, installation, and care by "riggers," who do the actual moving; a mosaic panel might weigh a thousand pounds or more. The lending museum doesn't exact rent, but other expenses mount—crating, transport, courier, insurance. The treasures gathered for *Lost Antioch* came from some two dozen institutions, including Dumbarton Oaks, the Virginia Museum of Fine Arts, the Detroit Institute of Arts, the University of Pennsylvania Museum, Smith College, and the Met. But just a few months before the show was set to open, Kondoleon still didn't know for sure whether the Louvre would let them have the Judgment.

She'd get on the phone with Metzger. "So, Catherine, how's Paris in the spring?" And with some version of that innocent overture she'd reprise the urgent question: Would the Louvre loan Judgment of Paris? Welu remembers it, too—the Louvre reluctant, ever requesting more information, never making it a firm no, never quite saying yes. For at least a year it went on like that, Kondoleon reduced to begging.

Finally, the way Kondoleon tells it, she sensed Metzger was put off from loaning Judgment by the prospect of accompanying the precious thing to the States and winding up alone in some anonymous hotel in some awful little American town. Well, Kondoleon cajoled her in one of their phone calls, "If you come yourself with the mosaic, you can come stay with me." And this gesture of hospitality, she says, helped bring Judgment to America. Lawrence Becker spent a week or two in Paris helping with the move. They didn't know just how it would work out, he says. "We were going in blind, not sure we could do it safely." As it happens, a small piece of the mosaic did break off and they had to go back and fix it.

What made this one mosaic vital to Kondoleon's plans was not only its artistry, but its origins in a largely intact Roman triclinium: Its three couches, arranged at one end of the room, invited guests to lean back, eat, drink, and talk. Communing together over philosophy, business, or politics, you could plan on a long evening of it in the triclinium. There, from your couch, you could look out over a central court adorned with endlessly absorbing mosaic images, whose echoes of Greek intellect, myth, and aesthetics compelled attention, inspired conversation, forged connection and good feeling. To re-create the Atrium House triclinium within the walls of the Worcester museum became the chief object of Kondoleon's ambitions.

Lawrence Becker doesn't remember a time when this wasn't central to their plans. Excavated in 1932, the triclinium included, we may recall from Part II, no fewer than five distinct mosaic panels, spanning almost four hundred square feet. There was the superb, almost wholly intact Drinking Contest of Herakles and Dionysus, already part of Worcester's collection. It was flanked by two small dancing figures, a maenad and a bacchante, devotees of Dionysus, on view in Baltimore since the 1930s. And there was Princeton's damaged Aphrodite and Adonis, its top half destroyed in antiquity when crushed by a wall laid atop it. At the center was the Judgment of Paris. The individual figural compositions were set off by gorgeous, intricately interwoven geometric and ornamental borders. Finally, along most of the room's periphery, lay large swaths of mosaic filler, a plain net-like pattern, something close to just-plain-floor, normally obscured by the dining couches set over it.

"On first encountering the room," wrote Kondoleon in one of the books given over to the exhibition,

> the guest must surely have been dazzled by the sheer density of ornamentation and figural forms. One is immediately conscious of the wealth required to commission these mosaics and the virtuosity of technique employed in the creation of painterly panels of tiny stone *tesserae*. Even today any one of these mosaics elicits a response of awe from museum visitors.

But it was not "any one" of them to which she called attention now, but all of them together:

> The assemblage of this picture gallery framed by multiple polychromatic borders was spectacular. When the guests were invited to enter this grand room, they crossed the threshold and proceeded toward the far end where they sat on one of the three dining couches arranged in a U-shaped configuration around the figural panels. . . .

Her focus was on the experience of the guests: "What exactly did the ancient visitor see?" she asked.

> One not only sees these spaces, one moves through them and acts in them. Clearly, the spectator plays a role, along with the mosaicist and house owner, in controlling the viewing process. Given the variety of producers, a variety of readings must be admitted

as possible. Any one interpretation might be tentative, but certainly there was much for the ancient visitor to see in this great room, much to prompt wonder and reflection.

Early in the 1930s, Atrium House had helped catapult mosaics into their starring role at Antioch. But now, decades later, its mosaics could evoke a sense of loss, too, a regret for how they'd been broken up and dispersed. Bringing them together again could seem like righting a wrong.

Princeton had photos, taken during the excavation, of the simple net-patterned filler mosaic that took up a third or more of the room. But it didn't have the mosaic itself; that, like many geometric borders, had been left behind, save for a few fragments of it consigned to the Hatay Archaeology Museum. So a full-scale mock-up of the pattern was used for the exhibition. Kondoleon asked Victoria I, who'd helped reimagine the interiors of other Roman houses, to work up a watercolor representing all that was known of the Atrium House triclinium, together with best guesses for what visitors could have seen—the mosaics, the walls flanking them, a columned portico and apse at one end decorated with generic sculptures. "It was very theatrical," says Victoria I. Aside from the mosaics themselves, Kondoleon would acknowledge, "the installation does not reproduce any particular setting or archaeological find." Rather, it was based on all she had learned from

> close observation of several house plans from Antioch in which dining rooms frequently opened onto porticoes that led to open courtyards and pools. Reclined diners thus could enjoy extended views through a columnar curtain into a pseudo-peristyle adorned with garden and fountain.

The mosaics, Peter Brown would write, were "like shimmering carpets that led the eye from room to room. They were the discreet visual equivalent of the classical chamber music to whose accompaniment the greats of Europe in the *ancien régime* went about their daily life."

For visitors in 2000 and 2001, then, some vestige of the mosaics' original setting had been restored. A measure of guesswork went into it, but guesswork enriched by the sort of inspiration artists and scientists similarly bring to the vast uncertainties of creative work.

Even with explanatory panels to remind them, foot-weary visitors lost to the show's light, color, and visual display might conceivably miss the archaeological point: restoring context to the mosaics. But scholars, including Claudia Barsanti, got it right away. In her angry 2012 lament she lauded the Atrium House installation from the previous decade as "a veritable tour de force" and Kondoleon's approach as "praiseworthy," helping undo "the unwitting damage that had been perpetrated by prior dismemberment." John R. Clarke, professor of art history at the University of Texas at Austin, was similarly impressed. In a review of the exhibition for *Art Bulletin*, he noted that Antioch, unlike Pompeii, had suffered "a curious oblivion," its famous mosaics, "cut from their architectural contexts and often displayed like pictures on a wall," doing little "to articulate the identity of ancient Antioch." Kondoleon's show had changed all that.

> When I exited the show at Baltimore and found myself in the museum's ample courtyard, [the mosaics on its walls, not part of the exhibition] looked strangely out of place; the exhibition had shown how they belonged on floors, where their job was to articulate domestic space. The exhibition had made its point about the viewing dynamics of floor mosaics. . . . [So had] five computer models of the church at Seleucia Pieria that helped the viewer understand the spaces of the church and the effects of its marble and mosaic decoration.

Peter Brown likewise saw how the exhibition made for a fuller way to experience ancient art:

> What we wish to find, nowadays, is a hint of the living social context of this art. To the historian of ancient Antioch, the mosaics are precious not only because they illustrate so vividly one of the grandest themes in the history of the arts—the end of the classical world and the onset of the Byzantine Middle Ages. They are valuable as well because they allow us to glimpse the studied commitment to

> the *dolce vita* of the handful of great families who, as landowners, controlled the wealth of the city's agrarian hinterland . . . and ran the city and its region on behalf of the Roman emperors.

The exhibition had brought something of them and their values to life.

—

A few years after the onset of the excavations, Rufus Morey cautioned that Antioch was "not a site that can be dug in five or ten years, but one that demands a systematic exploration no more limited in time or detail than that of Pompeii." Surely it couldn't be exhaustively explored in the eight short seasons that academic calendars, vicissitudes of climate, and international tensions left the Franco-American dig. The last serious on-site work was done in 1939. Doro Levi's book was published in 1947. Then the decades marched ahead up to the 1990s, with little or no archaeological progress in Antioch. As archaeologist Hatice Pamir noted, potential expeditions came under the auspices of Turkey's Law on the Protection of Cultural and Natural Heritage, whose "regulations may have discouraged" interest from abroad.

But a series of digs beginning in 1995 did open Antioch's fertile agricultural hinterlands to exploration. And in 2002, Pamir herself—today a professor at Antakya's Mustafa Kemal University, her doctoral dissertation focused on Seleucia Pieria, Antioch's port—began digging in Antioch proper. In part, she hoped to refine the still-indistinct map of the ancient city. She and her team traced city walls, surveyed the slopes of the mountains east of the city, studied aqueducts, cisterns, and reservoirs, went back for another look at Antioch's hippodrome. Beginning in 2010, she took up the study of an area just west of the city's "Main Street," today's Kurtuluş Street, near where the Parmenius torrent sweeps into the city, the area Jean Lassus had made his own three-quarters of a century before. Along the way, she was involved in the discovery of perhaps the largest mosaic on earth.

A wealthy local entrepreneur, Necmi Asfuroglu, had plans to put up a great five-star hotel on land well north of the Antakya city center at a site beside Kurtuluş Street. But then, exploratory digs of Parcel 4642 revealed baths and expanses of mosaic flooring, both richly figured and space-filling geometric, some areas rippled and distorted by past floods, some left almost intact. Among the latter was a stunning second-century mosaic depicting Pegasus, the winged horse of myth and legend; they had to go thirty feet below ground level to find it.

Early work on the hotel was halted. Building site became archaeological site. In the end, after almost a decade, the two were muscularly integrated. A towering modern hotel today extends over broad stretches of mosaic pavement, nine thousand square feet of it, all left where found. Structural columns were slotted into the site so as to spare the mosaics, which were cleaned and partially restored. Ramps, walkways, and viewing platforms were erected to bring visitors and hotel guests down among the mosaics. The experience is intimate and unforgettable.

After more than a half century of hibernation, Antioch's past was slipping into the archaeological light once more. New teams descended on the ancient city, taking up where the excavators of the 1930s left off, digging in new places, seeing in new ways, visions of the old city lighting up their imaginations as they had those of their predecessors.

CHAPTER TWENTY-ONE

Back in Antioch

In the book he wrote near the end of the dig, Rufus Morey tells of the ancient city, its mosaics, their excavation, and what they told of classical art's makeover into that of the Middle Ages. It is a vivid and illuminating account. But while he writes as art historian and even, to a degree, art popularizer, our Mr. Morey was no memoirist. He says next to nothing of how he felt about the excavation he'd launched and led, or of the team who'd worked at his direction. Save for a few brief visits, as in 1936, Morey had not much *been* to Antioch. He learned most of what he knew of the day-to-day life of the dig secondhand, from correspondence, reports, photos, and, once they were back in Princeton, the excavators themselves. With the war on and the dig shut down, he went on to other things. Always, Rome loomed large in his ideas and affections. In April 1945, he resigned his chair at Princeton and became cultural attaché to the U.S. embassy in Rome, in which role he helped repatriate looted art and preserve scholarly libraries. "He may have done more to heal the wounds inflicted by the war," his great admirer Erwin Panofsky wrote of him, "than any professional diplomat."

Morey's choice for the dig's first field director, Clarence Fisher, died in Jerusalem in July 1941 at age sixty-four. "He was a delicate and a sensitive man," an obituary said of him. Of late, he'd been less archaeologist, more given to his charities, like the Jerusalem YMCA and a school, Dar el-Awlad, for poor Arab orphans, many of them "wretched little basket-boys from the Suq in Jerusalem." For reasons unclear, Fisher received a full military funeral, a British flag draped across his coffin; had he perhaps clandestinely served Britain during the Great War? He was, said the obituary, "a gentle man of many good deeds," and no little mystery.

Shortly after Robert Schirmer's return from his one year on the dig, memorably depicted in the rambling, often playful letters he wrote his wife, the couple divorced. He was soon married again, to an author of historical romances. During World War II he served with the American Red Cross in France. But soon afterward, whatever remained of his verbal mischievousness was extinguished by cancer, in "one of its more rapidly developing and devastating forms," as a 1947 death notice put it.

George Elderkin retired from professorial chores in 1948. In later years, he gained some notoriety as the author of anti-Catholic tracts. In *The Roman Catholic Problem*, he made clear he saw little place for Catholics in American public life. His book was denounced as blasphemous by the Roman Catholic chaplain at Princeton, Father Hugh Halton, whom Elderkin denounced as "the fulminating Jupiter of the Aquinas Foundation" and charged with trying to turn the country's leading universities toward Catholicism. The editor of the *Princeton Alumni Weekly* addressed Elderkin in a public letter: Whatever Father Halton's excesses, "your activities are just about as embarrassing to Princeton as his are." Elderkin died in 1965, at age eighty-six, his death earning a respectful *New York Times* obituary: "Specialist in Hellenistic Art Participated in the First Antioch Excavations."

Doro Levi, after his return to Italy in 1945 and to the end of his life in 1991, enjoyed a long, respected career as excavator, at Phaistos in Crete, and Iasos in Turkey, among other sites. After *Antioch Mosaic Pavements*, he never returned to mosaics as a subject of study.

—

Many among the Princeton expedition's notable figures—many, that is, besides the Egyptian *reises* who oversaw the physical work of the dig—came and went. George Elderkin was all but banished after that first year, Robert Schirmer gave it only a year, and Clarence Fisher was gone after two. Many besides them—photographers, cataloguers, numismatists, graduate students, helpers of all kinds—figured in the dig for only a season or two, Antioch's influence on them light or limited set against the whole of their lives.

Not so Glanville Downey. Though in Antioch only that first eventful season of 1932, while still a graduate student, he contributed much to the scholarly understructure of the dig. Handicapped by a severe stutter, he would largely avoid the classroom during his career. But as scholar he was unimpeded and, as Morey would write of him, a natural. Antioch was his recurring subject. Even before the excavations shut down, he was publishing articles like "The Gate of the Cherubim at Antioch" and "Personification of Abstract Ideas in the Antioch Mosaics." By January 1940, he had several other Antioch-linked articles in the works, including one on the Seleucids, one on local topography.

Downey's first real job out of grad school was as a fine arts librarian at Yale—where, in the anxious months after Pearl Harbor, as we saw earlier, he seemed amused to report he'd been named to the firefighting squad. A little later he enlisted in the army, which took him to Sicily as one of the "Monuments Men," helping track down antiquities, archives, and other war-damaged art and cultural objects. Whatever else he did across a long span of years and academic posts, Downey never left behind the Antioch he'd tasted that first year on the dig. It was 1948 when, after many false starts, he started work on his *A History of Antioch in Syria*. When finally published in 1961, it was dedicated to Morey. Readers, he hoped, would "understand how deeply I regret that the book could not have been published before he died in 1955."

Almost as much as Morey, Sandy Campbell and Jean Lassus embodied the steady, stalwart line of care and personal responsibility that kept the excavations on track. Posing for "class pictures" taken each season, the two of them, in their mid-thirties, might be spotted standing in the back row together. Lassus was taller, hair slicked back and parted in the middle, shoulders thrown back, big smile, all personality. Campbell was maybe the easier to take of the two. The two young men grew close, at one point promising each other they'd one day return to Antioch to renew the excavation. Lassus wanted Campbell to know, he wrote him, in English, on January 26, 1937, "how much I appreciate your wishes and friendship. It is very precious, and perhaps not so frequent, to be always in good *amitié*, where you have to cooperate with a foreigner. Especially, I think, for archaeologists, the worst kind of people in the world, the only kind of wolves who love to eat each other."

Back from Antioch, Campbell lectured about the Princeton expedition at universities around the country. Later, after Pearl Harbor, he served with the U.S. Army Middle East Command—as well as, the evidence seems plain, with the OSS, wartime predecessor of the CIA. After the war, he helped found the American Levant Shipping Company (of which Adib Ishak would become director). In 1957, he joined the Trans-Arabian Pipeline Company, "Tapline," which pumped oil across Saudi Arabia to Lebanon and the Mediterranean.

At one point stopping in Antioch during the war, Campbell wrote Morey, describing Princeton's shrunken presence there. The concession was still nominally in force. A few men were working with a mosaic in Daphne. One day, he walked the five miles there, reminiscing of "when we used to flash past pedestrians in a fine station wagon." He supplied Morey with news of the "native staff," on whom they'd so relied, like Adib, Mr. and Mrs. Athanassiou, and William Gad Gabriel. He mentioned the "excellent guards," all from a single family, who had watched over vulnerable Princeton sites for the past dozen years.

And Campbell wondered out loud about returning after the war: Maybe it would be possible to initiate "a series of short summer excavations." The war was then at its height, Allied troops were battling their way up the Italian boot, forces were massing in England for the invasion of France. And Sandy Campbell was thinking back—and ahead—to Antioch.

Seventeen years later, in spring 1961, professor Carl Kraeling, whose compilation of historic references to Antioch Morey had counted on to help tell them where to dig in 1932, was just back from Beirut. There, he'd met with Campbell and had "a pleasant reunion." Their talk turned to archaeology. Campbell "planned to retire the following November; and then do a bit more archaeological field work" in Antioch, but worried that, at sixty-two, maybe he was too old. On the other hand, he had friends who might be willing to put up money toward the venture. And he still had all his old field records and notes from the 1930s. By spring 1963 he could be back in harness.

Kraeling was pleased to hear it. A man who's once "gotten dirt under his fingernails," it seemed to him, "never quite [loses] the skill of field work." He promised Sandy he "would bring the matter up in the old circle of the Antiochenes and Princetonians." He'd already tried out the idea on Glanville Downey and Kurt Weitzmann, another Princeton art historian, who were both receptive. "All that Sandy needs at this time is some kind of a green light."

Writing the following week to Campbell, Dick Stillwell expressed support:

> As to your doing the field work, why ever not? I am sure that you will not have forgotten your ancient cunning, or that you will have difficulty in getting your hand in once again. . . . I should like nothing better than to visit you again at Antioch and renew the memorable times we had in 1936 when Morey, Francis Taylor and others gathered in the excavation house.

By the sound of it, Antioch had a grip on Stillwell, too.

It wasn't only personal ambition or the luster of old mosaics that called them back. Historian Peter Brown, who would immerse himself in the Princeton excavation files, wrote how they brought him unnervingly close to "the foibles and limitations of an expedition—the touchiness of individual members, their moments of high-handedness, their imperturbability bordering upon insensitivity in a foreign environment." Yet what lingered was "the courage and the capacity for friendship" among them. As Clarence Fisher, Elderkin, and Campbell duked it out that first year, even cheerfully eccentric Robert Schirmer had felt the dig's claim on him: "Out here, it's like being married to 5 new people. We are so much together."

In 1961, just a week after seeing Kraeling in Beirut, Campbell was diagnosed with a brain tumor. Returning to the U.S., he underwent surgery, which seemed to go well enough. He stayed for a while in New York, then set off for Switzerland to recuperate. "And with this good news," he wrote Rensselaer Lee, then chair of Art and Archaeology, the "desire of continuing some work at Antioch has revived." He mentioned three prospects left from 1939—a paved area outside a church in Seleucia Pieria; shallow trenches on the Island he thought might lead to the great palace; and—yet another local farmer's alluring lead—"a mosaic inscription in his peanut patch."

But Campbell would never get to them. The cancer returned. He died in a Beirut hospital late in the evening of December 27, 1963. "I am sorry that we have lost our beloved late Mr. Campbell," Adib wrote Stillwell early the following month. "All his friends and relatives felt this terrible loss, but his name and smile and energy will never be forgotten by those who loved him."

Jean Lassus's odyssey was more tortuous than Campbell's. His letter recounting "the terrible things your family passed through" after the Germans invaded France in May 1940, Morey wrote him that September, made "distressing reading." He hoped that "this sort of thing" would be the last of Lassus's troubles.

On the eve of the war, students and faculty of the Université de Strasbourg in Alsace, at which Lassus had finally secured a position in the spring of 1938, had evacuated to the University of Clermont-Ferrand, in Auvergne, south of what became the armistice line. For a few years Lassus somehow managed an almost normal professional life, even overseeing a dig at nearby Gergovie, the site of a famous battle between the Gauls and Julius Caesar. Yet he was also a *résistante*, supplier of false papers to students seeking escape from German-occupied Alsace. In May 1944, the Gestapo arrested him and shipped him to Dachau. On the train packed with frightened souls that took him there, his sister told the story later, he tried to lighten its misery with tales of Antioch and archaeology. Any relief, though, was short-lived. Of the hundred people in his car, sixty-five died on the way. "*Monsieur le professor*," said the clerk at Dachau who inscribed him as prisoner 77019, "you know you are here to die?" A few months later, Lassus was sent on to Dora, the vast, underground slave-labor factory that made the V2 rockets fired at England during the war's final year. "The insolent power of this secret weapon horrified me," Lassus would write. "And for the only time during the war, I doubted our victory."

Improbably, Lassus survived.

After the war, he became rector of the French-Vietnamese university of Hanoi.

From 1955 to 1964, he was director of antiquities in Algeria. In 1957, Dick Stillwell wrote him of the recent deaths of Princeton's Baldwin Smith and Morey, adding: "I think often of the days—back in 1936—when we were together at Antioch, and to the excavations to which you contributed so greatly."

Lassus needed no reminder. Indeed, he had unfinished business with Antioch, too. In 1966, out of Algeria and now a professor at the Sorbonne in Paris, he applied to the Institute for Advanced Study at Princeton for a scholarly retreat. Stillwell had tracked down drawings and maps he'd been missing; Lassus needed them and other excavation records. With those in hand and a semester free to think and write, he could finally complete the work "entrusted to me by C. R. Morey and W. A. Campbell." He meant, of course, the Main Street dig, his excavations of the city's great colonnaded street.

Lassus arrived on a Pan Am flight at Kennedy Airport on September 24, 1967. His ambitious project, of course, was nowhere near finished when he left. But finish it he ultimately did. In 1972, forty years after arriving in Antioch, and after what a Princeton University Press editor acknowledged were "exasperating delays," early copies of his book, *Les Portiques d'Antioche*, fifth in the series of books on the yearslong expedition, reached him in France. "When I came back from Paris yesterday, I was truly stupefied," he wrote back in English. "The book has arrived. . . . [It] is truly beautiful," the printing, the quality of plans and pictures—a work of book art, he makes it sound, as much as one of scholarship. He professed anxiety that maybe it wasn't worth the abundance of care that had gone into it and the price it would fetch. He needn't have worried. To Princeton University

Press's own reviewer, he had revealed facets of the city's history "in a novel and vivid way." A French review called it "fascinating," a book that "makes us hope that one day the excavations will be reprised . . . and chronicled in a publication of similarly fine quality."

"I am free from a heavy scruple," Lassus wrote Stillwell a little later. "I don't like to let . . . things [remain] undone." He dedicated the book

> to the memory of William Alexander Campbell . . . the most tactful, gracious and effective of leaders and friends. For years, we worked together. Then, after the war, when we met again in Beirut, he dreamed we'd take up together our interrupted project. I wish to offer him now this portrait of our past efforts, this testimony of my fidelity.

They were young men during their Antioch days, Lassus, Campbell, and Downey, among others. They survived the war—in Lassus's case, barely—and went on to full lives and notable careers. But they never got Antioch out of their systems. In Antioch, they had come of age. In Antioch, they had dug into the same dirt in which, two millennia before, mosaicists had laid down their scenes of men, women, animals, and gods, their memorable compositions, their bold geometries.

I think these archaeologists of the 1930s bear a kinship with their artisanal forebears. For months at a time they were borne away from homes, offices, and seminar rooms to this place of fertility and urban vitality between the Syrian desert and the sea. Theirs, too, was a world of stone, wood, coarse cloth, trowels, baskets, pots, and drinking vessels, stashes of tesserae, mosaics peeking up from beneath the dirt or lined up beside a wall. Like the mosaicists of earlier times, their world was, for a time, one of objects, *things*, in all their irreducible physical substance. Might we count them, too, as honorary fellows of the Antioch Workshop?

The earthquake that struck Turkey and Syria in 2023, which destroyed most of Antakya and killed more than twenty thousand people in Hatay province alone, might seem to banish all thought of art, exploration, or beauty. But death and life are incommensurable; they cannot be neatly balanced against one another. The quake was all destruction and death. But it took nothing from the achievements of the early Antioch mosaicists. And nothing from those of the 1930s excavators, who uncovered the mosaic art they made that we today can savor with gratitude, pleasure, and respect.

ACKNOWLEDGMENTS

This book took shape during the COVID pandemic, which only aggravated the isolation that I, like many authors, submit to as occupational hazard. Friends, however, found ways to keep in touch, helping me to maintain equanimity. They included the *Passager* poets, Kendra and Kathleen, and their spouses, Jon and Danny, Rosanne and Steve, David Bergman and John Lessner; Tristine Skyler, Brandon Stickney, Amitabh Avasthi, and Haleema Aslam; Dottie and Peg from the farm, Isabelle, Patti Mac and Robin Henig, Elise and Katherine; and my neighbors up and down the block and across the alley.

Thanks especially go to Pam Mensch, who offered a ready ear, and sustained and caring interest, across this span of years; to Aaron Levin for his knowledgeable introduction to the world of archaeological digs; to Arthur Magida, for his lunchtime cheer, generosity, and good heart; to Harry, Rachele, and Laird, Duncan and Jessie, and my son, David. And to my wife, Sarah, for almost everything that matters.

Robert Messenger was the book's first editor at Simon & Schuster. I had fruitful conversations and correspondence with him until his departure in fall 2024. At that time, Emily Simonson took on the book, made it her own, and energetically guided it the rest of the way home. Thank you, Emily. Thanks also are due Rob Sternitzky, for his on-the-mark copyediting; Phil Metcalf, production editor; Lewelin Polanco, for her appealing interior design; Natalia Olinski for her smart design of a beautiful cover; and others behind the scenes whose efforts kick in at later points of a bookmaking process sometimes invisible to the author.

Thanks to the two Michaels at Inkwell Management—my agent, Michael Carlisle, and his capable colleague, Mike Mungiello—for stepping in at crucial moments in the book's genesis.

I wish to thank classical archaeologist Christopher "Kit" Moss, former publications editor with Princeton's Art and Archaeology Department, who genially advised me on the resources within the department and forwarded to me digital sites he thought might be useful to me—and invariably were.

Jim Garrett welcomed me to his home in Baltimore and shared with me documentary materials about his forebear, Robert Garrett.

Christine Kondoleon set aside time to talk, answer my queries, furnish leads, and share key materials I might not have stumbled on myself. Among these was what I've come to call the Peter Brown Compilation—sixty-two pages of extracts from Princeton's Antioch files, astutely culled by Shari Kenfield, then curator of the Art and Archaeology Department, for use by Professor Brown, the distinguished historian of late antiquity. Christine received this cache from Professor Brown while working on her *Lost Antioch* exhibition and passed it on to me in 2024. Art conservator Lawrence Becker, Kondoleon's colleague on *Lost Antioch*, gave me additional insights into this key exhibition's formative period, as did designer Victoria I.

Jim Welu, former director of the Worcester Art Museum, told me about the early days of his collaboration with Professor Kondoleon, his memories leavened and enriched by scoops of his homemade ice cream, hauled up from the basement of his house in Worcester in bountiful variety. Paula Artal-Isbrand took me behind the scenes at the museum and spoke to me at length about objects conservation in general and the Antioch mosaics in particular. Many thanks to all.

Jessica Arista, also a conservator, now at the Getty Villa in California, has over the years helped introduce me to her field, as both art and science. She was an early spur to my interest in the Antioch mosaics, first as an intern at the Worcester Art Museum, where she worked on the Dionysus and

Ariadne mosaic from Antioch. She was also kind enough to review parts of the manuscript.

I owe many thanks to Julia Gearhart and her colleagues, including Yichin Chen, for guiding me through the vast archival bounty of A & A's Visual Resources Collection; Julia knows *always*—if so improbable an assertion can be trusted—where *anything* can be found.

From almost the beginning of my work on Antioch, Jessica Savage has been there. An art history specialist with Princeton's Index of Medieval Art, she served as exemplary guide to the Index and its creator, Charles Rufus Morey, the dominant early force behind the Antioch dig. Jessica directed me to obscure materials, read and commented on early chapters of the book, and encouraged me along the way.

From the 2022 conference in Antakya, Turkïye, devoted to Antioch's mosaics, I owe thanks, often across multiple language barriers, to Hatice Pamir, Isil Isiklikaya, Marek Olszewski, Catherine Saliou, Ana Silkatcheva, and, on many counts, Katherine Dunbabin.

Finally, I wish to thank the three accomplished mosaicists who, beginning in 2014, helped introduce me to mosaics—Rick Shelley, Bonnie Fitzgerald, and Yulia Hanansen.

NOTES AND SOURCES

PRINCETON ARCHIVES

The Princeton-led excavations of Antioch spanned eight years. Before that came four years of organization and planning. Across the years since, the mosaics and other finds have been dispersed to museums in the U.S., France, and Turkïye. The records of this activity are today gathered up and maintained in a great archive, organized by the university's Art and Archaeology Department's Visual Resources Collection, or VRC. During the several years of my research it has been presided over by the extraordinarily knowledgeable and helpful Julia Gearhart and her staff. Many of its materials, probably most by now, are available online on a site maintained by a University of Chicago data service known as OCHRE.

Foremost in the VRC are the various dig records. These include daily diaries by the field director, yearly reports, a vast bank of photographs, mostly black-and-white, but some in color, maps, drawings, film footage, and much else, from the years of the dig and since, together furnishing a substantial part of the source material for *Uncovering Antioch*. Letters back and forth among Princeton archaeologists, donors, government officials, and others are normally found in its copious Correspondence file, broken down by year and author. Under the rubric of Additional Sources are the books published by Princeton University Press, all under the collective name of *Antioch-on-the-Orontes* and likewise available on the OCHRE site. These are Antioch I, covering the excavations of 1932, George W. Elderkin, ed.; Antioch II, 1933–1936, Richard Stillwell, ed.; Antioch III, 1937–1939,

Richard Stillwell, ed.; Antioch IV, in two parts, is devoted to ceramics and coins; Antioch V is Jean Lassus's *Les Portiques d'Antioche*, the story of its genesis running through *Uncovering Antioch* as a kind of countercurrent to the mosaics.

The digitization of these materials is a continuing one, paper records continually being transmuted into digital. Much of this has taken place during the time I have been working with them. Accordingly, in what follows, I do not distinguish digital materials from paper. (Among archival materials, it should be noted, are the Robert Schirmer Letters, about fifteen of them, dated from March 16 to May 17, 1932. These can be viewed at VRC, but at this writing are not available online.)

Other Princeton-area resources, distinct from VRC, and drawn on for this book, include:

Seeley G. Mudd Manuscript Library, with A&A departmental correspondence mostly from after the end of the dig, during and after World War II, and including correspondence to and from C. R. Morey, Fred Waagé, Glanville Downey, Robert Garrett, and others. Its holdings include a folder, "Refugee Applications," addressed to C. R. Morey from European refugees during the Nazi period.

Princeton University Library Special Collections: Among these are Princeton University Press papers that include Jean Lassus's correspondence with his editors about the book he worked on late in life that became *Les Portiques d'Antioche*, part V of *Antioch-on-the-Orontes*.

The *Institute for Advanced Study* is distinct from Princeton University, but just down the road. Its Levy Archive, presided over by Caitlin Rizzo, includes materials built around the scholarly stays of various expedition figures, including Jean Lassus, Glanville Downey, and Doro Levi. C. R. Morey's central role in widening the domain of the institute to the humanities is also represented here.

OTHER ARCHIVAL SOURCES

The Baltimore Museum of Art furnished records bearing on the museum's crucial involvement in the Antioch excavations, Robert Garrett's central role, news accounts, and issues of conservation. Despite difficulties imposed by a major renovation of museum spaces at the time, Sarah Dansberger, archivist and head librarian, was of enormous help.

Robert Garrett papers, a private collection made available through the courtesy of James Garrett, Baltimore.

Worcester Art Museum, Rebecca Morin, head librarian.

Fiske Kimball Records, Philadelphia Museum of Art, Library and Archives, courtesy Marge Huang.

Robert Bliss papers, Pusey Archives, Harvard University.

Robert Bliss and Royall Tyler papers, Dumbarton Oaks Museum, Carla Galfano, registrar and collections manager.

Dorothy Waagé Collection, Zhang Legacy Collections Center, Western Michigan University, courtesy Lynn Houghton. Dorothy Waagé's letters from the dig in Antioch to her parents in America cover two periods—April 18–August 20, 1937, and March 23–August 3, 1938.

PHONE AND IN-PERSON INTERVIEWS AND CORRESPONDENCE

Laura Albans, Jessica Arista, Paula Artal-Isbrand, Lawrence Becker, Andrew Campbell, Katherine Dunbabin, Andrea U. De Giorgi, James R. Garrett, Victoria I, Christine Kondoleon, Marilyn A. Lavin, Christopher Moss, Michael Padgett, Hatice Pamir, Michael Parrish, Jessica Savage, Alan Shapiro, Jennifer Stager, Alan Stahl, Frederick Waagé, James Welu.

MOSAICS

Not to be dismissed as a proper "source" for this book—and, indeed, a constant inspiration for the writing of it—are the mosaics themselves, many of which I viewed in the following locations: Princeton University; Baltimore Museum of Art; Worcester Art Museum; Institute for Advanced Study, Princeton, NJ; Getty Villa, Los Angeles; Hatay Archaeology Museum, Antakya, Türkiye; and Dumbarton Oaks Research Library and Collection, Washington, D.C., where several of the Antioch mosaics are set out as ordinary flooring, as true "pavements," trod upon by visitors, as of old.

Practically speaking, seeing the mosaics through black-and-white or color images, in books, prints, or online—that is, at several removes from their physical origins—is often necessary. But the pixels and fleeting images that inundate our lives today can, I think, mislead us into thinking we enjoy a richer experience than we do. As this book sometimes suggests, the mosaics are most revealing and satisfying in person, whether close-up or at a little distance. They catch the light. They seem more physically alive. They encourage one's touch, even where touching is proscribed.

NOTES

In these chapter notes and the bibliography that follows I aim to lead readers through the thick research understory of *Uncovering Antioch*. I don't presume to furnish one-to-one tracking for each individual fact or quote, though letters cited, and accounts built up from the excavation diaries, are often dated and credited within the text itself.

PART I

ONE: MR. MOREY

17 For Antioch and the post–World War I mandates, see Gelin, 2002; Goode, 2007; Khoury, 1987; Griswold, 2020; Rifaioğlue, 2014.

18 No full-scale biography of Morey exists, but much can be gleaned from Panofsky, 1955; Arndt, 2005; Taylor, 1955; Blair, 1957; Lee, 1955. For a sense of his intellect at work outside mosaics, see "Medievalist Looks at Modern Art," Baldwin Lecture, February 8, 1945, in manuscript, courtesy Jessica Savage. On Morey's family of origin see "Addie Charlotte Stone Morey," *Genesee Country Express and Advertiser*, March 23, 1939; obituary of Harry T. Morey, *New York Times*, January 26, 1936. On Morey's Index of Christian Art, see Hourihane, 2002.

21 The Renaissance cleric of whom Morey reminded his students was, according to Panofsky, Nicholas Albergati. But Arndt, 2005, p. 10, writes of Morey that "he bore a striking resemblance to Canon van der Paelen in Jan van Eyck's altarpiece." The images coming down to us of all three look much alike.

22 For the origins of the Antioch expedition, Christopher Moss's unpublished "The 'Prehistory' of the Antioch Excavation" was helpful. See also Morey's "The Excavation of Antioch-on-the Orontes," *Proceedings of the American Philosophical Society* 76, no. 5 (1936): pp. 637–51, reprinted by the Baltimore Museum of Art, May 1937. For more on the stubbornly recurring case of the Antioch Chalice, see chapter 14, "The Making of the Medieval," and chapter 20, "Off the Wall." For early French surveys of the Near East, see Provost, 2016, and Clive Foss, "Dead Cities of the Syrian Hill Country," *Archaeology* 49, no. 5 (September–October 1996): pp. 48–53.

TWO: HARD MONEY

23 The years from 1927 to 1932 during which the Antioch expedition went from bare suggestion to going concern is exhaustively covered in the VRC files, from which most of Morey's correspondence with would-be donors, and within Art and Archaeology, are drawn. See also the Fiske Kimball Records.

24 For Robert Garrett, see Cindy Kelly, 2001. Garrett's travels to the Near East in 1899–1900 are based in part on letters furnished by James R. Garrett of Baltimore; a more informal account appears also in the *Triennial Record of the Class of 1897*, no. 2 (Princeton University, 1900). A sense of how Garrett was regarded later in life comes from a book of tributes presented to him on his eightieth birthday in 1950, courtesy of James R. Garrett; Baltimore Museum of Art materials on Robert Garrett and the museum's role in the expedition were furnished by Sarah Dansberger, the museum's head librarian and archivist; see also Garrett, "Recollections of a Collector," 1949.

32 For the Worcester Art Museum in the origins of the Antioch expedition, see Welu, 2005; VRC files, especially for Francis Taylor, Morey, and Robert Garrett. For "a snag on the Antioch proposition," see handwritten, undated letter, on letterhead of Mrs. Francis Henry Taylor, from Francis Taylor to Morey, Worcester Art Museum archives, which concludes: "I do not give up hope. . . ."

34 The bad news from Philadelphia plays out in the VRC files and the Fiske Kimball Records.

37 The Baltimore Museum of Art's response to the Depression and its eventual signing-on to the Antioch excavation is drawn in part from executive committee meeting minutes and other museum records.

THREE: EXCAVATION'S EVE

40 For Clarence Fisher, see "Clarence S. Fisher," *Biblical Archaeologist*, 1941; "Clarence Fisher: An Unknown Achievement," *Expedition*, 1979; McCurry, 2017; Glueck, 1941; for more on Fisher before Antioch, see also Eric H. Cline, "Please Accept My Resignation," excerpted from *Digging Up Armageddon*, 2020. For Fisher's "skilled Egyptian foremen," the Qufts, see Doyon, 2018.

45 References to George Wicker Elderkin as composer of Protestant hymns can be found on the online site Hymnary.org.

FOUR: ABOARD *EXCALIBUR*

48 For the *Excalibur*, see "Remembering the Classic Liners of Yesteryear," ssmaritime.com, with photos of the ship and passenger appointments.

49 For Antioch in literature, see Perkins, 1946; Wallace, 1880; "Rev. Jacob Randolph 'Jake' Perkins," Find a Grave; Gore Vidal's novel *Julian* (Little, Brown, 1962) is about Julian the Apostate, and includes fictional letters by Julian, Libanius, and other historical figures.

50 On the struggle among the generals following the death of Alexander, see Romm, 2012.

52 On Libanius, see Norman, 2000; Downey, 1959.

54 On Malalas, see Liebeschuetz, 2004; Downey, 1961, pp. 38–40.

55 On the Kraeling indices, see Kraeling's October 5, 1931, letter to Morey, as well as Morey's November 12, 1931, letter to Fiske Kimball, to which is attached a copy of the Kraeling index, both in VRC.

PART II

FIVE: POINTS OF ORIGIN

59 Fisher's early months in Antioch, before the arrival of the Princeton team and then after, are told mainly through his 1932 excavation diary.

60 For a substantial notice on Prost, who died on May 26, 1936, see Jouguet, 1936. His death in a car accident is mentioned in a footnote to an article by C. L. Woolley in the *Journal of Hellenic Studies* 58, pt. 1 (1938). Robert Schirmer's letters, VRC, also refer to Prost.

60 For Antioch at the time of the 1930s excavations, see, for example, Morton, 1936; Weulersse, 1934; black-and-white photos in VRC, viewable online on the OCHRE site.

62 For more on Antioch's flooding woes, see chapter 12, "Omphalos."

64 *"one must remind oneself"*: Jean Lassus, "Report on the Fall Campaign, 1934," VRC.

64 *"God knows, no one really knows anything about ancient Antioch"*: Robert Schirmer Letters, March 25, 1932. For a photo of Schirmer at work see Redford, 2014, p. 225.

66 Antioch's hippodrome, stony vestiges of which remain aboveground today: For the 1925 filming of *Ben Hur*, with its chariot race in Antioch's hippodrome, see John W. Harding, "Re-Inventing Antioch," excerpted on the Hollywood History Online site, from Harding's *The Ben-Hur Murders: Inside the 1925 Hollywood Games* (Pulp Hero Press, 2019).

69 On Fisher-Prost meeting: Fisher's 1932 diary, VRC.

72 *"found the automobile and truck waiting for us"*: This is from the first in a series of reports Elderkin wrote Morey from Antioch from March 19 to May 31, 1932, VRC.

74 Private baby language and thirties slang in Schirmer's letters: I have cross-checked three of Schirmer's pet usages—"eekish," "gadge," and "bumbly"—in H. L. Mencken's *The American Language*, abridged fourth edition (Knopf, 1982)—but find no sign of them there. I suspect Schirmer's wordplay is more private language than thirties slang.

79 Aphrodite and Adonis, in Ovid's telling: The translation is that of A. D. Neville in a 1986 Oxford University Press edition.

79 *simply called the Roman Villa*: See Lawrence Becker and Christine Kondoleon, "The Atrium House Triclinium: Archaeology, Iconography, Technique, and Style," in Becker and Kondoleon, 2005, p. 17.

SIX: THE JUDGMENT OF PARIS

82 For the Judgment, see Becker and Kondoleon, 2005, p. 17. The account of its discovery comes from Fisher's 1932 excavation diary.

84 Jean Lassus's account of the Louvre's valuation of the Judgment of Paris appears in Lassus, 1982, pp. 253–54; his doubts about breaking up the room-wide mosaic appears on p. 254; Elderkin's "I did entertain secretly" appears in the sixth of his regular reports to Morey, on May 12, 1932.

92 Morey's "cogent, clear-eyed study" to Garrett is dated November 16, 1932.

SEVEN: BY THE SIDE OF THE ROAD IN AIN-DJAMOUS

93 Spellings of the Yakto district differ; one variant is Ain-Jamoos.

93 *the first hills rise up*: Jean Lassus, "La Mosaïque de Yakto," in *Antioch-on-the Orontes I*, which also refers to Claude Prost's early role.

94 For flavor and understanding of Jean Lassus's long, eventful life, see Pralong, 2005; Le Glay, 1991; Souville, 1979. Lassus wrote widely of his archaeological and other adventures over the years, often slipping into the personal. He is the author of a 1973 memoir, *Souvenirs d'un Cobaye*. Here and elsewhere, translations from Lassus's French are by the author. (But in his Antioch correspondence Lassus did sometimes write in English.)

94 For more on the topographic border and *Megalopsychia*, see Étienne Michon, "Lettre de M. Morey relative à la découverte à Daphné (Syrie) d'une mosaïque avec le plan d'Antioche," *Comptes rendus des séances de l'Academie des Inscriptions et Belles-Lettres* 77, no. 1 (1933): pp. 26–27; Saliou, 2020; Tracey Elizabeth Eckersley, "Putting Christians on the Map: Topographic Mosaics from Late Antique Jordan as Representations of Authority and Status" (doctoral dissertation, University of Louisville, 2016), p. 160; Downey, 1941; Downey, 1945; Downey, 1961, pp. 30–32; Balty, 2000.

101 *Thorn Puller of Yakto*: See Kondoleon, 2000, p. 176, and Redford, 2014, p. 243.

EIGHT: DAPHNE AND APOLLO

102 The Ovid translation is that of A. D. Melville, in Ovid, *Metamorphoses* (Oxford University Press, 1986).

102 For Daphne, see Poccardi, 2020; Wilber, 1938; entry for Daphne in William Smith, ed., *Dictionary of Greek and Roman Geography* (John Murray, 1854); Downey, 1961, pp. 29–30.

103 *"Chief among the glories"*: See A. F. Norman's translation of Oration 11, which is studded with ebullient references to Daphne.

105 Lassus's account of Campbell's visit to his office appears in Lassus, 1982.

NINE: *LA FOUILLE DE MOSAÏQUES*

110 Factory efficiency experts: Such as Frederick Winslow Taylor, whose ideas were very much in the air of the 1930s, subject of my 1997 book, *The One Best Way*.

112 *"The obvious impulse"*: Jean Lassus, "Report on the Fall Campaign, 1934," VRC.

113 *"The roadway was open to the sky"*: Downey, *Antioch in the Age of Theodosius the Great*, 1962, pp. 17–18.

114 *"To respond to my concerns"*: Lassus, 1972, p. 5.

114 *"Main Street Dig"*: See Lassus, 1972; and chapter 12, "Omphalos."

114 *"an amazing effect on the visitors"*: Lassus to Campbell, sixteen-page letter, in English, on Committee letterhead, beginning, "The fall campaign is now finished." Its first page is undated, but subsequent pages suggest it was written over the course of days or weeks in December 1934.

TEN: DIVVYING UP THE SPOILS

117 "Eh bien, *I will take this one"*: Mallowan, 1999, p. 174.

119 For Seyrig, see, for example, Stetié, 2016, and Jérôme Bocquet, "Henri Seyrig, un gaulliste dans la décolonisation," *Syrie* 3, 2016, pp. 49–91. Seyrig's irritation with the Americans emerges in Stucky, 2016.

124 *"A catastrophe has befallen us"*: Campbell to Morey, April 10, 1935.

125 Group photos: For one of those cited, with Morey, see Redford, 2014, p. 245. For "class photo" of Fisher, Campbell, Lassus, his wife and child, and in the foreground, "Thorn Puller," see Redford, p. 243.

ELEVEN: BUFFET SUPPER

127 *"missed the train"*: Tassel, 2000.

128 *"picturesque native house"*: The author of this document, ANT_AM F-50-08 in the Princeton archives, does not appear on either its handwritten or typed version, but is likely Dick Stillwell, who visited the dig in the summer of 1936. For an image of the house, see Redford, 2014, p. 238.

128 *"a dish towel is something for dishes only"*: Dorothy Waagé to her parents, March 23, 1938, Waagé Letters.

129 *necessary order and routine*: See Redford, 2014, p. 161, for 1936 photo giving a taste of the day-to-day at the field headquarters.

132 For Honolulu sale, see *Honolulu Advertiser*, April 17, 1938; *Honolulu Academy of Arts Bulletin*, December 1938.

135 For Buffet Supper, see Lassus to Campbell, May 22, 1937; Redford, 2014, p. 193, for a view of the mosaic while still in the ground; see also, for example, Cimok, 1994, pp. 44–45; Sandra Knudsen, "Dining as a Fine Art: Tablewares of the Ancient Romans," in Kondoleon, 2000, pp. 181–84; John H. D'Arms, "The Culinary Reality of Roman Upper-Class Convivia: Integrating Texts and Images," *Comparative Studies in Society and History* 46, no. 3 (2004): 428–50.

135 *two hundred tesserae to depict the pig's foot*: My count.

TWELVE: OMPHALOS

137 *Louisa Dresser*: See Welu, 2005, pp. 11–12.

138 *"event which loomed largest"*: Dorothy Waagé to her parents, May 15, 1938, Waagé Papers.

138 *It took lives. But it also proved* interesting *to the archaeologists*: Lassus writes how the flooding illuminated "one of those disasters of which the history of Antioch is so full." The 2023 earthquake, an incomparably more deadly disaster, likewise lends immediacy to the quake-fraught history of the ancient city.

140 *"No emperor shied away"*: De Giorgi, 2016, p. 54.

142 *"axial rupture"*: Lassus, 1967, p. 60.

142 *"scar line"*: Brown, 2001.

142 *"As one walked along the avenue"*: Downey, 1962, p. 21.

THIRTEEN: OUT OF ANTIOCH

144 My account of the deteriorating political situation in Antioch and the city's absorption by Turkey is drawn from VRC correspondence, 1938 and 1939; as well as by the 1938 letters of Dorothy Waagé at Western Michigan. See also "'Hatay Belongs to Us': Defining Community in the Sanjak of Alexandretta, 1915–1940," honors thesis by Mary E. Tezak, Vanderbilt University, 2020; Khoury, 1987, chapter 19, "The Loss of the Sanjak"; Juliette Desplat, "Archaeological Business as Usual? Digging in the Hatay in the 1930s," UK National Archives blog, February 2, 2018; Khadduri, 1945.

145 *Kemalist Turks wore Western clothes*: Khoury, 1987, p. 505.

152 *"Perhaps because it is autumn"*: Mallowan, p. 202.

153 The Cyprus alternative seems to crop up first in Morey's letter to Francis Taylor on February 20, 1939, in response to the question of "Where we are going to dig next year if we leave Antioch?"

155 Gridlock out of Antioch: See Redford, 2014, p. 253.

PART III

FOURTEEN: THE MAKING OF THE MEDIEVAL

160 *"completely changed the situation"*: Morey, "The Antioch Mosaics at Baltimore," *Museum Quarterly of the Baltimore Museum of Art* 11 (1937): p. 4. See also "City Acquires Collection of Hellenistic Mosaics," Baltimore *Sun*, October 6, 1936.

161 *no cut-and-dried solution*: "Restoration of the Mosaics," in two parts, R. J. McKinney and Roland Wehrheim, *Museum Quarterly of the Baltimore Museum of Art* 11 (1937): pp. 5–7.

161 For the Worcester exhibition, see *The Dark Ages*, 1937.

163 For Antioch Chalice and the Holy Grail, see Juliette Wood; letters in the Worcester Art Museum archives, including Francis Henry Taylor to Robert Woods Bliss, October 28, 1937; Taylor to Robert Woods Bliss, November 8, 1937; Anson Phelps Stokes to Taylor, November 9, 1937; Taylor to Stokes, November 18, 1937.

164 For transition from Greco-Roman to medieval art, see Milliken, 1947; Lassus, *The Early Christian and Byzantine World*, 1967.

166 *"It is not to Rome"*: Marquand, 1910, pp. 357, 360.

167 *the soil of Strzygowski's ideas*: See reference to Strzygowski in foreword to *Antioch-on-the-Orontes, I, The Excavations of 1932*, ed. G. W. Elderkin (Princeton University Press, 1934); Morey's review of *Early Christian Art* by O. M. Dalton, *Art Bulletin*, March 1927; Marquand, 1910; Britt, 2011; Christopher S. Wood, 2017. For a taste of Strzygowski in English, see "The Origin of Christian Art," *Burlington Magazine for Connoisseurs* 20, no. 195, December 1911. Morey, together with Ernst E. Herzfelt and W. R. W. Koehler, wrote a 1942 obituary of Strzygowski, in *Speculum*, vol. 17, 1942, pp. 460–61, in which they discern tendrils of National Socialist thought in Strzygowski's later work.

168 *"current problems . . . would be solved"*: Morey to Dana C. Munro, December 4, 1928, VRC.

168 *"every stage of which is illustrated"*: Morey, 1935.

FIFTEEN: THE THREE HUNDRED

172 2022 conference: Homage to Antioch Mosaics: "Current Stand and Perspectives," Hatay Mustafa Kemal University, Antakya, June 13–19, 2022.

173 *diamond-edged scribe*: Mark T. Wypyski and Lawrence Becker, "Glassmaking Technology at Antioch: Evidence from the Atrium House Triclinium and Later Mosaics," in *The Arts of Antioch*, ed., Lawrence Becker and Christine Kondoleon (Princeton University Press, 2005), p. 115.

173 *"My photograph . . . was taken"*: Lassus, 1935.

174 *accomplished American mosaicist*: The artist, Erin Adams, is featured in JoAnn Locktov and Leslie Plummer Clagett, *The Art of Mosaic Design: A Collection of Contemporary Artists* (Quarry Books, 1998).

176 *Consider the Erotes*: See Neuenfeldt, 2009.

177 *"At least a part of the value"*: See Downey, "Personification of Abstract Ideas in the Antioch Mosaics," *Transactions of the American Philological Association*, vol. 69 (1938).

177 *Dionysus*: See da Silva, 2021; Yamaç, 2011.

179 *"salient elements"*: Lavin, 1963, p. 276.

179 For geometric patterns in the Antioch mosaics, see Sheila Campbell, 1988; for "never, in the course of my career," see Lassus, 1982, p. 255; for 523 vs. 197 tesserae, see Sheila Campbell, 1988, p. 19; for Dionysus and Ariadne see Becker and Kondoleon, 2005, pp. 182–89; for "its mesmerizing assortment of geometric patterns," see Belis, 2016, p. 46.

SIXTEEN: DORO IN AMERICA

184 Account of Levi based on Laviosa, 1993; Balty 2001; Capristo, 2013; Guarnieri, 2023. For the Blisses and Levi, see correspondence among Royall Tyler, Mildred Barnes Bliss, and Robert Bliss, Dumbarton Oaks archives; and Bliss papers, Harvard University Archives. For young Levi, see Begg, 2002; Guarnieri, 2023; Robert Pounder, review of Ian Begg, *Lost Worlds of Ancient and Modern Greece: Gilbert Bagnani*, in *Bryn Mawr Classical Review*, September 2, 2021. See also Athanasios A. Rodopoulos, dir., *Doro Levi: Adventure in Archaeology*, video documentary, Italian Archaeological School at Athens, 1989.

190 Doro Levi's papers at the Institute for Advanced Study include correspondence between Abraham Flexner and Robert Bliss, and between Baldwin Smith and Frank Ayedlotte, mostly about efforts to support Levi in America.

195 For responses to Levi's book, see Lévêque, 1949; Hopkins, 1948; Balty, 2001.

SEVENTEEN: ANONYMOUS HANDS

197 For the themes of this chapter generally, see Parrish, 1997; Dunbabin 1979, 1999, 2001; da Silva, 2016; Toynbee, 1950; Lavagne, 1998.

199 *"Beautiful work by anonymous hands"*: da Silva, 2016, p. 221.

200 Opora, Agros, and Oinos: Morey, "The Antioch Mosaics at Baltimore," *Museum Quarterly of the Baltimore Museum of Art* 11 (1937): p. 3. This catalogue of possibilities inspires a seeming improbable comparison with an early Bob Dylan song, "Who Killed Davey Moore?" In it, Dylan asks who is to blame for the death of Moore, a thirty-year-old boxer. Was it his

opponent, "whose fists laid him low"? Or the referee who didn't stop the fight? Or the crowd, screaming for blood? Was it his manager, "puffing on a big cigar"? Or "the boxing writer / Pounding print on his old typewriter"? In Dylan's song, each denies responsibility for Davey Moore's death, whereas in our recital of candidate creators of mosaics we might imagine each angling for a share of the credit. Either way, the easy answer—that blame or credit owes to a single individual—seems dubious.

202 *off by only two millimeters*: Lawrence Becker and Christine Kondoleon, "The Atrium House Triclinium: The Archaeological Record," in Becker and Kondoleon, 2005, p. 31.

202 On mosaicists at work: *"l'artiste et l'artisan se confondent"*: Lassus, 1936, p. 38; "done by the artist in charge": Morey, 1938, p. 40; "the communal production of the overall work": Dunbabin, 2001, p. 272; "the practice . . . was not lonely": da Silva, 2016, p. 223; Jerash trough of tesserae: Licthenberger and Raja, pp. 1005–7; "ignominious function": Lavin, 1963, p. 181; "products of secondary quality": Levi, 1947, p. 7.

208 *"whose spirit is too narrow"*: Lavagne, 1998, p. 443.

209 *its "looping cables"*: Coleman, 2018.

210 *"most magical form of art"*: Account built up from Elizabeth James's notes from her 2022 Weitzmann Lecture at Princeton and supplementary email to the author.

EIGHTEEN: ANTIQUE STONES

214 *cranks and winches*: "Moving the Mosaics," video, Davis Museum at Wellesley College, June 1, 2016.

216 *neighborhood children had broken into*: Jean Labatut to Baldwin Smith, February 3, 1949, VRC.

216 *"a very serious problem of storage"*: Baldwin Smith to J. Jaujard, June 24, 1949, VRC.

217 Villanova sale: Account drawn from "Dick" and "Gene" correspondence in VRC files.

220 *"some specialist"*: Account of mosaic conservation drawn from Artal-Isbrand, 2001, 2005; interviews with Artal-Isbrand, Lawrence Becker, and Jessica Arista; see also Giroire, 2014; Gael de Guichen and Roberto Nardi, "Mosaic Conservation: Fifty years of Modern Practice," keynote address delivered at ninth conference of the International Committee for the Conservation of Mosaics, November 2005. See also Katherine Becker, 2012.

222 *"Opinions may differ"*: "Restoration of the Mosaics," in two parts, R. J. McKinney and Roland Wehrheim, *Museum Quarterly of the Baltimore Museum of Art* 11 (1937): pp. 5–7.

NINETEEN: FOR SALE OR TRADE

224 Oklahoma State mosaic sale: VRC, November 1949–February 1950. See also Tyler Jo Smith, "From Antioch to Oklahoma: The Cilicia Mosaic Rediscovered," *Mosaic: The Journal of Asprom* 38 (2011): pp. 9–16.

226 *"gave 50 feet of floor"*: Maas, 2010, p. 220.

227 *"practically no house"*: Levi, 1947, p. 1.

228 *"spot-lit the normally darkened spaces"*: Leyerle, 2018, p. 269. See also J. N. D. Kelly, 1995; and Leyerle, 2001. Levi, 1947, p. 1, observed of Libanius that he heard in the homilies of Chrysostom "a pitiless scourging of the folly of luxury and the turpitude of vice."

228 *"not one single whole block"*: John J. Dobbins, "The Houses of Antioch," in Kondoleon, 2000, p. 52.

228 *"uneven walled structure"*: Perkins, 1946, p. 95.

229 For Worcester-Getty mosaic sale, see Worcester Art Museum correspondence, Fall 1970. See also "Mosaic Floor with Animals," chapter 7 of Belis, 2016, pp. 46–49.

230 *"curiously peripatetic"*: Padgett, 1996.

230 Michigan State mosaic sale: VRC, March–October 1965. See also "Campaign for a Better Art Museum," Michigan State University publication, title uncertain, about 2000.

232 *"hauled out of the earth"*: Brown, 2001.

232 *"the core objective"*: Griswold, 2020.

TWENTY: OFF THE WALL

234 Account of the Kondoleon exhibition is based largely on interviews and correspondence with Christine Kondoleon, Lawrence Becker, Victoria I, Paula Artal-Isbrand, Alan Shapiro, Michael Padgett, and James Welu; Kondoleon, 2000; Becker and Kondoleon, 2005; publicity materials issued by the three museums involved.

237 *"necessary to define"*: Lassus. 1983, p. 254.

237 *"the laurels generally go"*: Diane Favro, review of Kondoleon, *Domestic and Divine, Studies in Iconography*, vol. 18, 1997, pp. 237–40. (For setting her on course in her study of Cypriot archaeology, Kondoleon would, in *Domestic and Divine*, thank A. H. S. Megaw; this is the same Megaw who,

almost seventy years before, importuned the Princeton archaeological team to turn its attentions to Cyprus.)

241 *"On first encountering"*: Kondoleon, "Mosaics of Antioch," in Kondoleon, 2000, pp. 62–77.

242 *"like shimmering carpets"*: Brown, 2001, sect. 2.

243 *"When I exited the show"*: Clarke, 2003.

243 *"What we wish to find"*: Brown, 2001, sect. 2.

244 *"regulations may have discouraged"*: Hatice Pamir, "Architectural Research in Antioch-on-the-Orontes and Its Vicinity, 2002–12," in Redford, 2014, p. 80.

244 Museum Hotel and Pegasus mosaic account based on A. J. P. Artemel, "Perched Over 2000-year-old Roman Mosaics and Ruins, This Hotel Takes a Bold Approach to Historic Preservation," *ArchDaily*, May 11, 2019; text 7, about the Museum-Hotel, from the Hatay Archaeology Museum, Antakya; tour of the hotel and its mosaics.

TWENTY-ONE: BACK IN ANTIOCH

246 *"He may have done more"*: Panofsky, 1955, p. 489.

246 *"a delicate and a sensitive man"*: Glueck, 1941.

247 *"rapidly developing and devastating forms"*: *Princeton Alumni Weekly*, October 24, 1947.

247 For Elderkin's Catholic problem, see Koppel S. Pinson, review of George W. Elderkin, *The Roman Catholic Problem*, and two other books, *Jewish Social Studies* 17, no. 2 (1955): p. 159; "Father Halton: The Stormy Petrel," *Harvard Crimson*, November 9, 1956.

248 For Downey, see his correspondence with Morey, VRC; and with Dr. Aydelotte, Institute for Advanced Study; and, in the Mudd Library, correspondence of A. M. Friend and Paul Sachs.

248 Campbell: For his obituary, see *Dartmouth Alumni Magazine*, March 1964. Campbell's son, Andrew, writes, in an email to the author, how his father, "normally a reserved person . . . would light up when talking about how the excavations kept giving and giving." In her 1995 Haskins Lecture, art historian Phyllis Pray Bober spoke of Campbell as "a romantic figure to all of us [at Wellesley] because he had once been a 'Wobbly' on the West Coast and had a Lawrence of Arabia aura, owing to his recent undercover activities" during World War II.

249 *"a pleasant reunion"*: See Carl Kraeling to Richard Stillwell, May 10, 1961; *"Why ever not?"*: Stillwell to Campbell, May 16, 1961; *"foibles and*

limitations": Brown, 2001; *"continuing some work at Antioch"*: Campbell to Rensselaer Lee, September 11, 1961.

251 *Lassus's odyssey*: See Lassus, *Souvenirs d'un Cobaye*, 1973; Christine Kondoleon tells of hearing about Lassus's experience on the train to Dachau from Lassus's sister; for overview of those years, see Jean Strauss, biographical note on Lassus, in Federation des Societés d'Histoire & d'Archéologie d'Alsace; letters from Lassus to Stillwell, February 25, 1940, and a torn and tattered one to Morey, July 16, 1940, tell of his early experiences during the war.

252 Lassus's application for a place at the Institute for Advanced Study in 1966 is represented in papers drawn from his IAS file. Something of his later experiences with publishing *Portiques* is drawn from Princeton University Press papers in Special Collections.

253 *"free from a heavy scruple"*: Lassus to Stillwell, July 9, 1972, Princeton University Press.

253 *"this testimony of my fidelity"*: Lassus, *Portiques*, p. 13.

BIBLIOGRAPHY

(See references to *Antioch* I–V, published by Princeton University Press, under Princeton Archives, above.)

"'Antioch is a city geologically and environmentally complex and without parallel.'" (An interview with Andrea de Giorgi, retwittered on X, formerly Twitter, September 29, 2023.)

Arndt, Richard T. (2005). "The Humanist at Large: Charles Rufus Morey in Rome." In *The First Resort of Kings: American Cultural Diplomacy in the Twentieth Century*, Potomac Books.

Artal-Isbrand, Paula (2001). "Mosaic Conservation at the Worcester Art Museum." *Objects Specialty Group Postprints* 8, pp. 136–49.

——— (2005). "The Mosaic Conservation Campaign: Three Case Studies." In *The Arts of Antioch: Art Historical and Scientific Approaches to Roman Mosaics and a Catalogue of the Worcester Art Museum Antioch Collection*. Edited by Lawrence Becker and Christine Kondoleon. Princeton University Press, pp. 81–114.

Balty, Janine (2000). "Les Mosqaïques de Daphné: découverte, première études, problems de datation." *Syria* 97, pp. 71–83.

——— (2001). "Doro Levi, *Antioch Mosaic Pavements*: Cinquante Ans Après." *Byzantion* 71, no. 2, pp. 303–24.

——— (2004). "Les Mosaíques d'Antioche: Style et Rayonnement." *Topoi, Orient-Occident*, Supplément 5, 2004, Antioche de Syrie.

——— (2006). Review of Lawrence Becker and Christine Kondoleon, eds. *The Arts of Antioch: Art Historical and Scientific Approaches to Roman Mosaics and a Catalogue of the Worcester Art Museum Antioch Collection*. In *L'Antiquité classique*, Tome 75, 2006, pp. 654–55.

Barsanti, Claudia (2012). "The Fate of the Antioch Mosaic Pavements: Some Reflections." *Journal of Mosaic Research* 5, pp. 25–42.

Beach, C. Clarke (1937). "Mosaics from Ancient Antioch: Treasures Recovered in Syria to Go on View Tuesday at the Museum." Baltimore *Sun*, May 16.

Becker, Katherine (ca. 2012). "Preserving Archaeological Mosaic Pavements: A Discussion of Context and Access." *Chronika*, Institute for European and Mediterranean Archaeology, pp. 51–64.

Becker, Lawrence, and Christine Kondoleon, eds. (2005). *The Arts of Antioch: Art Historical and Scientific Approaches to Roman Mosaics and a Catalogue of the Worcester Art Museum Antioch Collection*. Worcester Art Museum.

Begg, Ian (2002). "Greece 1921–1924 in the Bagnani Archives." *Scripta Mediterranea* XXIII, p. 55.

Belis, Alexis (2016). *Roman Mosaics in the J. Paul Getty Museum*. J. Paul Getty Museum.

Blair, David F., Jr. (1957). "The Morey School: A Great Medieval Scholar Lives on in Art History." *Princeton Alumni Weekly*, March 15.

Blanc-Bijon, Véronique (2016). "Comment Travaillaient les Mosastes dans l'Antiquité." *Territoria della Cultura* 25, pp. 16–41.

Bouchier, E. S. (1921). *A Short History of Antioch, 300 B.C.–A.D. 1268*. Basil Blackwell.

Bowersock, G. W. (2006). *Mosaics as History: The Near East from Late Antiquity to Islam*. Belknap Press.

Brands, Gunnar (2010). "Hellenistic Antioch on the Orontes: A Status Quo." In *Anadolu ve Çevresinde Ortaçağ* 4 (Ankara), pp. 1–18.

Britt, Karen C. (2011). "These Stones Still Speak: The Progress of Research on Late Roman and Early Byzantine Mosaic Pavement in the Eastern Mediterranean." *Journal of Art Historiography*, no. 5, December.

Brown, Peter (1989). *The World of Late Antiquity, A.D. 150–750*. W. W. Norton.

_____ (2001). "Charmed Lives," *New York Review of Books*, April 12. Review of *Antioch: The Lost Ancient City*, exhibition and accompanying catalogue.

_____ (2008). "The Voice of the Stones." Review of *Mosaics in History*, by G. W. Bowersock, *New York Review of Books*, April 17.

Butler, Howard Crosby (1900). "Report of an American Archaeological Expedition in Syria, 1899–1900." *American Journal of Archaeology* 4, no. 4 (October–December): pp. 415–40.

Cabouret, Bernadette (1999). "Sous Les Portiques d'Antioche." *Syria: Archéologie, Art et Histoire* 76, pp. 127–50.

Caillet, Jean-Pierre (1993). *L'Évergétisme monumental chrétien en Italie et á ses Marges*. École Française de Rome.

Campbell, Sheila (1979). "Roman Mosaic Workshops in Turkey." *American Journal of Archaeology* 83, no. 3 (July): pp. 287–92.

——— (1988). *The Mosaics of Antioch*. Pontifical Institute of Mediaeval Studies.

Campbell, William Alexander (1934). "Archaeological Notes: Excavations at Antioch-on-the-Orontes." *American Journal of Archaeology* 38 (April–June): pp. 201–6.

——— (1936). "Archaeological Notes: The Third Season of Excavation at Antioch-on-the-Orontes." *American Journal of Archaeology* 40 (January–March): pp. 1–10.

——— (1938). "Archaeological Notes: The Fourth and Fifth Seasons of Excavations at Antioch-on-the-Orontes." *American Journal of Archaeology* 42 (April–June): pp. 205–17.

——— (1940). "Archaeological Notes: The Sixth Season of Excavation at Antioch-on-the-Orontes." *American Journal of Archaeology* 44, no. 4 (October–December): pp. 417–27.

Capristo, Annalisa (2013). "Italian Intellectuals and the Exclusion of Their Jewish Colleagues from Universities and Academies." *Telos* 164 (Fall): pp. 63–95.

Cimok, Fatih (1994). *Antioch on the Orontes*. Rev. 2nd ed. A Turizm Yayinlari.

"Clarence S. Fisher" (1941). *The Biblical Archaeologist* 4, no. 3 (September): p. 48. No author.

"Clarence Fisher: An Unknown Achievement" (1979). *Expedition* 21, no. 2 (Winter). No author.

Clarke, John R. (2001). Review of Christine Kondoleon, *Antioch: The Lost Ancient City*. *Bryn Mawr Classical Review*, January 7.

——— (2003). "Finding Lost Antioch: Exhibition, Catalogue, Programs." *Art Bulletin*, March 2003, pp. 185–88.

Cline, Eric H. (2020). *Digging Up Armageddon: The Search for the Lost City of Solomon*. Princeton University Press.

Coleman, Kathleen Mary (2018). "Later Roman Mosaics at the Institute for Advanced Study." Institute for Advanced Study. www.ias.edu/ideas/coleman-mosaics.

Crowfoot, J. W. (1942). Review of *The Mosaics of Antioch* by C. R. Morey. *Journal of Hellenic Studies* 62, pp. 109–10.

Crowther, Benjamin (2018). Review of Ross Burns, *Origins of the Colonnaded Streets in the Cities of the Roman East*. *Bryn Mawr Classical Review*.

Cuno, James (2008). *Who Owns Antiquity?: Museums and the Battle over Our Ancient Heritage.* Princeton University Press.

_____ (2009). *Whose Culture? The Promise of Museums and the Debate over Antiquities*. Princeton University Press.

The Dark Ages: Loan Exhibition of Pagan and Christian Art in the Latin West and Byzantine East. Worcester Art Museum, February 20–March 21, 1937.

Da Silva, Gilvan Ventura (2016). "The Rapports between 'Techné' and 'Paideia' in the Roman Empire: Reading the Antiochene Mosaics." *Acta Scientiarium Education* 38, no. 3 (July–September): pp. 219–29.

_____ (2021). "Images of the Feast in Antioch: Reflections about Dionysus' Mosaics in Domestic Settings." *Mythos* 15.

Dauphin, Claudine (1980). "Mosaic Pavements as an Index of Prosperity and Fashion." *Levant* 12, no. 1 (July): pp. 112–34.

De Giorgi, Andrea U (2015). Review of *The Princeton Excavations in Antakya*, Scott Redford, ed. *Journal of Roman Archaeology* 28, pp. 873–76.

_____ (2016). *Ancient Antioch: From the Seleucid Era to the Islamic Conquest.* Cambridge University Press.

De Giorgi, Andrea U., and A. Asa Eger (2021). *Antioch: A History*. Routledge.

Downey, Glanville (1941). "Ethical Themes in the Antioch Mosaics." *Church History* 10, no. 4 (December): pp. 367–76.

_____ (1945). "The Pagan Virtue of Megalopsychia in Byzantine Syria." *Transactions and Proceedings of the American Philological Association* 76, pp. 279–86.

_____ (1959). "Libanius' Oration in Praise of Antioch (Oration XI)." Translated with introduction and commentary. *Proceedings of the American Philosophical Society* 103, no. 5 (October): pp. 652–86.

_____ (1961). *A History of Antioch in Syria, from Seleucus to the Arab Conquest.* Princeton University Press.

_____ (1962). *Ancient Antioch.* Princeton University Press.

_____ (1962). *Antioch in the Age of Theodosius the Great*. University of Oklahoma Press.

Doyon, Wendy (2018). "The History of Archaeology through the Eyes of Egyptians." In *Unmasking Ideology in Imperial and Colonial Archaeology*. Ed., Bonnie Effros and Guolong Lai. Cotsen Institute of Archaeology Press, UCLA.

Dunbabin, Katherine, M.D. (1979). "Technique and Materials of Hellenistic Mosaics." *American Journal of Archaeology* 83, no. 3 (July): pp. 265–77.

——— (1999). "Mosaics and Their Public." In *La Mosaïque Gréco-Romaine VII*, Tome 2. Institut National du Patrimoine, Tunis.

——— (2001). *Mosaics of the Greek and Roman World*. Cambridge University Press.

Dyson, Stephen L. (1998). "The Triumph of the Establishment: Classical Archaeology between the Wars." In *Ancient Marbles to American Shores*. University of Pennsylvania Press.

Fabrikant, Geraldine (2005). "Mosaic Restoration as Performance Art. *New York Times*, August 29.

Felch, Jason, and Ralph Frammolino (2011). *Chasing Aphrodite: The Hunt for Looted Antiquities at the World's Richest Museum*. Houghton Mifflin Harcourt.

Fisher, Steve. "C.S. Fisher" (his grandfather), on Steve Fisher's website, eightpointfive.net.

Foss, Clive (1996). "Dead Cities of the Syrian Hill Country." *Archaeology*, September–October, pp. 48–53.

Fox, Georgia (2011). Review of L. Becker and C. Kondoleon, eds., *The Arts of Antioch. Journal of American Institute for Conservation* 50, no. 2 (Fall/Winter): pp. 161–63.

"Francis Henry Taylor, 54, Dies; Head of Museum of Art, 1939–1954." *New York Times*, November 22, 1954.

Garrett, Robert (1914). *Topography and Itinerary.* Part I of *Publications of an American Archaeological Expedition to Syria in 1899–1900*. Century Co.

——— (1949). "Recollections of a Collector." *Princeton University Library Chronicle* 10, no. 3 (April): pp. 103–16.

Gelin, Mathilde (2002). *L'Archéologie en Syrie et au Liban À l'Epoque du Mandat (1919–1946): Histoire et Organisation.* Librairie orientaliste P. Geuthner.

Getty Conservation Institute and Israel Antiquities Authority (2003). "Illustrated Glossary, Mosaics in Situ Project." December.

Ginouves, René (1975). Review of Jean Lassus, *Antioch-on-the-Orontes, V, Les Portiques d'Antioche*. Princeton University Press, 1972. In *Syria* 52, nos. 3–4, pp. 298–301.

Giroire, Cecile (2014). "Les Mosaiques d'Antioche du Louvre, Nouvelle Presentation." In *Revue Archéologique*, Nouvelle Série, Fasc.1, pp. 136–42.

Glueck, Nelson (1941). "Clarence Stanley Fisher in Memoriam." *Bulletin of the American Schools of Oriental Research*, no. 83 (October): pp. 1–4.

Goode, James F. (2007). *Negotiating for the Past: Archaeology, Nationalism, and Diplomacy in the Middle East, 1919–1941*. University of Texas Press.

Griswold, Sarah (2020). "Locating Archaeological Expertise: Debating Antiquities Norms in 'A' Mandates, 1918–1926." In *Experts et expertise dans les mandates de la société des nations: figures, champs, outils*. Ed., Philippe Bourmaud, Norig Neveu, and Chantall Verdeil. Presses de l'Italco.

Guarnieri, Patrizia (2023). *Intellectuals Displaced from Fascist Italy*. 2nd ed. Firenze University Press.

Hopkins, Clark (1948). "Antioch Mosaic Pavements." *Journal of Near Eastern Studies* 7, no. 2 (April): pp. 91–97.

Hourihane, Colum (2002). "'They Stand on His Shoulders': Morey, Iconography, and the Index of Christian Art." In *Insights and Interpretation: Studies in Celebration of the Eighty-fifth Anniversary of the Index of Christian Art*. Ed., Colum Hourihane. Department of Art and Archaeology, Princeton Unviersity.

Huskinson, Janet (2002). "Three Antioch Dining Rooms." *Mosaic* 29, pp. 21–23.

_____ (2003). "Theatre, Performance and Theatricality in Some Mosaic Pavements from Antioch." *Bulletin of the Institute of Classical Studies* 46, no. 1 (December): pp. 131–65.

_____ (2004). "Surveying the Scene: Antioch Mosaic Pavements as a Source of Historical Evidence." In *Culture and Society in Later Roman Antioch*. Ed., Isabella Sandwell and Janet Huskinson. Oxbow Books.

James, Elizabeth (2022). "A Glass Dream: Byzantine Wall Mosaics and the Alchemy of Making." Unpublished raw notes for Weitzmann Lecture at Princeton. Courtesy of the author.

Jones, Frances F. (1981). "Antioch Mosaics in Princeton." *Record of the Art Museum, Princeton University* 40, no. 2, pp. 2–26.

Jones, Tom B. (1978). *In the Twilight of Antiquity*. University of Minnesota Press.

Jouguet, Pierre (1936). "Claude Prost." *Bulletin de L'Institut Français d'Archéologie Orientale* 36, pp. 125–27.

Kamm, Henry (1986). "Ancient Town of Mythology and Mosaics." *New York Times*, September 21.

Kelly, Cindy (2001). "Maps, Manuscripts and Mosaics: Robert Garrett's Road to Antioch." Unpublished manuscript. "Antioch at 70" symposium, Baltimore, October 13.

Kelly, J. N. D. (1995). *Golden Mouth: The Story of John Chrysostom, Ascetic, Preacher, Bishop*. Baker Books.

Khadduri, Majid (1945). "The Alexandretta Dispute." *American Journal of International Law* 39, no. 3 (July): pp. 406–25.

Khoury, Philip S. (1987). *Syria and the French Mandate: The Politics of Arab Nationalism, 1920–1945*. Princeton University Press.

Kolarik, Ruth (2009). "Mosaics from Antioch: Chronological Implications for Other Regions?" In *Mosaics of Turkey and Parallel Developments in the Rest of the Ancient and Medieval World: Questions of Iconography, Style and Technique from the Beginnings of Mosaics until the Late Byzantine Era*. Ed., M. Şahin. Eleventh International Conference on Ancient Mosaics, Bursa, Turkey.

Kondoleon, Christine (1995). *Domestic and Divine: Roman Mosaics in the House of Dionysos*. Cornell University Press.

——— (2000). *Antioch: The Lost Ancient City*. Princeton University Press and Worcester Art Museum.

Lassus, Jean (1933). "La Mosaïque de Yakto." In *Antioch I*, pp. 114–56.

——— (1935). "Dans les Rues d'Antioche." In *Bulletin d'etudes orientales*, pp. 121–24.

——— (1936). "Les Mosaïques d'Antioche." *Comptes rendus des séances de l'Académie des Inscriptions et Belles-Lettres*, pp. 33–42.

——— (1967). "Antioche, Fouilles Profondes, 1934–1938." *Comptes rendus des séances de l'Académie des Inscriptions et Belles-Lettres*, pp. 45–75.

——— (1967). *The Early Christian and Byzantine World*. McGraw-Hill.

——— (1972). *Antioch-on-the-Orontes V: Les Portiques d'Antioche*. Princeton University Press.

——— (1973). *Souvenirs d'un Cobaye*. Editions Alsatia.

——— (1982). "Le Fouilleur et les Mosaïques." In *Mosaïque: Recueil d' Hommages à Henri Stern*. Editions Recherche sur les Civilisations, pp. 253–58.

Lavagne, Henri (1978). "Histoire de la Mosaique." In *Annuaires de l'École pratique des hautes études*. 4e section, Sciences historiques et philologiques, pp. 431–45.

Lavin, Irving (1963). "The Hunting Mosaics of Antioch and Their Sources: A Study of Compositional Principles in the Development of Early Mediaeval Style." *Dumbarton Oaks Papers* XVII, pp. 179–286.

Laviosa, Clelia (1993). "Doro Levi, 1898–1991." *American Journal of Archaeology* 97, no. 1 (January): pp. 165–66.

Lee, Rensselaer W. (1955). "Charles Rufus Morey, 1877–1955." *Art Bulletin* 37, no. 4 (December): pp. iii–vii.

Le Glay, Marcel (1991). "Jean Lassus (1903–1990)." In *Antiquités africaines* 27, pp. 7–9.

Lévêque, Pierre (1949). Review of Doro Levi, *Antioch Mosaic Pavements*. *Bulletin de Correspondance Hellénique* 73, pp. 490–91.

Levi, Doro (1947). *Antioch Mosaic Pavements*, 2 vols. Princeton University Press.

Leyerle, Blake (2001). "Theatrical Shows and Ascetic Lives: John Chrysostom's Attack on Spiritual Marriage." University of California Press.

_____ (2018). "Imagining Antioch, or the Fictional Space of Alleys and Markets." In *Antioch II: The Many Faces of Antioch: Intellectual Exchange and Religious Diversity, CE 350–450*. Ed., Silke-Petra Bergjan and Susanna Elm. Mohr Siebeck. (This *Antioch II* should not be confused with Richard Stillwell, ed., *Antioch II*, from the original expedition.)

Lichtenberger, Achim, and Rubina Raja (2017). "Mosaicists at Work: The Organisation of Mosaic Production in Early Islamic Jerash." *Antiquity* 91, no. 358 (August): pp. 998–1010.

Liebeschuetz, J. H. W. G. (1972). *Antioch: City and Imperial Administration in the Later Roman Empire*. Clarendon Press.

_____ (2004). "Malalas on Antioch." *Topoi Orient-Occident*, suppl. 5, pp. 143–53.

Ling, Roger (1998). *Ancient Mosaics*. Princeton University Press.

_____ (2001). "Roman Mosaics: A Success Story of Classical Archaeology." A review article. *American Journal of Archaeology* 105, no. 2 (April): pp. 325–29.

Maas, Michael (2010). *Readings in Late Antiquity: A Sourcebook*. 2nd ed. Routledge.

Mallowan, Agatha Christie (1999). *Come, Tell Me How You Live*. HarperCollins.

Marquand, Allan (1910). "Styzygowski and His Theory of Early Christian Art." *Harvard Theological Review* 3, no. 3 (July): pp. 357–65.

Maynard, W. Barksdale (2012). "Dig of the Century." *Princeton Alumni Weekly*, March 7.

McCurry, Grace K. M. (2017). "Excavated from the Archives: Recovering the Contributions of Cyrus Ashton Rollins Sanborn to Expeditions in Egypt, 1915–1921." Masters thesis in Middle Eastern Studies. Harvard University.

Milliken, William M. (1947). "Christian and Byzantine Art in America." *Journal of Aesthetics and Art Criticism* 5, no. 4 (June): pp. 256–68.

Molacek, Elizabeth M., and Dylan K. Rogers (2021). "The Mosaics of the Boat of Psyches: Reexamining Identity in Antoch." In *A Quaint & Curious Volume: Essays in Honor of John J. Dobbins*, ed., Dylan K. Rogers and Claire J. Weiss. Archaeopress, pp. 168–96.

Morey, C. R. (1924). "The Sources of Mediaeval Style." *Art Bulletin* 7, no. 2 (December): pp. 35–50.

_____ (1927). Review of *East Christian Art*, by O. M. Dalton. *Art Bulletin* 9, no. 3 (March): pp. 275–78.

——— (1932). "Antioch on the Orontes: French Authorities Select Princeton Art Department to Excavate Ancient Syrian Metropolis." *Princeton Alumni Weekly*, January.

——— (1933). "The Excavation of Antioch." *Bulletin of the Worcester Art Museum* 24, no. 3 (Autumn): pp. 50–55.

——— (1934). Foreword. In *Antioch-on-the-Orontes*. Vol. 1. Ed., George W. Elderkin. Princeton.

——— (1935). "The Excavation of Antioch-on-the-Orontes." *Parnassus* 7, no. 4 (May): pp. 9–12.

——— (1936). "The Excavation of Antioch-on the Orontes," read April 24, before American Philosophical Society. Reprinted by Baltimore Museum of Art, May 1937.

——— (1937). "The Antioch Mosaics at Baltimore." *Museum Quarterly of the Baltimore Museum of Art* 11.

——— (1938). *The Mosaics of Antioch*. Longmans, Green.

Morton, H. V. (2002). *In the Steps of St. Paul*. Da Capo Press, 2002. (Originally published in 1936.)

Morvillez, Éric (2020). "Revisiter les archives des missions franco-américaines de Princeton: le cas de la residence de Yakto prês d'Antioche." *Syria* 97, pp. 85–112.

Moss, Christopher (2001). "The 'Prehistory' of the Antioch Excavation: Butler and Morey at Princeton." Unpublished paper delivered at symposium, "Antioch at 70: An Excavation and Its Impact." Baltimore Museum of Art, October 13.

Nelson, Robert (2022). "Atypical Patrimony: Collecting Byzantine Art in American University Museums." *24th International Congress of Byzantine Studies*, vol. 1. Proceedings of the Plenary Sessions, pp. 47–60.

Neuenfeldt, Lori P. (2009). "Eros and Erotes in the Late Antique Mosaics of Antioch." M.A. thesis, Florida State University.

Norman, A. F. (2000). *Antioch as a Centre of Hellenic Culture as Observed by Libanius*. Liverpool University Press.

Padgett, J. Michael (1996). "The Collections of Ancient Art: The Early Years." *Record of the Art Museum, Princeton University* 55, no. 1/2, pp. 107–24.

Pamir, Hatice, and Nilüfer Sezgin (2016). "The Sundial and Convivium Scene on the Mosaic from the Rescue Excavation in a Late Antique House of Antioch." *Adalya* 19, no. 19, pp. 251–80.

Panofsky, Edwin (1955). "Charles Rufus Morey (1877–1955)." *American Philosophical Yearbook*, pp. 482–91.

Parrish, David (1997). "Essai d'identification d'un atelier de mosaïstes à Antioche-sur-l'Oronte." In *Actes du VIIIème Colloque international pour l'étude de la mosaïque antique et médiévale*. Ed., D. Paunier and C. Schmidt. Cahiers d'archéologie romande.

Pedone, Sylvia (2012). "The Jewels in the Mosaics of Antioch: Some Visual Examples of Late Antique and Byzantine Luxury." *Rivista degli studi orientali*. Nuova Serie, vol. 85, Fasc. 1/4, pp. 391–410.

Perkins, J. R. (1946). *Antioch Actress: A Novel of Pagan against Christian*. Bobbs-Merrill.

Poccardi, Grêgoir (2020). "La topographie archêologique du faubourg de Daphnê." *Syria* 97, pp. 13–26.

Pralong, Annie (2005). "Homage á Jean Lassus." *École pratique des hautes études, section des sciences religieuses, Annuaire.* Tome 114, pp. 299–303.

Provost, Samuel (2016). "Les deux missions de Paul Perdrizet et Henri Seyrig en Syrie et leurs prolongements (1924–1928)." *Syria*, HS III, pp. 33–47.

Redford, Scott, ed. (2014). *Antioch on the Orontes: Early Explorations in the City of Mosaics.* Koc Universitesi.

Rifaioğlue, Mert Nezih (2014). "The Historic Urban Core of Antakya under the Influence of the French Mandate, and Turkish Republican Urban Conservation and Development Activitities." *Megaron* 9, no. 4, pp. 271–88.

Robinson, Thomas A. (2009). *Ignatius of Antioch and the Parting of the Ways: Early Jewish-Christian Relations.* Hendrickson.

Rodopoulos, Athanasios A. (1989). *Doro Levi: Adventure in Archaeology*. Documentary film. Italian Archaeological School at Athens.

Romm, James (2012). *Ghost on the Throne: The Death of Alexander the Great and the Bloody Fight for His Empire*. Vintage Books.

Saliou, Catherine, "Bains et histoire urbaine. L'exemple d'Antioche sur l'Oronte dans l'Antiquité," dans M.-Fr. Boussac, S. Denoix, Th. Fournet, B. Redon (dir.), *25 siècles de bain collectif en Orient (Proche-Orient, Égypte et péninsule Arabique), Actes du colloque de Damas*, 2009, Le Caire, 2014, pp. 657–85.

——— (2020). "De la Mosaïque au Dictionnaire Topographique: Les Legends de la Bordure Topographique de la Mosaïque de Megalopsychia." *Syria* 97, pp. 113–25.

——— (2020). "Liaisons Dangereuses: textes et archéologie." In *Histoire urbaone de l'Orient romain tardif*. In six parts, April 9 to June 1.

——— (2020). "À la Recherche du Forum de Valens: Jean Lassus au Travail." In *Histoire urbaine de l'Orient romain tardif*, OpenEdition, August.

Sandwell, Isabella, and Janet Huskinson, eds. (2004). *Culture and Society in Later Roman Antioch*. Oxbow Books.

Scheibelreiter-Gail, Veronika (2012). "Inscriptions in the Late Antique Private House: Some Thoughts about their Function and Distribution." In *Patrons and Viewers in Late Antiquity*. Ed., Stine Birk and Birte Poulsen. Aarhus University Press.

Schenck, Edgar C. (1938). "Mosaic from Daphne." *Honolulu Academy of Arts Bulletin*, December, pp. 35–44.

Schmidtke, Sabine, ed. (2018). *Studying the Near and Middle East at the Institute for Advanced Study, Princeton, 1935–2018*. Gorgias Press.

Schoolman, Edward (2017). "Luxury, Vice, and Health." *Studies in Late Antiquity* 1, no. 3 (Fall): pp. 225–53.

Seyrig, H. (1959). "René Dussaud." *Syria*, tome 36, fascicule 102, pp. 1–7.

Smith, Tyler Jo (2011). "From Antioch to Oklahoma: The Cilicia Antioch Rediscovered," *Mosaic* 38, pp. 9–16.

Smyth, Craig Hugh, and Peter M. Lukehart, eds. (1993). *The Early Years of Art History in the United States.* Department of Art and Archaeology, Princeton University.

Souville, Georges (1979). "Homage à Jean Lassus." *Antiquités africaines* 14, pp. 9–10.

Stahl, Alan M. (2017). "New Archaeology from Old Coins: Antioch Reexamined." In *European Archaeology as Anthropology*. Ed., Pam J. Crabtree and Peter Bogucki. University of Pennsylvania Press, pp. 227–46.

Starkey, Elizabeth (1972). "A Talk with Bayard Dodge." *Aramco World* 23, no. 4 (July/August): pp. 11–17.

Stétié, Salah (2016). "Cher Henri: Quelques souvenirs familiers d'Henri Seyrig." *Syria* 3, pp. 393–97.

Stillwell, Richard (1961). "Houses of Antioch." *Dumbarton Oaks Papers*, vol. 15, pp. 45–57.

Straus, Leon (1994). "Lassus Jean." Fédération des Sociétés d'Histoire & d'Archéologie d'Alsace.

Strong, Donald, and David Brown (1979). *Roman Crafts*. Duckworth.

Strzygowski, Josef (1911). "The Origin of Christian Art." *Burlington Magazine for Connoisseurs*, December.

Stucky, Rolf A. (2016). "Henri Seyrig et les archéologues suisses en Syrie et au Liban." *Syria* 3, pp. 251–65.

Sweetman, Rebecca J. (2007). Review of *The Arts of Antioch* by L. Becker and C. Kondoleon. *Classical Review* 57, no. 1 (April): pp. 217–19.

Tassel, Janet (2000). "Antioch Revealed." *Harvard Magazine*, November 1.

Taylor, Francis Henry (1955). "Charles Rufus Morey, 1877–1955." *College Art Journal* 15, no. 2 (Winter): pp. 139–42.

Toynbee, J. M. C. (1950). "Some Notes on Artists in the Roman World." *Latomus,* Société d'Études Latines de Bruxelles, July–September, pp. 295–302.

Veyne, Paul, ed. (1987). *A History of Private Life. I. From Pagan Rome to Byzantium.* Transl. Arthur Goldhammer. Belknap Press of Harvard University.

Wages, Sara M. (1986). "A Note on the Dumbarton Oaks *Tethys* Mosaic." *Dumbarton Oaks Papers*, vol. 40, pp. 119–28.

Wallace, Lew (1996). *Ben Hur: A Tale of the Christ*. Wordsworth Editions, 1996. (Originally published 1880.)

Watts, Edward J. (2020). *The Final Pagan Generation: Rome's Uncertain Path to Christianity*. University of California Press.

Weisgall, Deborah (2000). "Reading a Civilization through Its Ancient Shards." *New York Times*, November 19.

Welu, James R. (2005). "From Antioch to Worcester: The Pursuit of an Ancient City." In *The Arts of Antioch*. Ed., Lawrence Becker and Christine Kondoleon. Worcester Art Museum.

Weulersse, Jacques (1934). "Antioche: Essai de géographie urbaine." *Bulletin d'Études Orientales* 4, pp. 27–79.

Wilber, Donald N. (1938). "The Plateau of Daphne: The Springs and the Water System Leading to Antioch." In Stillwell, ed., *Antioch II*.

——— (1986). *Adventures in the Middle East: Excursions and Incursions*. Darwin Press.

"William Alexander Campbell" (1964). Obituary. *Dartmouth Alumni Magazine*, March.

Wood, Christopher S. (2017). "Strzygowski and Riegl in America." *Journal of Art Historiography*, no. 17, December.

Wood, Juliette (2008). "The Great Chalice of Antioch: On a Quest for the Holy Grail from Antioch to America and Back Again." Online account based on her book *Eternal Chalice: The Enduring Legend of the Holy Grail*. Tauris.

Woolley (1938). "Excavations at Minna." *Journal of Hellenic Studies* 58, pt. 1, pp. 1–30.

Yamaç Inanç (2011). "The Dionysus Cult in Antioch." *Proceedings of the 15th Symposium on Mediterranean Archaeology*, vol. II, March 3–5. Ed., M. P. Militello and H. Öniz. Archaeopress, pp. 677–83.

ILLUSTRATION CREDITS

TEXT

16 Antioch Excavation Collection, Department of Art and Archaeology, Princeton University

30 Wikimedia Commons/Bulgarian Archives State Agency

41 Library of Congress/Bain News Service

62 Antioch Excavation Collection, Department of Art and Archaeology, Princeton University

66 Wikimedia Commons/Aankoop met steun van de Mondriaan Stichting, het Prins Bernhard Cultuurfonds, het VSBfonds, het Paul Huf Fonds/ Rijksmuseum Fonds en het Egbert Kunstfonds

67 Antioch Excavation Collection, Department of Art and Archaeology, Princeton University

68 Antioch Excavation Collection, Department of Art and Archaeology, Princeton University

83 No Credit

83 Antioch Excavation Collection, Department of Art and Archaeology, Princeton

88 Wikimedia Commons/Antakya Archaeological Museum

96 Antioch Excavation Collection, Department of Art and Archaeology, Princeton University

106 Antioch Excavation Collection, Department of Art and Archaeology, Princeton University

121 Antioch Excavation Collection, Department of Art and Archaeology, Princeton University

121 No Credit

129 Antioch Excavation Collection, Department of Art and Archaeology, Princeton University
156 Antioch Excavation Collection, Department of Art and Archaeology, Princeton University
160 Courtesy of the Author
182 The J. Paul Getty Museum, Villa Collection, Malibu, California, 70.AH.96
183 Guggenheim Foundation
198 Antioch Excavation Collection, Department of Art and Archaeology, Princeton University
198 No Credit
209 Antioch Excavation Collection, Department of Art and Archaeology, Princeton University
219 Antioch Excavation Collection, Department of Art and Archaeology, Princeton University; Worcester Museum, Excavation of Antioch and Vicinity funded by the bequests of the Reverend Dr. Austin S. Garver and Sarah C. Garver
219 No Credit

INSERT

1 Wikimedia Commons/Carole Raddato
2 Antioch Excavation Collection, Department of Art and Archaeology, Princeton University
3 Antioch Excavation Collection, Department of Art and Archaeology, Princeton University
4 Antioch Excavation Collection, Department of Art and Archaeology, Princeton University
5 Antioch Excavation Collection, Department of Art and Archaeology, Princeton University
6 Antioch Excavation Collection, Department of Art and Archaeology, Princeton University
7 Antioch Excavation Collection, Department of Art and Archaeology, Princeton University
8 Antioch Excavation Collection, Department of Art and Archaeology, Princeton University
9 Sarah Merrow
10 Dumbarton Oaks Research Library and Collection, Byzantine Collection, Washington, D.C.

11 Antioch Excavation Collection, Department of Art and Archaeology, Princeton University
12 Baltimore Museum of Art; Antioch Subscription Fund
13 Wikimedia Commons/Following Hadrian
14 Wikimedia Commons/CC Dosseman
15 Wikimedia Commons/CC Dosseman
16 Wikimedia Commons/CC Dosseman
17 Wikimedia Commons/CC Dosseman

INDEX

NOTE: Page numbers in *italics* refer to photos and figures.

ABOUT THE AUTHOR

ROBERT KANIGEL is the author of *The Man Who Knew Infinity*, *Eyes on the Street*, *The One Best Way*, *Hearing Homer's Song*, and six other nonfiction books—in biography, history, history of science, and memoir. He has been a finalist for the National Book Critics Circle Award and the Los Angeles Times Book Prize and a recipient of a National Endowment for the Humanities Public Scholar award as well as a Guggenheim fellowship. He spent earlier lives as a mechanical engineer, a professor of science writing at MIT, and a freelance writer of magazine articles, essays, and reviews. An avid cyclist and amateur mosaicist, he lives in Baltimore.

ABOUT THE AUTHOR